LMSW Exam Prep 2024-2025: UPDATED All in One ASWB Masters Study Guide for The Licensed Master Social Worker Certification. LMSW Review Material Plus 650 LMSW Practice Test Questions.

ISBN: 978-1-964079-42-4

Disclaimer: This publication, including all contents therein, is provided for informational and educational purposes only and is not intended as a substitute for professional advice, diagnosis, or treatment. It is designed to assist in preparing for the Licensed Master Social Worker (LMSW) exam. However, it does not guarantee passage of the exam. The authors and publishers have made every effort to ensure the accuracy and completeness of the information contained in this book as of the date of publication but assume no responsibility for errors, omissions, or for outcomes resulting from the use of the information provided herein.

The views and opinions expressed in this book are those of the authors and do not necessarily reflect the official policy or position of any certification boards, academic institutions, or governmental agencies. This book may contain references to specific statutes, laws, and ethical guidelines that are subject to change and interpretation. The reader is encouraged to review the most current version of all relevant statutes, laws, and guidelines when preparing for the LMSW exam and practicing social work.

The use of this book does not create an educator-student or any professional relationship between the reader and the authors or publishers. Furthermore, the authors and publishers disclaim all liability to any person or entity for any loss or damage caused, or alleged to be caused, directly or indirectly by the use, application, or interpretation of the information contained herein.

It is the responsibility of the reader to comply with all laws and ethical standards applicable to the practice of social work in their jurisdiction. This book should be used as a complement to, not a replacement for, formal education, practical training, and professional licensure requirements.

TABLE OF CONTENTS

INTRO:

Welcome to the journey towards becoming a Licensed Master Social Worker (LMSW). This book is your companion on the path to not just passing an exam but embracing a profession that has the power to change lives, including your own. You're embarking on a noble quest, and it's okay to feel a mix of excitement and nervousness. After all, it's a significant step towards fulfilling your dream of making a meaningful difference in the world.

In these pages, you'll find everything you need to prepare for the LMSW exam. We've distilled complex ideas into simple, understandable language, ensuring you grasp the key concepts without getting bogged down by jargon. From the history and fundamentals of social work to the ethical frameworks guiding the profession, and onto the intricacies of human behavior and social environments, this guide covers the essential knowledge required for the exam.

But it's not just about passing a test. It's about laying the foundation for your future career. This guide is structured to provide not only the theoretical knowledge you need but also practical insights and strategies to apply this knowledge effectively in real-world scenarios. We've included practice questions, case studies, and real-life examples to bridge the gap between theory and practice, making your learning experience as relevant and engaging as possible.

We understand the road to becoming a licensed social worker is challenging. There will be moments of doubt and hurdles to overcome. That's why this book also serves as a source of encouragement. Remember, every great journey begins with a single step, and by picking up this guide, you've already taken that step. Your dream is not just possible; it's within reach. The effort you put in now will pay dividends for years to come, in the lives you'll touch and the change you'll inspire.

So, let's get started. Together, we'll navigate the breadth of knowledge and practice that defines social work, equipping you with the tools you need to succeed on the exam and beyond. Your journey to becoming a Licensed Master Social Worker begins now, and we're here to guide you every step of the way. Welcome to the first day of your future.

UNDERSTANDING THE FOUNDATION OF SOCIAL WORK:

The history of social work is rich with significant milestones that trace the evolution of the field from its informal beginnings to its establishment as a professional discipline. These developments have profoundly influenced contemporary social work practice, embedding core values, ethics, and methodologies that guide social workers today.

Informal Beginnings

Social work's roots can be traced back to charitable and philanthropic efforts in the 19th century. Early forms of social work were often tied to religious and moral initiatives aimed at alleviating poverty and addressing social injustices. The Industrial Revolution and urbanization created widespread social problems that led to the emergence of organized efforts to help those in need, including the Charity Organization Society (COS) founded in London in 1869, which aimed to coordinate charitable activities and promote self-help among the poor.

Establishment of Settlement Houses

A pivotal milestone was the establishment of settlement houses in the late 19th and early 20th centuries, such as Toynbee Hall in London (1884) and Hull House in Chicago (1889), founded by Jane Addams and Ellen Gates Starr. These community-based centers aimed to improve social conditions in urban areas by providing education, recreational activities, and social services. Settlement houses played a crucial role in the development of social work by emphasizing direct community involvement and advocating for social reform.

Professionalization and Education

The early 20th century saw efforts to professionalize social work, marked by the establishment of formal social work education. In 1898, Columbia University offered the first social work training program. The establishment of the National Association of Social Workers (NASW) in 1955 further solidified social work's status as a profession, setting ethical standards and promoting continued professional development.

The New Deal and Expansion of Social Services

The Great Depression and the New Deal in the 1930s expanded the role of social workers, as government-funded programs required skilled professionals to administer aid and services. This period underscored the importance of social work in addressing economic and social crises, leading to an expansion of social services and an increased recognition of social work as an essential profession.

Civil Rights Movement and Social Justice

The civil rights movement of the 1960s and subsequent social justice movements greatly influenced social work, emphasizing the profession's commitment to advocacy, equality, and human rights. Social work's ethical foundation in social justice was strengthened during this period, leading to a greater focus on systemic change and empowerment.

Contemporary Social Work Practice

These historical developments have had a lasting impact on contemporary social work practice. Today, social workers are not only involved in individual and family services but also play critical roles in community organizing, policy advocacy, and social reform. The profession's ethical standards, emphasizing respect for all persons, social justice, and professional integrity, trace back to these milestones. Furthermore, the evolution of social work education, with a focus on evidence-based practice and interdisciplinary collaboration, prepares social workers to meet complex social challenges.

The history of social work reflects a dynamic evolution from charitable acts to a professional and academic discipline deeply involved in the fabric of societal well-being. These milestones underscore the profession's resilience, adaptability, and unwavering commitment to social justice and human rights, shaping the principles that guide social workers in their practice today.

The evolution of social work ethics and values is a testament to the profession's responsiveness to changing societal contexts and challenges. This journey, from the profession's informal roots to its current structured ethical frameworks, highlights a continuous effort to align practice with core humanistic values and social justice principles. Understanding this evolution provides insight into contemporary ethical practice and the profession's commitment to serving as a moral compass in addressing human needs and rights.

Early Foundations

The earliest social work activities were inherently ethical, grounded in the desire to alleviate suffering and address social injustices. Rooted in charity and philanthropy, these efforts were guided by moral principles of benevolence and compassion. The settlement house movement, with pioneers like Jane Addams, introduced a commitment to social reform, emphasizing the dignity and worth of every individual and the importance of community and societal wellbeing.

Professionalization and the Codification of Ethics

As social work transitioned into a formal profession, there was a growing recognition of the need for a codified ethical framework to guide practice. The establishment of social work education and professional associations facilitated the development of ethical codes and standards. In 1955, the National Association of Social Workers (NASW) in the United States was formed, and it played a pivotal role in defining social work ethics through the creation of the NASW Code of Ethics. This code articulated the profession's core values, ethical principles, and standards, serving as a guide for ethical decision-making in practice.

Influence of Social Movements

The civil rights movement, feminist movements, and other social justice movements of the 20th century significantly influenced social work ethics. These movements brought to the forefront issues of equality, autonomy, and rights, leading to an expanded emphasis on social justice, empowerment, and advocacy in social work ethics. The profession's commitment to challenging social inequalities and discrimination became more pronounced, reflecting a broader understanding of social work as a vehicle for societal change.

Contemporary Ethical Practice

Today, contemporary ethical practice in social work is characterized by a complex, nuanced understanding of the interplay between individual, community, and societal wellbeing. The current NASW Code of Ethics, with subsequent revisions, reflects this complexity, emphasizing:

- **Respect for diversity and cultural competence**: Recognizing the importance of understanding and respecting cultural differences and working effectively in multicultural contexts.
- **Client self-determination**: Upholding the right of clients to make their own choices and control their own lives, within the bounds of ethical practice.
- **Confidentiality**: Protecting clients' privacy and confidentiality, with a clear understanding of the exceptions and legal obligations that may require disclosure.
- **Professional boundaries**: Maintaining appropriate professional relationships and boundaries to protect the interests of clients.
- **Advocacy and social justice**: Advocating for social change to address social, economic, and environmental injustices that affect clients and communities.

Implications for Contemporary Practice

The evolution of social work ethics and values underscores the profession's adaptability and its proactive stance in responding to societal changes and ethical challenges. Contemporary social workers must navigate complex ethical dilemmas that reflect the intricacies of modern societies, such as technological advances in communication, increased awareness of global interconnectivity, and evolving understandings of identity and human rights. Social workers are expected to engage in continuous ethical reflection, education, and dialogue to navigate these challenges effectively.

The history of social work ethics provides a foundation from which social workers can draw strength and guidance as they confront contemporary issues. It reinforces the profession's commitment to advocating for the vulnerable and marginalized and to upholding the dignity and worth of all individuals. By grounding practice in this rich ethical tradition, social workers continue to play a crucial role in advancing societal wellbeing and justice.

The NASW (National Association of Social Workers) Code of Ethics serves as the foundational ethical framework guiding social work practice. Established to outline the primary mission, values, ethical principles, and ethical standards of the profession, the Code is integral to ensuring social workers conduct themselves in a manner that is both ethical and effective. This in-depth analysis explores the significance of the NASW Code of Ethics across various dimensions of social work practice.

Mission and Core Values

The NASW Code of Ethics begins with a declaration of the profession's primary mission: to enhance human well-being and help meet the basic human needs of all people, with particular attention to the needs and empowerment of people who are vulnerable, oppressed, and living in poverty. Central to this mission are six core values that underpin social work ethics:

1. **Service**: Commitment to helping people in need and addressing social problems.
2. **Social Justice**: Pursuit of social change, particularly for vulnerable and oppressed individuals, to ensure equal rights, opportunities, and social justice.

3. **Dignity and Worth of the Person**: Respect for the inherent dignity and worth of every individual, acknowledging their right to self-determination.
4. **Importance of Human Relationships**: Recognition of the critical importance of human relationships in creating change and enhancing well-being.
5. **Integrity**: Behaving in a trustworthy manner, being honest, and responsible.
6. **Competence**: Practicing within one's areas of expertise and continually developing professional knowledge and skill.

Ethical Principles

Derived from the core values, the Code outlines ethical principles that provide general ethical guidance:

- **Service**: Social workers prioritize service to others over self-interest.
- **Social Justice**: They challenge social injustice, focusing on issues of poverty, unemployment, discrimination, and other forms of social injustice.
- **Dignity and Worth of the Person**: They respect every person's unique qualities and cultural and ethnic diversity.
- **Importance of Human Relationships**: They understand that relationships are an important vehicle for change.
- **Integrity**: They act honestly and responsibly.
- **Competence**: They practice within their areas of expertise and contribute to the knowledge base of the profession.

Ethical Standards

The Code further delineates specific ethical standards, which are detailed rules of conduct that social workers must adhere to. These standards are divided into several sections, addressing social workers' ethical responsibilities to clients, colleagues, in practice settings, as professionals, to the social work profession, and to the broader society. Key standards include confidentiality, informed consent, conflicts of interest, cultural competence, supervision and consultation, public participation, and policy practice.

Significance to Social Work Practice

The NASW Code of Ethics is significant for several reasons:

- **Guidance for Professional Conduct**: It offers comprehensive guidelines for addressing ethical issues and dilemmas in social work practice, ensuring that professionals act in the best interests of their clients and the community.
- **Professional Identity and Unity**: The Code helps define the values and principles that unite social workers, regardless of their specific fields of practice or geographical location, fostering a strong professional identity.
- **Accountability**: By establishing clear ethical standards, the Code holds social workers accountable to the public and their peers, promoting trust in the profession.
- **Educational Tool**: It serves as a foundational document in social work education, helping students and practitioners understand the ethical obligations of their profession.
- **Legal and Organizational Framework**: Although not a legal document, the Code influences legal and organizational policies related to social work, guiding the development of ethical policies within agencies and institutions.

The NASW Code of Ethics is a cornerstone of social work practice, embodying the profession's commitment to integrity, justice, and the dignity of all individuals. It provides a comprehensive framework for navigating the complex ethical challenges that social workers encounter, ensuring that their practice is guided by a deep commitment to serving society and upholding the values that define social work. Through adherence to the Code, social workers affirm their dedication to the ethical principles that underpin their critical role in advancing individual and societal well-being.

Navigating ethical dilemmas and maintaining professional boundaries are central challenges in social work practice, requiring a thoughtful, principled approach. Social workers often encounter complex situations that necessitate careful analysis and decision-making to uphold the profession's ethical standards. Here are strategies to help candidates identify, analyze, and resolve ethical dilemmas, alongside tips for maintaining professional boundaries.

Identifying Ethical Dilemmas

1. **Recognize Conflicting Values or Principles**: Ethical dilemmas often arise when there are conflicts between personal values, the values and ethics of the profession, and legal or organizational policies.
2. **Consult the NASW Code of Ethics**: Familiarity with the Code helps identify whether an issue constitutes an ethical dilemma, based on the profession's established values and principles.
3. **Seek Supervision and Consultation**: When uncertain, seeking advice from supervisors or more experienced colleagues can provide clarity and additional perspectives on the ethical dimensions of a situation.

Analyzing Ethical Dilemmas

1. **Gather All Relevant Information**: Obtain a comprehensive understanding of the situation, including all involved parties' perspectives and the potential consequences of different actions.
2. **Consider the Ethical Principles Involved**: Reflect on the core ethical principles affected by the dilemma, such as client self-determination, confidentiality, and the duty to do no harm.
3. **Use Ethical Decision-Making Models**: Apply structured frameworks or models to systematically analyze the dilemma. Models such as the NASW's Ethical Decision-Making Model guide social workers through considering ethical standards, legal implications, and the potential impact on all stakeholders.

Resolving Ethical Dilemmas

1. **Evaluate Options and Outcomes**: Weigh the potential outcomes of various courses of action, considering which options best uphold the ethical principles at stake.
2. **Make a Decision and Act**: Based on this evaluation, make a decision that aligns with ethical standards and is in the best interest of the client, taking action in a responsible and informed manner.
3. **Reflect and Learn**: After the situation has been resolved, reflect on the decision-making process and the outcome. This reflection is crucial for professional growth and for improving ethical decision-making in future scenarios.

Maintaining Professional Boundaries

1. **Understand Boundaries**: Recognize the importance of professional boundaries in protecting both the client's and the social worker's well-being and the therapeutic relationship.
2. **Be Mindful of Dual Relationships**: Avoid dual relationships that could impair professional judgment or increase the risk of harm to the client. When dual relationships are unavoidable, take steps to protect clients' interests.
3. **Set Clear, Consistent Limits**: From the outset of the client-social worker relationship, establish clear, consistent limits regarding the nature and scope of the professional relationship.
4. **Seek Supervision**: Regular supervision helps social workers navigate complex relationships and scenarios that may pose boundary challenges.
5. **Educate on Boundaries**: It's also essential to educate clients about the purpose and importance of boundaries, fostering a mutual understanding of professional limits.

By employing these strategies, candidates and practicing social workers can navigate ethical dilemmas with confidence and maintain professional boundaries effectively. This approach not only upholds the integrity of the profession but also ensures the delivery of ethical, client-centered care.

CORE CONTENT AREAS:

Understanding major theories of human growth and development across the lifespan is crucial for social work practice. These theories offer frameworks for assessing and interpreting clients' behaviors, experiences, and life stages, enabling social workers to provide more effective and empathetic support. Here's an exploration of several key theories and their relevance to social work.

Psychoanalytic Theories

Freud's Psychosexual Stages: Sigmund Freud proposed that personality develops through five stages of psychosexual development. Each stage is characterized by the erogenous zone that is the focus of the libido. Understanding these stages helps social workers recognize the roots of some behaviors and emotional challenges.

Erik Erikson's Psychosocial Development Theory: Erikson expanded Freud's theories into the psychosocial domain, suggesting that personality develops through eight stages from infancy to adulthood, each characterized by a psychological crisis. This theory is particularly relevant to social work, offering insights into clients' challenges and resilience at different life stages.

Cognitive Development Theories

Jean Piaget's Theory of Cognitive Development: Piaget's theory outlines four stages of cognitive development from infancy to adolescence, emphasizing how children construct an understanding of the world around them at each stage. Social workers can use this theory to gauge children's and adolescents' ability to understand and interact with their environments.

Lev Vygotsky's Sociocultural Theory: Vygotsky emphasized the role of social interaction and culture in cognitive development, introducing the concept of the Zone of Proximal Development (ZPD). This theory underscores the importance of social context in development, guiding social workers in leveraging community and cultural resources to support clients' growth.

Behavioral and Social Learning Theories

B.F. Skinner's Behaviorism: Skinner's theory focuses on observable behaviors and how they're influenced by reinforcement and punishment. Understanding behaviorism allows social workers to apply behavioral modification techniques to help clients change harmful behaviors.

Albert Bandura's Social Learning Theory: Bandura proposed that people learn from one another through observation, imitation, and modeling. This theory highlights the influence of role models and social context, reinforcing the social worker's role in providing positive examples and fostering supportive environments.

Humanistic Theories

Abraham Maslow's Hierarchy of Needs: Maslow's theory posits that humans are motivated by a hierarchy of needs, from basic physiological needs to self-actualization. This framework helps social workers assess what needs must be addressed first to support clients in achieving higher-level growth and fulfillment.

Carl Rogers' Person-Centered Theory: Emphasizing empathy, unconditional positive regard, and congruence in therapeutic relationships, Rogers' theory aligns closely with social work values, guiding practitioners in creating supportive, empowering client relationships.

Ecological Systems Theory

Urie Bronfenbrenner's Ecological Systems Theory: This theory describes individuals' development within the context of systems of relationships that form their environment, structured from immediate settings like family and school to broader social and cultural contexts. It's instrumental for social workers in assessing the various environmental factors affecting clients and in planning interventions that address multiple layers of influence.

Relevance to Social Work Practice

These theories inform social work practice by providing frameworks for understanding clients at different life stages and within the contexts of their environments. They guide assessments, interventions, and the development of empathetic, supportive relationships with clients. By applying these theoretical perspectives, social workers can tailor their approaches to meet clients' specific developmental, cognitive, and emotional needs, facilitating more effective support and advocacy across the lifespan.

The impact of diversity, oppression, and social injustice on the well-being of individuals and communities is profound and multifaceted, influencing mental, emotional, physical, and economic health. Social workers play a critical role in addressing these impacts, leveraging their unique position to advocate for social justice, provide support, and foster empowerment among those affected. Understanding the dynamics of these issues and the strategies for intervention is essential for effective social work practice.

Impact of Diversity, Oppression, and Social Injustice

Mental and Emotional Health: Experiences of discrimination, marginalization, and systemic inequality can lead to increased rates of stress, anxiety, depression, and other mental health challenges. The constant strain of navigating a prejudiced society can result in trauma and a pervasive sense of vulnerability among affected individuals.

Physical Health: There is a well-documented correlation between experiences of oppression and adverse physical health outcomes. This can manifest in higher rates of chronic diseases, such as hypertension and diabetes, partly due to the stress of systemic inequities and limited access to quality healthcare and nutritious food.

Economic Well-being: Oppression and social injustice significantly impact economic opportunities, contributing to poverty, housing instability, and employment discrimination. These economic barriers limit individuals' and communities' ability to access essential resources, further entrenching cycles of disadvantage.

Community Cohesion: Discrimination and injustice can erode the fabric of communities, leading to divisions and a breakdown of social supports. Conversely, communities that experience shared forms of oppression can also develop strong bonds and resilience through shared struggle.

Social Worker's Role

Advocacy: Social workers advocate for policy changes at the local, state, and national levels to address systemic inequality and promote social justice. This can involve lobbying for laws that ensure equal rights, participating in social justice movements, and working to dismantle discriminatory practices in various sectors.

Support and Empowerment: Providing direct support to individuals and communities affected by oppression is a key part of social work. This includes counseling services, crisis intervention, and connecting clients with resources. Empowerment-focused practice encourages clients to discover their strengths and capacities to advocate for themselves and their communities.

Cultural Competence: Social workers must continually strive to understand the diverse cultural backgrounds of the clients they serve. This includes recognizing how culture intersects with experiences of oppression and working to provide services that are respectful, culturally sensitive, and inclusive.

Education and Training: Part of the social worker's role involves educating others about the impacts of oppression and social injustice on individuals and communities. This can extend to clients, other professionals, and the public, fostering a broader understanding of these issues and the need for systemic change.

Community Engagement and Development: Social workers engage in community organizing and development to strengthen community cohesion and resilience. By facilitating community-driven initiatives, social workers help build collective power and support community-based solutions to social injustice.

In addressing diversity, oppression, and social injustice, social workers not only support the well-being of individuals and communities but also contribute to the broader project of building a more equitable and just society. The profession's commitment to social justice mandates a proactive, informed, and compassionate approach to these challenges, embodying the core values and ethical principles of social work.

The ecological systems theory and the person-in-environment (PIE) perspective offer comprehensive frameworks for understanding how individuals' social and psychological functioning is intricately linked to their environmental contexts. These approaches underscore the dynamic interactions between a person and their surroundings, emphasizing that well-being cannot be fully understood without considering the broader environmental influences. This holistic understanding is crucial for guiding social work assessment and intervention.

Ecological Systems Theory

Developed by Urie Bronfenbrenner, the ecological systems theory conceptualizes individuals within a series of nested environmental systems that interact with and influence each other. These systems range from the immediate, like families and schools (microsystem), to the more distant, such as societal attitudes and policies (macrosystem). The theory identifies several key layers:

- **Microsystem**: The immediate settings where individuals spend their lives, including family, school, workplace, and peer group. Direct interactions within these settings profoundly affect a person's development.
- **Mesosystem**: The interconnections between microsystems, such as the relationship between a child's school and their family life.
- **Exosystem**: External environmental settings that indirectly affect the individual, such as a parent's workplace policies or community health services.
- **Macrosystem**: The broader socio-cultural context, including societal norms, laws, and cultural values.
- **Chronosystem**: The dimension of time, reflecting the impact of both life transitions and historical events on individual development.

Person-in-Environment (PIE) Perspective

The PIE perspective in social work focuses on assessing individuals within the context of their social environments. It highlights the importance of understanding a person's interactions with their various social systems and how these systems support or hinder their well-being. The PIE approach is particularly attuned to identifying sources of stress, support, and resilience within an individual's environment, allowing for more targeted interventions.

Guiding Social Work Assessment and Intervention

Assessment: Both the ecological systems theory and the PIE perspective inform social work assessments by encouraging a broad view of the client's life. Social workers gather information not only about clients' psychological and physical health but also about their family dynamics, community connections, workplace conditions, and any relevant societal factors. This comprehensive assessment identifies the multifaceted influences on individuals' well-being.

Intervention: Interventions are designed to address challenges across multiple environmental levels. For example, a social worker might provide individual therapy for psychological issues (microsystem), facilitate a support group to build social connections (mesosystem), advocate for policy changes to improve community health services (exosystem), or engage in community education to shift harmful societal attitudes (macrosystem). The ecological perspective and PIE guide social workers in prioritizing interventions that not only address immediate concerns but also work towards systemic change.

Empowerment and Advocacy: Central to these approaches is the empowerment of clients to navigate their environments more effectively and the advocacy for environmental changes to better support individual and community well-being. Social workers empower clients by developing their skills and capacities, facilitating access to resources, and supporting their engagement with social systems.

By integrating the ecological systems theory and the PIE perspective, social work practice acknowledges the complexity of human development and functioning within the context of environmental systems. This comprehensive approach enables social workers to develop more nuanced assessments and interventions, ultimately supporting individuals in achieving optimal social and psychological functioning.

Comprehensive assessment techniques are pivotal in social work practice, enabling practitioners to develop a holistic understanding of clients' circumstances, strengths, and needs. These assessments guide the planning and implementation of interventions, tailored to support clients effectively. Key comprehensive assessment techniques include the biopsychosocial approach, risk assessments, and needs assessments.

Biopsychosocial Approaches

Overview: The biopsychosocial approach is a holistic method of assessment that considers biological, psychological, and social factors affecting an individual's health and well-being. This model reflects the understanding that well-being is a complex interplay of various dimensions.

Application in Social Work:

- **Biological**: Assesses physical health, genetic vulnerabilities, or biological factors influencing health and behavior. It may involve collaborating with healthcare providers to understand medical conditions and their implications.
- **Psychological**: Evaluates mental health status, emotional well-being, coping mechanisms, and cognitive functions. It includes understanding the client's perceptions, beliefs, and personality traits that influence their psychological health.
- **Social**: Considers the impact of social environments on the individual, including family dynamics, social support networks, community resources, and cultural influences. It assesses the quality of the client's social interactions and their effect on well-being.

Implications: This approach enables social workers to devise interventions that address the multifaceted nature of clients' needs, ensuring a more comprehensive and effective response to their situations.

Risk Assessments

Overview: Risk assessments are specialized evaluations aimed at identifying factors that may pose a threat to an individual's safety or well-being. These include the risk of harm to oneself or others, vulnerability to exploitation, or risk stemming from environmental conditions.

Application in Social Work:

- **Identifying Risk Factors**: Involves gathering information to identify potential risks, such as substance abuse, domestic violence, self-harm, or neglect.
- **Evaluating the Severity and Immediacy of Risk**: Determines the level of threat and the urgency of intervention required.
- **Developing Safety Plans**: Based on the assessment, social workers collaborate with clients and, when appropriate, their families or support systems, to develop safety plans. These plans outline steps to mitigate risks, including accessing emergency services, utilizing support networks, and implementing coping strategies.

Implications: Risk assessments are critical for preventing harm and ensuring the safety and security of clients, especially those who are most vulnerable.

Needs Assessments

Overview: Needs assessments aim to identify the specific needs of individuals or communities to inform the development of targeted, effective services and interventions.

Application in Social Work:

- **Gathering Data on Client Needs**: Involves comprehensive data collection to understand the client's current situation, including health, housing, employment, education, and social support.
- **Prioritizing Needs**: Not all needs can be addressed simultaneously. Prioritization involves determining which needs are most pressing and which interventions could have the most significant impact.
- **Resource Identification**: Identifies resources and services that can meet the identified needs, taking into account availability, accessibility, and suitability for the client or community.

Implications: Needs assessments ensure that interventions are client-centered and resource-efficient, directly addressing the most critical areas to improve clients' quality of life.

These comprehensive assessment techniques are interconnected, often used in combination to provide a thorough understanding of clients' situations. By employing these methods, social workers can develop nuanced, holistic interventions that effectively support clients' well-being and foster positive change in their lives.

Developing effective intervention strategies and treatment plans is a pivotal component of social work practice, requiring a thoughtful, informed approach based on comprehensive assessments. Here's a guide to help candidates navigate this process:

Understanding Comprehensive Assessments

Comprehensive assessments gather detailed information about a client's situation, including their strengths, needs, challenges, and the context of their environment. Effective intervention strategies stem from a deep understanding of these assessments, utilizing the biopsychosocial approach, risk assessments, and needs assessments to inform planning.

Steps for Developing Intervention Strategies and Treatment Plans

1. **Integrate Assessment Findings**: Begin by integrating findings from the comprehensive assessments to construct a holistic picture of the client's situation. Consider biological, psychological, social, and environmental factors that might affect their well-being and capacity for change.
2. **Identify Goals with the Client**: Collaborate with the client to identify short-term and long-term goals. Goals should be SMART (Specific, Measurable, Achievable, Relevant, and Time-bound) and aligned with the client's values, preferences, and cultural background.
3. **Prioritize Needs**: Based on the comprehensive assessment, prioritize the client's needs, focusing first on those that are most pressing or pose a risk to the client's safety or well-being.
4. **Select Appropriate Intervention Strategies**: Choose intervention strategies that are evidence-based and best suited to the client's unique circumstances and goals. This could include psychotherapy, community resources mobilization, advocacy, or other supports. Consider the client's cultural and environmental context when selecting interventions.
5. **Plan for Service Coordination**: Many clients require a range of services to meet their needs fully. Plan for coordination among various service providers, including healthcare professionals, community services, and support groups, to ensure a comprehensive approach.
6. **Develop a Treatment Plan**: Formalize the intervention strategies into a treatment plan. The plan should detail the goals, chosen interventions, responsible parties (including the client and social worker), and timelines. Ensure the plan is flexible to accommodate changes in the client's situation or progress.

7. **Implement the Plan**: Implement the treatment plan, maintaining open communication with the client and any other involved service providers. Monitor the client's progress and adjust the plan as necessary.
8. **Evaluate and Adjust**: Regularly evaluate the effectiveness of the intervention strategies and the client's progress towards their goals. Use feedback from the client, your observations, and any quantitative measures available to make informed adjustments to the plan.

Best Practices for Effective Intervention Strategies

- **Client-Centered Approach**: Keep the client's preferences, goals, and well-being at the center of the intervention planning process.
- **Cultural Competence**: Ensure interventions are culturally appropriate and sensitive to the client's background.
- **Evidence-Based Practices**: Utilize interventions with a strong evidence base, adapting them to the client's unique context.
- **Interdisciplinary Collaboration**: Work collaboratively with other professionals to provide holistic support to the client.
- **Ethical Considerations**: Adhere to social work ethical principles in all stages of intervention planning and implementation.

Effective intervention strategies and treatment plans are dynamic, evolving based on ongoing assessment, client feedback, and progress towards goals. By following these guidelines, candidates can develop the skills necessary to create and implement effective, ethical, and client-centered treatment plans that facilitate positive outcomes for clients.

Incorporating evidence-based practices (EBPs) into intervention planning is pivotal for ensuring the effectiveness and efficacy of social work interventions. EBPs are interventions that have been scientifically tested and proven to produce positive outcomes. The use of such practices is central to contemporary social work, emphasizing the profession's commitment to providing the highest standard of care and ensuring clients receive interventions that are not only ethical but also have a strong likelihood of success.

Foundation in Research

EBPs are grounded in rigorous research and clinical expertise, ensuring that interventions are based on the most current, comprehensive knowledge available. By relying on methods that have been systematically tested and validated, social workers can make informed decisions about client care, reducing the reliance on intuition or outdated practices.

Enhancing Client Outcomes

The primary goal of incorporating EBPs into intervention planning is to enhance client outcomes. When interventions are based on solid evidence, clients are more likely to experience improvements in their well-being, whether the focus is on mental health, behavioral changes, or social functioning. This aligns with the social work mandate to prioritize client welfare and work towards the most effective solutions for client challenges.

Ethical Imperative

The NASW Code of Ethics underscores the importance of competence in social work practice. Using EBPs is part of this ethical mandate, as it ensures social workers are employing the most effective, researched methods available. This adherence to professionalism and competence upholds the integrity of the profession and the trust placed in it by the public and clients alike.

Empowering Practitioners

EBPs empower social workers by providing a framework for understanding complex client issues and identifying effective interventions. This knowledge base aids in the critical evaluation of intervention options, enhancing the practitioner's confidence in their clinical decisions. Furthermore, it facilitates a process of lifelong learning, as EBPs evolve with new research findings, encouraging social workers to stay current with developments in the field.

Facilitating Funding and Support

In many contexts, the use of EBPs can facilitate access to funding and support from governmental and non-governmental organizations. Evidence of effectiveness is often a requirement for funding social services programs, making the integration of EBPs essential for securing resources necessary to deliver high-quality client care.

Strategies for Incorporating EBPs

1. **Continuous Education**: Social workers should engage in ongoing education and professional development to stay informed about emerging EBPs relevant to their areas of practice.
2. **Critical Appraisal**: Develop skills in critically appraising research literature to discern the quality and applicability of studies supporting EBPs.
3. **Client Engagement**: Involve clients in the decision-making process, discussing the evidence supporting potential interventions and considering their preferences and values.
4. **Adaptation and Flexibility**: While EBPs provide a strong foundation, they may need to be adapted to fit the unique cultural, social, and individual context of each client. Flexibility and cultural competence are essential in this process.

The incorporation of evidence-based practices into intervention planning is not merely a recommendation; it is a cornerstone of effective, ethical, and responsible social work practice. By prioritizing EBPs, social workers ensure that their interventions are grounded in the best available evidence, thereby maximizing the potential for positive client outcomes and advancing the profession's commitment to excellence.

Effective direct practice in social work revolves around a core set of skills that enable social workers to engage with clients meaningfully, conduct thorough assessments, implement appropriate interventions, and evaluate outcomes. These skills are critical for fostering positive change and supporting clients through various challenges.

Engagement

Building Rapport: The foundation of effective social work practice is the ability to build rapport with clients. This involves demonstrating empathy, active listening, and genuine concern for the client's well-being. Establishing a trusting relationship enables clients to feel safe and understood, which is crucial for effective collaboration.

Cultural Competence: Understanding and respecting the cultural backgrounds and identities of clients are essential for meaningful engagement. Social workers must be adept at navigating cultural nuances and incorporating culturally responsive approaches into their practice.

Communication Skills: Effective communication, both verbal and non-verbal, is vital in establishing and maintaining engagement with clients. This includes being clear, concise, and using language that is accessible to clients, as well as being an attentive listener.

Assessment

Holistic Understanding: Effective assessment requires a comprehensive approach, considering the biopsychosocial aspects of a client's situation. Social workers must gather information about the client's physical health, psychological well-being, and social environment to understand fully the factors affecting their situation.

Critical Thinking: Social workers must employ critical thinking to analyze the information gathered during the assessment phase. This involves identifying patterns, evaluating the impact of various factors on the client's life, and discerning underlying issues that may need addressing.

Strengths-Based Perspective: A strengths-based perspective focuses on the client's resources, capabilities, and resilience, rather than just problems or deficits. Identifying strengths helps in building client confidence and forming the basis for empowerment and positive change.

Intervention

Evidence-Based Practice: Choosing interventions that are supported by research evidence ensures the likelihood of their effectiveness. Social workers must be knowledgeable about current evidence-based practices relevant to their client's issues and be skilled in applying these practices appropriately.

Creativity and Flexibility: While evidence-based practices provide a foundation, social workers also need to be creative and flexible in their approach. Tailoring interventions to meet the unique needs and circumstances of each client is essential for their success.

Advocacy: Advocacy is a critical skill in social work intervention. Social workers often need to advocate on behalf of their clients to access resources, services, or rights that are essential for their well-being.

Evaluation

Outcome Measurement: Effective evaluation requires the ability to measure outcomes and assess the impact of interventions. This involves selecting appropriate tools and methods to evaluate progress towards goals.

Reflective Practice: Social workers must engage in reflective practice to evaluate the effectiveness of their interventions. This includes self-reflection on one's practice, seeking feedback from clients and colleagues, and being willing to adjust approaches based on outcomes.

Documentation: Accurate and thorough documentation of the assessment, intervention, and evaluation processes is essential. Documentation not only provides a record of the client's journey but also supports accountability and continuous improvement in practice.

Incorporating these essential skills in direct practice enables social workers to provide high-quality, client-centered support. Through ongoing learning and development in these areas, social workers can enhance their effectiveness and make a meaningful difference in the lives of those they serve.

In indirect practice, social workers extend their influence beyond individual and family interventions to address broader societal issues through policy analysis, advocacy, and community organizing. This macro-level practice focuses on creating systemic change to improve social conditions, promote social justice, and ensure that vulnerable populations have access to necessary resources and services. Here's an outline of the roles social workers play in these key indirect practice areas:

Policy Analysis

Understanding and Evaluating Policies: Social workers in policy analysis examine existing policies to understand their impact on social issues, service delivery, and the populations they serve. They evaluate policies for effectiveness, equity, and alignment with social justice principles.

Research and Data Utilization: Utilizing research skills and data analysis, social workers identify gaps in policies and gather evidence to support policy improvements. They contribute to the evidence base that informs policy development and reform.

Policy Development: Social workers actively participate in developing policies at local, state, and national levels. They use their understanding of social issues and service delivery systems to contribute to creating policies that address societal needs and promote well-being.

Advocacy

Individual and Systemic Advocacy: Advocacy efforts can be directed at both individual and systemic levels. Social workers advocate for individuals and groups to access services, rights, and resources, while systemic advocacy focuses on changing laws, policies, and practices that affect larger populations.

Coalition Building: By building coalitions with other organizations, groups, and stakeholders, social workers amplify their advocacy efforts. Coalitions allow for sharing resources, strategies, and influence to achieve common goals.

Public Awareness: Social workers raise public awareness about social issues, injustices, and the need for policy changes. Through campaigns, public speaking, and media engagement, they educate the public and mobilize community support for social change.

Community Organizing

Engagement and Mobilization: Social workers engage and mobilize community members around common issues or goals. They facilitate the process of identifying community needs, strengths, and aspirations, encouraging active participation from community members.

Capacity Building: Social workers assist communities in developing the skills, knowledge, and resources needed to advocate for themselves and effect change. This includes leadership development, organizational skills, and networking.

Sustainable Change: The goal of community organizing is to achieve sustainable change that empowers communities and addresses systemic issues. Social workers support communities in developing strategies for long-term success, ensuring that changes are enduring and self-sustaining.

The Significance of Indirect Practice

The roles social workers play in indirect practice areas are critical to advancing the profession's commitment to social justice and systemic change. Through policy analysis, advocacy, and community organizing, social workers address the root causes of social issues, working towards creating a more equitable and just society. These efforts complement direct practice by ensuring that broader systemic factors that affect individuals' lives are addressed, demonstrating the profession's holistic approach to well-being and social justice.

Indirect practice highlights the versatility of social work, showcasing how skills in analysis, communication, leadership, and collaboration are utilized to effect change at macro levels. Social workers in these roles exemplify the profession's core values, advocating for policies and systems that uphold the dignity and rights of all individuals, particularly those who are marginalized and vulnerable.

Integrating micro, mezzo, and macro practice approaches allows social workers to address the complex and interconnected issues facing individuals and communities comprehensively. This holistic strategy acknowledges that personal problems are often rooted in broader social issues, necessitating interventions at multiple levels. Here's an illustration of how social workers might integrate these approaches to address a hypothetical scenario involving youth homelessness:

Scenario: Youth Homelessness

Youth homelessness is a multifaceted issue that impacts individuals and communities. It can stem from various factors, including family conflict, abuse, systemic poverty, and lack of affordable housing.

Micro-Level Intervention

At the micro level, social workers engage directly with homeless youth, offering individual counseling and support services. They assess each youth's specific needs, which might include mental health support, substance abuse treatment, or assistance with education and job training. By building trust and rapport, social workers help youth address personal challenges and develop skills for independence.

Example: A social worker might work with Alex, a homeless teenager, providing one-on-one counseling to address trauma and developing a personalized plan to help Alex complete their education.

Mezzo-Level Intervention

Mezzo practice focuses on groups, organizations, and communities. In addressing youth homelessness, social workers might develop or participate in programs that offer transitional housing, life skills training, and educational support for homeless youth. They collaborate with schools, non-profit organizations, and community groups to create supportive environments that foster youth development and resilience.

Example: The social worker could establish a support group for homeless youth within a community center, providing a space for social support, life skills workshops, and connections to local resources.

Macro-Level Intervention

Macro practice involves engaging with policies, systems, and societal structures. Social workers advocate for policy changes to address the root causes of youth homelessness, such as poverty, lack of affordable housing, and insufficient mental health services. They might lobby for increased funding for homeless services, advocate for policies that make education and job training more accessible to homeless youth, and work to raise public awareness about the issue.

Example: The social worker might collaborate with a coalition of agencies to advocate for a city ordinance that increases funding for homeless shelters and services targeted at youth.

Integration of Approaches

The integration of micro, mezzo, and macro approaches provides a comprehensive strategy to tackle youth homelessness:

- **Individual Needs and Systemic Change**: While working directly with homeless youth (micro) to address immediate needs and personal development, the social worker simultaneously engages in community programs (mezzo) that broaden the support network for these youth. At the macro level, advocating for systemic changes ensures that the structural issues contributing to homelessness are addressed, potentially preventing future cases.
- **Feedback Loops**: Insights gained from direct practice with individuals (micro) inform advocacy efforts at the macro level, ensuring that policies reflect the real needs of affected youth. Conversely, changes at the macro level, such as improved access to housing or mental health services, directly benefit individuals and groups at the micro and mezzo levels.
- **Collaboration and Coalition Building**: Engaging with community organizations, policymakers, and other stakeholders (mezzo and macro) creates a unified front against youth homelessness, pooling resources and knowledge for greater impact.

Integrating micro, mezzo, and macro practices allows social workers to address not just the symptoms but the root causes of issues like youth homelessness. This comprehensive approach underscores the profession's commitment to individual well-being and social justice, demonstrating the unique value social workers bring to tackling societal challenges.

Building and sustaining effective professional relationships is foundational to social work practice. These relationships, whether with clients, colleagues, or within the broader professional community, are crucial for delivering quality care, facilitating collaboration, and enhancing the overall impact of social interventions. Here are key strategies for developing these essential connections:

With Clients

Establish Trust and Rapport: The bedrock of effective social work relationships is trust. Demonstrate reliability, confidentiality, and respect. Actively listen and show genuine interest in the client's experiences and feelings. Establishing rapport involves being empathetic, consistent, and patient, creating a safe space for clients to share openly.

Clear Communication: Maintain open lines of communication. Be clear about the goals, processes, and limitations of the social work intervention. Use language that is accessible and avoid jargon, ensuring that clients fully understand the information shared.

Cultural Sensitivity and Competence: Acknowledge and respect the cultural backgrounds and identities of clients. Educate yourself about the cultural contexts of your clients and integrate culturally responsive approaches into your practice. Being culturally competent also means being aware of your own biases and how they might impact your work.

Empowerment: Focus on empowering clients by highlighting their strengths and capacities. Encourage self-determination where appropriate, supporting clients in making their own decisions and building their confidence to manage their situations effectively.

With Colleagues

Professional Respect and Courtesy: Treat colleagues with respect and professionalism. Recognize the value of diverse perspectives and skills that different professionals bring to the team. Politeness and respect foster a positive working environment.

Effective Collaboration: Work collaboratively by sharing information, resources, and insights. Participate actively in team meetings, respect different professional roles, and be open to feedback. Collaboration enhances the quality and continuity of client care.

Conflict Resolution: Address conflicts promptly and constructively. Openly discuss issues, listen to others' perspectives, and work towards mutually beneficial solutions. Maintaining professional relationships despite disagreements is crucial for effective teamwork.

Continuous Learning: Engage in lifelong learning and professional development. Share knowledge and experiences with colleagues, contributing to a learning culture within your workplace. Continuous learning promotes professional growth and enhances the collective expertise of the team.

Within the Professional Community

Networking: Build a broad network of professional contacts within the social work field and related disciplines. Attend conferences, workshops, and professional meetings to connect with other professionals. Networking facilitates the exchange of ideas, resources, and support.

Advocacy and Leadership: Take on advocacy and leadership roles within professional associations and the broader social work community. Advocate for policies and practices that advance the profession and improve client outcomes. Leadership roles enhance your professional profile and contribute to the growth of the field.

Ethical Practice: Adhere strictly to the ethical guidelines and professional standards of social work. Ethical practice builds trust, respect, and credibility among clients, colleagues, and within the broader professional community.

Self-Care and Professional Boundaries: Practicing self-care and maintaining professional boundaries are essential for sustaining long-term professional relationships. Manage work-related stress effectively and set clear boundaries to prevent burnout, ensuring you can provide the best possible service to clients and collaborate effectively with colleagues.

Building and sustaining effective professional relationships in social work requires a commitment to ethical practice, continuous learning, and the development of interpersonal skills. These relationships enhance the social worker's ability to make a meaningful difference in the lives of individuals and communities, promoting social well-being and justice.

Identifying potential conflicts of interest and maintaining professionalism in the face of ethical challenges are critical aspects of social work practice. Social workers must navigate complex relationships and decisions, ensuring that their actions are in the best interest of their clients and uphold the integrity of the profession. Here's guidance on recognizing conflicts of interest and strategies for maintaining professionalism.

Identifying Potential Conflicts of Interest

Understanding Conflicts of Interest: A conflict of interest occurs when a social worker's personal, professional, or financial interests could influence or appear to influence their judgment or actions in their professional role. Recognizing these conflicts involves self-awareness and an understanding of the ethical principles that guide social work.

Common Sources of Conflicts: Potential conflicts can arise from various sources, including dual relationships (personal relationships with a client), accepting gifts or favors from clients or service providers, private interests that could affect professional judgment, or situations where the social worker's advocacy roles for different clients conflict.

Regular Self-Assessment: Social workers should engage in ongoing self-assessment and reflection to identify any personal biases, preferences, or situations that may lead to conflicts of interest. Being mindful of how one's actions and decisions might be perceived is crucial in identifying potential conflicts.
Consultation and Supervision: Regular consultation with supervisors or colleagues can help in identifying potential conflicts of interest. Discussing complex cases and ethical dilemmas in supervision or peer consultation provides additional perspectives and guidance.

Maintaining Professionalism

Adherence to Ethical Standards: Familiarity with and adherence to the NASW Code of Ethics or relevant professional ethical standards is fundamental. These standards provide guidance on managing dual relationships, confidentiality, informed consent, and other ethical considerations.

Transparent Communication: If a potential conflict of interest is identified, it should be disclosed to all affected parties as soon as possible. Transparency in acknowledging and addressing conflicts reinforces trust and professionalism.

Establishing Boundaries: Maintaining clear professional boundaries is essential in preventing conflicts of interest. This includes setting limits on relationships with clients, ensuring that personal and professional lives remain separate, and avoiding situations where personal interests could influence professional judgment.

Decision-Making Protocols: Develop and follow decision-making protocols that prioritize clients' interests and welfare. This may include ethical decision-making models that provide a structured approach to evaluating and addressing ethical dilemmas and conflicts of interest.

Documentation: Documenting the process of identifying, disclosing, and managing conflicts of interest is crucial. This documentation can provide a record of the social worker's efforts to address the conflict ethically and transparently.

Seeking Guidance: When facing ethical challenges, seek guidance from ethics committees, professional associations, or legal counsel. These resources can provide advice and support in navigating complex ethical situations.

Professional Development: Engage in continuous professional development focused on ethics and boundary issues. Workshops, training, and education on ethics can enhance social workers' ability to identify and manage conflicts of interest effectively.

By being proactive in identifying potential conflicts of interest and employing strategies to maintain professionalism, social workers can navigate ethical challenges while upholding the core values and principles of the profession. This not only protects the interests of clients but also preserves the integrity and trustworthiness of the social work profession.

Confidentiality, informed consent, and client rights are foundational principles that anchor ethical social work practice. These principles uphold the dignity and autonomy of clients, foster trust, and ensure that social workers' interventions are conducted within an ethical framework that respects individuals' privacy, autonomy, and decision-making capacity. Delving into each principle highlights its centrality to social work ethics and practice.

Confidentiality

Confidentiality refers to the obligation of social workers to protect private information shared by clients during the course of their professional relationship. It is essential for establishing trust, as clients often share sensitive and personal information with the expectation that it will not be disclosed without their permission.

Key Aspects:

- **Legal and Ethical Boundaries**: Confidentiality is mandated by legal statutes and ethical guidelines. Social workers must be knowledgeable about the laws and regulations governing confidentiality in their jurisdiction and the specific circumstances under which confidentiality might be legally breached, such as imminent risk of harm to the client or others.

- **Transparency**: Clients should be informed about the limits of confidentiality, including the specific situations in which confidential information may need to be disclosed, such as reporting child abuse or threats of violence.

Informed Consent

Informed consent is the process by which clients are fully informed about the services they will receive, the risks and benefits of those services, alternative options, and the right to refuse or withdraw consent at any time. Informed consent respects clients' autonomy and right to make decisions about their own treatment.

Key Aspects:

- **Clarity and Comprehension**: Information provided to clients must be clear, accurate, and presented in a manner that is understandable to them, taking into account language barriers, literacy levels, and cognitive abilities.
- **Voluntariness**: Consent must be given voluntarily, without coercion or undue influence. Social workers must ensure that clients understand they have the right to refuse or withdraw consent without penalty.

Client Rights

Client rights encompass a broad range of entitlements related to autonomy, respect, privacy, and access to services. These rights are fundamental to ethical social work practice and include the right to be treated with dignity and respect, the right to privacy, the right to access one's own records, and the right to receive competent and ethical care.

Key Aspects:

- **Empowerment and Participation**: Clients have the right to be active participants in all aspects of their care, including assessment, planning, and intervention. Social workers empower clients by involving them in decision-making processes and respecting their choices and preferences.
- **Non-discrimination**: Social workers must provide services equitably, without discrimination based on race, ethnicity, gender, sexual orientation, age, religion, or any other characteristic. Ensuring equality of access and treatment is central to client rights.

Centrality to Ethical Practice

Together, these principles form the bedrock of ethical social work practice. They guide social workers in navigating the complexities of their roles with integrity and respect for the inherent worth of every individual. By adhering to these principles, social workers:

- Build and maintain trust with clients, essential for effective helping relationships.
- Protect clients' autonomy and right to self-determination.
- Foster ethical, transparent, and accountable practice.

Social workers must continually engage in self-reflection, education, and consultation to navigate the nuances of confidentiality, informed consent, and client rights, ensuring their practice not only complies with ethical and legal standards but also promotes the well-being and dignity of those they serve.

SPECIALIZED PRACTICE AREAS:

Child welfare systems are complex networks designed to protect children from abuse, neglect, and exploitation, while ensuring their well-being and development. These systems operate at multiple levels, involving local, state, and federal agencies, and are supported by a range of policies, laws, and practices. The role of social workers within these systems is multifaceted, emphasizing the protection, advocacy, and support of children and their families. Below is a comprehensive overview of the structure, function, and the pivotal role of social workers within child welfare systems.

Structure

Child welfare systems typically consist of a variety of components working in concert, including:

- **Government Agencies**: At the federal level, agencies like the Administration for Children and Families (ACF) provide guidance, funding, and standards. State and local child protective services (CPS) agencies are responsible for the direct implementation of child welfare services.
- **Legal and Judicial Systems**: Courts play a critical role in decisions related to child custody, placement, and the termination of parental rights. Family courts, juvenile courts, and specialized child welfare courts are integral to the legal framework protecting children.
- **Community-Based Services**: Non-profit organizations, community groups, and foster care providers offer support services such as foster care, adoption services, family preservation programs, and counseling.

Function

The primary functions of child welfare systems include:

- **Investigation of Abuse and Neglect**: CPS agencies are responsible for investigating reports of child abuse and neglect. This involves assessing the child's immediate safety, the risk of future harm, and the needs of the child and family.
- **Protection and Placement**: When necessary, child welfare agencies take steps to protect children from harm. This may involve removing children from their homes and placing them in foster care, kinship care, or residential treatment facilities.
- **Family Support and Reunification**: Many child welfare efforts focus on supporting families to resolve issues that led to intervention. The goal is often to reunify children with their families whenever it is safe to do so.
- **Permanent Placement**: When reunification is not possible or safe, child welfare systems seek permanent placements for children, including adoption or guardianship arrangements.

Role of Social Workers

Social workers are central to the operation and efficacy of child welfare systems. Their roles include:

- **Assessment and Investigation**: Social workers assess reports of abuse and neglect, conducting home visits and interviews to determine the safety and well-being of children.
- **Case Management**: They develop and implement case plans tailored to the needs of the child and family, coordinating a range of services aimed at addressing issues of abuse, neglect, and family dysfunction.
- **Advocacy**: Social workers advocate for the rights and needs of children within the child welfare system, the legal system, and the broader community. They work to ensure that children have access to necessary services and that their best interests are represented in legal proceedings.
- **Support and Counseling**: Providing emotional support and counseling to children and families affected by abuse, neglect, or the child welfare process itself is a crucial role of social workers. They help families access resources, improve parenting skills, and resolve conflicts.
- **Foster Care and Adoption Services**: Social workers recruit, train, and support foster and adoptive families, ensuring that children placed in these homes receive appropriate care. They also facilitate the process of adoption when it becomes the goal for permanency.

Social workers within child welfare systems embody a commitment to child safety, family support, and the promotion of positive outcomes for vulnerable children. Their work is characterized by ethical practice, cultural competence, and a deep understanding of the dynamics affecting children and families in crisis.

Through their dedicated efforts, social workers play an indispensable role in protecting children and fostering environments where they can thrive.

Family dynamics are intricate systems of relationships and interactions influenced by various factors, including individual personalities, cultural backgrounds, socioeconomic status, and life experiences. These dynamics significantly impact the well-being of family members and their ability to cope with challenges. Social workers play a critical role in supporting families through the application of tailored intervention strategies that address complex family dynamics and promote well-being. Understanding these complexities and effectively intervening requires a multifaceted approach.

Understanding Family Dynamics

Family dynamics are shaped by numerous factors:

- **Roles and Relationships**: Each family member plays specific roles that may evolve over time. Understanding these roles and how they impact family interactions is crucial.
- **Communication Patterns**: Communication styles within a family can either facilitate understanding and cohesion or lead to misunderstandings and conflict.
- **Boundaries**: Healthy family dynamics often involve clear but flexible boundaries that respect individuals' autonomy while maintaining closeness and support.
- **Cultural and Societal Influences**: Families are influenced by their cultural backgrounds and societal norms, which shape their values, traditions, and coping mechanisms.

Challenges in Family Dynamics

Families may face various challenges that disrupt their dynamics and overall well-being:

- **Transitional Life Events**: Events like births, deaths, marriages, or divorces can significantly alter family dynamics and roles.
- **Mental Health Issues**: A family member's mental health challenges can affect the entire family system, requiring adjustments and coping strategies.
- **Substance Abuse**: Substance abuse can lead to a breakdown in communication, trust, and role fulfillment within the family.
- **Economic Stress**: Financial difficulties can strain family relationships, often leading to stress, conflict, and changes in family roles.

Intervention Strategies

Social workers employ various intervention strategies to support families in addressing challenges and promoting well-being:

- **Family Therapy**: This involves engaging the entire family in therapy sessions to improve communication, resolve conflicts, and change dysfunctional patterns. Techniques may vary depending on the therapeutic model, such as structural family therapy, which focuses on restructuring the family system.
- **Strengths-Based Approach**: Emphasizing the strengths and resources of a family empowers them to overcome challenges. This approach builds on existing family competencies and supports resilience.
- **Parenting Education**: Providing parents with skills and knowledge on effective parenting techniques can help improve family dynamics, especially in managing behavioral issues or navigating developmental stages.
- **Support Groups**: Facilitating or connecting families with support groups allows them to share experiences, receive peer support, and learn from others facing similar challenges.
- **Cultural Competence**: Tailoring interventions to respect and integrate families' cultural values and traditions is essential for effective support. Understanding cultural norms around family structure, communication, and problem-solving is crucial.

- **Collaboration with Other Services**: Many families may require comprehensive support that spans beyond psychosocial interventions. Collaborating with educational, medical, and financial services ensures a holistic approach to addressing the family's needs.

Best Practices

- **Holistic Assessment**: Conduct comprehensive assessments that consider all aspects influencing family dynamics, including individual needs, environmental factors, and social supports.
- **Client-Centered Planning**: Involve family members in developing intervention plans to ensure they are tailored to the family's specific needs and goals.
- **Confidentiality and Ethics**: Maintain ethical standards and confidentiality, especially when working with multiple family members, to build trust and support effective interventions.
- **Ongoing Evaluation**: Continuously evaluate the effectiveness of interventions, adjusting strategies as needed to meet the evolving needs of the family.

Supporting families in navigating the complexities of their dynamics requires sensitivity, creativity, and a deep understanding of the factors that influence family interactions. By applying targeted intervention strategies, social workers can help families address challenges, strengthen relationships, and promote a nurturing environment that supports the well-being of all family members.

Understanding common mental health disorders, their symptoms, and the available treatment modalities is crucial for social workers to provide comprehensive support to clients. Below is an overview designed to equip candidates with essential knowledge in this area.

Common Mental Health Disorders

1. **Depression**: Characterized by persistent sadness, loss of interest in activities, feelings of hopelessness, changes in appetite or weight, sleep disturbances, and sometimes thoughts of suicide.
2. **Anxiety Disorders**: Includes generalized anxiety disorder (GAD), panic disorder, social anxiety disorder, and specific phobias. Symptoms include excessive worry, restlessness, difficulty concentrating, and physical symptoms like rapid heartbeat and dizziness.
3. **Bipolar Disorder**: Marked by extreme mood swings that include emotional highs (mania or hypomania) and lows (depression), changes in sleep patterns, activity levels, and behavior.
4. **Schizophrenia**: A disorder that affects a person's ability to think, feel, and behave clearly. Symptoms include delusions, hallucinations, disorganized thinking, and reduced social engagement.
5. **Post-Traumatic Stress Disorder (PTSD)**: Can develop after exposure to a traumatic event. Symptoms include flashbacks, severe anxiety, nightmares, and uncontrollable thoughts about the event.
6. **Obsessive-Compulsive Disorder (OCD)**: Characterized by unwanted and intrusive thoughts (obsessions) and repetitive behaviors (compulsions) the person feels driven to perform.
7. **Eating Disorders**: Including anorexia nervosa, bulimia nervosa, and binge-eating disorder. Symptoms vary but revolve around severe disturbances in eating behaviors and related thoughts and emotions.

Treatment Modalities

1. **Psychotherapy**:
    - **Cognitive Behavioral Therapy (CBT)**: Focuses on identifying and changing negative thought patterns and behaviors.
    - **Dialectical Behavior Therapy (DBT)**: A form of CBT that teaches mindfulness, emotional regulation, distress tolerance, and interpersonal effectiveness.

- **Psychodynamic Therapy**: Explores unconscious patterns and past experiences to understand present behavior.
- **Family Therapy**: Addresses family dynamics and improves communication to support the individual's mental health.

2. **Medication**: Often used in combination with psychotherapy for disorders such as depression, bipolar disorder, and schizophrenia. Common types include antidepressants, anti-anxiety medications, mood stabilizers, and antipsychotics.
3. **Support Groups**: Provide a space for individuals to share experiences, offer mutual support, and learn coping strategies in a group setting.
4. **Lifestyle Modifications**: Encouraging healthy habits such as regular physical activity, adequate sleep, a nutritious diet, and stress management techniques can support mental health treatment.
5. **Integrated Care**: Combines psychiatric and medical treatment, especially important for individuals with co-occurring mental and physical health conditions.

Social Workers' Role

- **Assessment**: Conduct comprehensive assessments to identify mental health needs, including the use of standardized tools and clinical interviews.
- **Referral**: Facilitate access to mental health professionals for diagnosis and treatment, understanding when to refer to psychiatrists, psychologists, or specialized therapists.
- **Advocacy**: Advocate for clients to ensure they receive appropriate services, including navigating healthcare systems and addressing barriers to care.
- **Support and Education**: Provide psychoeducation to clients and families about mental health conditions and treatment options, enhancing understanding and coping strategies.
- **Case Management**: Coordinate care across different providers and services, ensuring a holistic approach to treatment and support.

Empowering social work candidates with knowledge about common mental health disorders and treatment modalities enhances their ability to support clients effectively. By integrating this knowledge with their practice, social workers can contribute significantly to the mental and emotional well-being of those they serve.

Substance abuse, encompassing a range of issues related to the misuse of alcohol, drugs, and other substances, presents significant challenges for individuals, families, and communities. Effective assessment and intervention require a nuanced understanding of the complexities involved, utilizing evidence-based practices to support recovery and well-being. Here's a comprehensive overview of techniques and strategies in this crucial area of social work practice.

Substance Abuse Assessment Techniques

Assessment in substance abuse is multifaceted, aiming to understand the extent of substance use, its impact on the individual's life, and any co-occurring disorders that may need to be addressed. Key assessment techniques include:

1. **Structured Interviews**: Utilizing standardized instruments such as the Addiction Severity Index (ASI) or the Substance Abuse Subtle Screening Inventory (SASSI) to gather comprehensive information on substance use and its consequences.
2. **Screening Tools**: Brief tools like the Alcohol Use Disorders Identification Test (AUDIT) or the Drug Abuse Screening Test (DAST) help quickly identify individuals who may require a more thorough assessment or immediate intervention.
3. **Biological Testing**: Urine, blood, hair, or breath tests can provide objective data on recent substance use, though results should be interpreted in the context of clinical findings and self-reports.

4. **Psychosocial Assessment**: Exploring the individual's history, mental health status, family dynamics, social supports, and any environmental factors that contribute to or mitigate substance use.
5. **Co-occurring Disorders Assessment**: Since substance abuse often co-occurs with mental health conditions, it's vital to assess for disorders such as depression, anxiety, or PTSD, which may require integrated treatment.

Intervention Strategies

Effective interventions for substance abuse draw on a range of evidence-based practices tailored to the individual's needs, preferences, and circumstances. Key strategies include:

1. **Cognitive Behavioral Therapy (CBT)**: Helps individuals recognize and change maladaptive thought patterns and behaviors related to substance use, developing coping strategies to deal with triggers and cravings.
2. **Motivational Interviewing (MI)**: A client-centered approach that enhances motivation to change by exploring ambivalence and supporting self-efficacy. MI is particularly effective in the early stages of addressing substance abuse.
3. **Medication-Assisted Treatment (MAT)**: Combines behavioral therapy with medications to treat substance use disorders, particularly effective for opioid, alcohol, and nicotine dependence. Common medications include methadone, buprenorphine, and naltrexone.
4. **Contingency Management (CM)**: Involves providing tangible rewards to reinforce positive behaviors such as abstinence. CM has shown effectiveness, especially in treating stimulant use disorders.
5. **12-Step Facilitation Therapy**: Encourages participation in self-help groups like Alcoholics Anonymous (AA) or Narcotics Anonymous (NA), promoting abstinence and recovery through a structured program.
6. **Family Therapy**: Addresses substance abuse within the context of family dynamics, improving communication, and supporting recovery as a shared goal.
7. **Dual Diagnosis Treatment**: For individuals with co-occurring substance use and mental health disorders, integrated treatment approaches that address both conditions simultaneously are critical for effective care.

Social Workers' Role

Social workers play a pivotal role in both the assessment and treatment of substance abuse, including:

- **Conducting Comprehensive Assessments**: Utilizing a combination of interviews, screening tools, and psychosocial assessments to understand the scope of the substance use disorder and related issues.
- **Developing Treatment Plans**: Collaborating with clients to create individualized treatment plans that incorporate appropriate intervention strategies, with an emphasis on client strengths and resources.
- **Facilitating Referrals and Access to Services**: Connecting clients with specialized treatment services, support groups, and community resources to support their recovery journey.
- **Providing Ongoing Support**: Offering counseling, support, and advocacy throughout the treatment process, including addressing any barriers to care and supporting relapse prevention efforts.

Incorporating evidence-based practices in the assessment and intervention of substance abuse is essential for promoting recovery and enhancing the well-being of individuals affected by substance use disorders. Social workers, with their holistic and client-centered approach, are uniquely positioned to provide comprehensive care that addresses the multifaceted needs of those they serve.

Social workers in healthcare settings play a vital and diverse role, bridging clinical care and social support to address the holistic needs of patients. Their work spans various domains, including direct patient care, advocacy, discharge planning, and coordination of care, among others. By addressing the psychosocial determinants of health, social workers significantly impact patient care, outcomes, and well-being. Below is an outline of their roles and responsibilities, highlighting the breadth of their impact in healthcare settings.

Direct Patient Care

1. **Psychosocial Assessments**: Conduct comprehensive assessments to identify patients' psychosocial needs, strengths, and challenges, considering factors like mental health, family dynamics, and social support systems.
2. **Counseling and Support**: Provide emotional support and counseling to patients and families dealing with chronic illness, terminal diagnoses, and other health-related stressors, facilitating coping and adaptation.
3. **Crisis Intervention**: Respond to crises by providing immediate support, assessment, and intervention to patients and families in acute distress, often related to diagnoses, patient behaviors, or end-of-life issues.

Care Coordination and Discharge Planning

1. **Interdisciplinary Collaboration**: Work as part of interdisciplinary healthcare teams to ensure that patient care plans are comprehensive, integrating medical and psychosocial care components.
2. **Discharge Planning**: Develop and coordinate discharge plans that ensure safe transitions from hospital to home or other care settings. This includes arranging for necessary community resources, follow-up care, and support services.
3. **Resource Linkage**: Connect patients and families with community resources and services, such as home health care, medical equipment, transportation, and financial assistance programs, to support recovery and well-being.

Advocacy and System Navigation

1. **Patient Advocacy**: Advocate for patients' rights, preferences, and needs within the healthcare system, ensuring that care decisions respect patients' autonomy and values.
2. **System Navigation**: Assist patients and families in navigating complex healthcare systems, helping them understand their healthcare options, insurance benefits, and rights.
3. **Policy Advocacy**: Engage in policy advocacy to address systemic issues in healthcare access, quality, and equity, promoting reforms that improve patient care and outcomes.

Education and Prevention

1. **Patient and Family Education**: Provide education on managing chronic conditions, medication adherence, and preventive health practices, empowering patients to take an active role in their healthcare.
2. **Community Outreach and Education**: Participate in community outreach programs to raise awareness of health issues, preventive care, and available healthcare services, targeting at-risk populations.

Research and Continuous Improvement

1. **Evidence-Based Practice**: Implement and advocate for evidence-based interventions and programs that improve patient care and outcomes, staying informed about the latest research in health and social work.
2. **Quality Improvement**: Participate in quality improvement initiatives to enhance healthcare services and practices, including patient satisfaction, safety, and care coordination efforts.

Ethical and Cultural Competence

1. **Ethical Decision-Making**: Navigate complex ethical dilemmas related to patient care, confidentiality, and end-of-life decisions, guided by professional ethical standards.
2. **Cultural Competence**: Deliver culturally competent care that respects the diverse backgrounds, cultures, and beliefs of patients and families, addressing health disparities and promoting equity.

Social workers in healthcare settings contribute significantly to the holistic care of patients, addressing not only their medical needs but also the psychosocial factors that influence health and well-being. Through their diverse roles and responsibilities, social workers enhance the quality of patient care, support effective healthcare delivery, and advocate for systems that meet the needs of all individuals, particularly the most vulnerable. Their work underscores the critical intersection of health and social support, emphasizing the importance of a comprehensive approach to healthcare.

Social workers play a pivotal role in supporting individuals and families navigating the complexities of chronic illness, disability, and end-of-life care. Their involvement is critical for addressing the multifaceted psychosocial challenges that accompany these experiences, ensuring that clients receive comprehensive support that respects their dignity, preferences, and needs. Here's an exploration of the roles, interventions, and ethical considerations social workers prioritize in these contexts.

Psychosocial Interventions

Holistic Assessments: Social workers conduct thorough assessments to understand the psychosocial impact of chronic illness, disability, or terminal illness on individuals and their families. These assessments consider factors like mental health, family dynamics, social support, financial concerns, and coping mechanisms.

Counseling and Emotional Support: Providing counseling and emotional support is central to helping clients and families manage the psychological and emotional challenges posed by chronic illness, disability, and end-of-life situations. Social workers offer a safe space for expression, facilitating coping strategies, grief counseling, and adjustment processes.

Resource Navigation and Advocacy: Social workers guide clients and families through the healthcare system, helping them access needed services such as home health care, rehabilitation, palliative care, or hospice services. They advocate for the client's needs and rights, ensuring access to quality care and support services.

Advance Care Planning: In end-of-life care, social workers assist individuals and families in making informed decisions about future care preferences, living wills, and durable powers of attorney. They ensure discussions about advance care planning are conducted sensitively, respecting clients' values and wishes.

Family Support and Intervention: Social workers engage families in the care process, offering interventions that promote healthy family dynamics, improve communication, and support family members in their caregiving roles. They facilitate family meetings and provide education on the nature of the illness or disability and its implications.

Support Groups: Facilitating or connecting individuals and families with support groups offers mutual support, shared experiences, and coping strategies. These groups can be disease-specific or focused on broader issues such as caregiving or grief.

Ethical Considerations

Autonomy and Self-Determination: Respecting the autonomy and self-determination of clients, especially in making decisions about their care and end-of-life preferences, is fundamental. Social workers ensure that clients have the information needed to make informed decisions and support clients' rights to direct their own care.

Confidentiality: Maintaining confidentiality is crucial, particularly given the sensitive nature of information shared by clients and families in these contexts. Social workers navigate confidentiality while coordinating care and communicating with healthcare teams.

Cultural Competence: Understanding and respecting the cultural, spiritual, and religious values of clients and their families is essential, especially in end-of-life care. Social workers approach these conversations with sensitivity and openness to diverse beliefs and practices.

Ethical Dilemmas: Social workers often face ethical dilemmas, such as conflicts between a client's wishes and family desires or healthcare team recommendations. Navigating these dilemmas requires a deep understanding of ethical principles, consultation with colleagues, and sometimes, ethical review boards.

Advocacy for Quality of Life: Advocating for interventions and policies that enhance the quality of life for individuals with chronic illnesses, disabilities, and those receiving end-of-life care is a key ethical responsibility. This includes advocating for pain management, palliative care services, and policies that support the rights and dignity of these populations.

Social workers in chronic illness, disability, and end-of-life care settings provide essential psychosocial support and interventions that address the complex needs of clients and their families. By focusing on holistic, client-centered care, and navigating the ethical considerations inherent in these contexts, social workers ensure that clients receive compassionate, comprehensive support through challenging times. Their work underscores the profound impact psychosocial factors have on health, well-being, and the human experience at every stage of life.

PREPARING FOR THE EXAM:

Developing effective study habits and creating optimized study schedules are crucial skills for candidates preparing for exams or engaging in any form of academic or professional learning. These practices enhance the efficiency of study sessions, improve retention, and reduce the stress associated with preparation. Here are strategies to equip candidates with the knowledge to maximize their learning potential.

Understanding Learning Styles

Begin by identifying your learning style—visual, auditory, reading/writing, or kinesthetic—as this will influence the most effective study methods for you. Tailoring study activities to align with your learning style can enhance comprehension and retention.

Setting Clear Objectives

Define clear, achievable goals for each study session to maintain focus and direction. Objectives should be specific, measurable, attainable, relevant, and time-bound (SMART). This approach ensures that study sessions are productive and aligned with overall learning goals.

Developing a Study Schedule

1. **Assessment of Available Time**. Start by assessing your weekly schedule to identify available study times. Be realistic about how much time you can dedicate to studying each day, considering other commitments.
2. **Prioritization**: Prioritize subjects or topics based on their complexity and your level of proficiency. Allocate more time to areas that require additional focus.
3. **Breaks and Downtime**: Schedule short breaks to prevent burnout and enhance retention. The Pomodoro Technique, involving focused study intervals followed by short breaks, can be particularly effective.
4. **Consistency and Routine**: Aim for consistency in your study schedule. Studying at the same times each day can help establish a routine that enhances focus and productivity.
5. **Flexibility**: While consistency is key, your schedule should also allow for some flexibility to accommodate unexpected events or shifts in focus based on progress.

Effective Study Habits

1. **Active Learning**: Engage with the material actively through summarizing, questioning, and teaching concepts to others. Active engagement facilitates deeper understanding and retention.
2. **Variety in Study Techniques**: Incorporate a variety of study techniques, such as flashcards, quizzes, mind maps, and practice tests, to cater to different aspects of learning and maintain interest.
3. **Organization**: Keep study materials organized and accessible. Use notebooks, folders, or digital tools to categorize notes, assignments, and resources by subject or topic.
4. **Healthy Lifestyle Choices**: Adequate sleep, nutrition, and physical activity significantly impact cognitive function and learning efficiency. Ensure these basic needs are met to optimize study effectiveness.
5. **Mindfulness and Stress Management**: Incorporate mindfulness or stress management practices, such as meditation or deep breathing exercises, to maintain mental clarity and focus during study sessions.
6. **Seek Support When Needed**: Don't hesitate to seek clarification or assistance from instructors, peers, or study groups when facing difficulties. Collaborative learning can offer new insights and reinforce understanding.

Regular Review and Adjustment

Regularly review your study progress and adjust your schedule and strategies as needed. Reflection enables you to identify what is working well and areas that require changes, ensuring continuous improvement in your study approach.

Equipping candidates with these strategies not only prepares them for successful exam outcomes but also fosters lifelong learning skills that are valuable in any academic or professional endeavor. By developing effective study habits and a personalized study schedule, learners can navigate their educational journeys with confidence and efficiency.

Effective test-taking strategies and managing exam anxiety are essential skills that can significantly impact performance. Here's a comprehensive guide to navigating exams confidently, focusing on approaches to various question types and tips for anxiety management.

Strategies for Different Types of Exam Questions

Multiple-Choice Questions:

- **Read Carefully**: Read the question and all options thoroughly before answering. Look for keywords and be wary of absolutes like "always" or "never."
- **Eliminate Clearly Wrong Answers**: Narrow down your choices by eliminating options you know are incorrect, increasing your chances if you need to guess.
- **Look for Clues**: Sometimes, one option can give a clue about another. Pay attention to these subtle hints.

True/False Questions:

- **Watch for Qualifiers**: Words like "all," "none," "always," and "never" can often indicate a statement is false, whereas "usually," "often," "sometimes," and "generally" suggest it may be true.
- **Consider Each Part**: If a statement has two parts connected by "and," both must be true for the statement to be true. If one part is false, the entire statement is false.

Short Answer/Essay Questions:

- **Outline Before Writing**: Spend a minute planning your answer. Jot down key points you want to cover to ensure a coherent and comprehensive response.
- **Stay on Topic**: Answer the question directly and avoid veering into unrelated information, no matter how well you know it.

- **Introduction and Conclusion for Essays**: If writing an essay, include a brief introduction that outlines your main points, and a conclusion that wraps up your argument or analysis.

Problem-solving/Mathematical Questions:

- **Show Your Work**: Even if you can do the math in your head, write down your steps. This can help you catch mistakes and is often required for full credit.
- **Review Formulas**: Make sure you understand how and when to use formulas. Familiarize yourself with any formulas provided during the exam or those you're expected to know.

Managing Exam Anxiety

Preparation:

- **Start Early**: Begin your review well in advance of the exam to avoid last-minute cramming, which can exacerbate anxiety.
- **Simulate Exam Conditions**: Practice under exam conditions. Use timed sessions and refrain from using your notes to adjust to the pressure.

Mindfulness and Relaxation Techniques:

- **Deep Breathing**: Practice deep, abdominal breathing before and during the exam to calm your nervous system.
- **Visualization**: Visualize success. Imagine yourself answering questions confidently and calmly.
- **Progressive Muscle Relaxation**: Tense and then relax different muscle groups to release physical tension.

Strategic Approach During the Exam:

- **Read Instructions Carefully**: Take the time to read instructions thoroughly to avoid misunderstandings that could cause anxiety.
- **Tackle Easier Questions First**: Answer questions you're confident about first to build momentum and calm nerves.
- **Budget Your Time**: Keep an eye on the time, but don't obsess over it. If you're stuck on a question, move on and come back to it later if time allows.

Positive Mindset:

- **Affirmations**: Use positive affirmations to bolster your confidence. Remind yourself of your preparation and ability.
- **Avoid Catastrophic Thinking**: Remind yourself that a single exam will not define your future. Focus on doing your best.

Physical Well-being:

- **Sleep Well**: Ensure you get a good night's sleep before the exam. Sleep impacts memory, concentration, and stress levels.
- **Eat and Drink Wisely**: Have a nutritious meal before the exam and stay hydrated to ensure your brain is functioning at its best.

By adopting these test-taking strategies and managing anxiety effectively, candidates can enhance their performance, demonstrating their knowledge and skills more accurately under exam conditions.

Creating a full-length practice exam that mirrors the format, content, and difficulty level of the actual Licensed Master Social Worker (LMSW) exam is an essential step in preparing candidates for the real test. While I can't generate a complete practice exam in this single response, I can guide you through the structure of such an exam and outline types of questions that would be appropriate. This framework can serve as a blueprint for developing comprehensive practice exams.

Exam Structure Overview

The actual LMSW exam typically consists of multiple-choice questions that cover a broad range of topics relevant to social work practice. A full-length practice exam should include 170 questions, mirroring the actual exam structure, with questions distributed across four primary content areas:

1. **Human Development, Diversity, and Behavior in the Environment** (20-25%)
2. **Assessment and Intervention Planning** (20-25%)
3. **Direct and Indirect Practice** (20-25%)
4. **Professional Relationships, Values, and Ethics** (20-25%)

Sample Questions Framework

Below is a framework outlining sample questions for each primary content area, designed to simulate the actual exam's format and challenge level.

Human Development, Diversity, and Behavior in the Environment

1. **Question**: Which theory posits that identity development occurs through the resolution of conflicts across eight stages of life?
    - A) Piaget's stages of cognitive development
    - B) Erikson's psychosocial stages
    - C) Kohlberg's stages of moral development
    - D) Freud's psychosexual stages
    - **Answer**: B) Erikson's psychosocial stages

Assessment and Intervention Planning

2. **Question**: A social worker is conducting an assessment for a client presenting with symptoms of depression. Which of the following is the MOST important for determining the severity of the client's depression?
    - A) Family history of mental illness
    - B) Client's educational background
    - C) Duration and intensity of symptoms
    - D) Client's employment status
    - **Answer**: C) Duration and intensity of symptoms

Direct and Indirect Practice

3. **Question**: In motivational interviewing, expressing empathy and supporting self-efficacy are essential components. Which of the following techniques best demonstrates these principles?
    - A) Advising the client without asking permission
    - B) Arguing against the client's limitations
    - C) Reflective listening
    - D) Establishing authority as an expert
    - **Answer**: C) Reflective listening

Professional Relationships, Values, and Ethics

4. **Question**: A social worker discovers that a colleague has been falsifying client records. According to the NASW Code of Ethics, what is the FIRST action the social worker should take?
    - A) Report the colleague to the licensing board
    - B) Discuss the issue directly with the colleague
    - C) Ignore the behavior, as it's a matter of professional discretion
    - D) Inform the supervisor or employer of the colleague's actions
    - **Answer**: B) Discuss the issue directly with the colleague

Tips for Effective Practice Exam Use

- **Timed Sessions**: Simulate the actual exam environment by timing your practice session. This helps with time management skills.

- **Review Explanations**: After completing the practice exam, review the explanations for both correct and incorrect answers to deepen your understanding.
- **Identify Weak Areas**: Use the results to identify areas where further study is needed, allowing you to focus your preparation more effectively.
- **Repeat Practice**: Taking multiple practice exams can help build confidence and improve test-taking skills over time.

Creating and utilizing a full-length practice exam that accurately reflects the structure and content of the LMSW exam is an invaluable tool for candidates, providing a realistic test-taking experience and helping identify areas for further study and improvement.

Providing detailed explanations for both correct and incorrect answer choices can significantly enhance candidates' learning and understanding. Below, I'll demonstrate this approach using the previously outlined sample questions from the practice exam framework.

Human Development, Diversity, and Behavior in the Environment

1. **Question**: Which theory posits that identity development occurs through the resolution of conflicts across eight stages of life?
    - **Correct Answer**: B) Erikson's psychosocial stages
        - **Explanation**: Erik Erikson's theory of psychosocial development identifies eight stages from infancy to adulthood, each characterized by a specific conflict that contributes to a person's identity development. Successfully resolving these conflicts leads to healthy personality and social relationships. Erikson's model is widely recognized for its emphasis on psychosocial challenges across the lifespan, making it a foundational theory in understanding human development within social work.
    - **Incorrect Choices**:
        - A) Piaget's stages of cognitive development focus on the evolution of cognitive processes from infancy through adolescence, not specifically on identity development.
        - C) Kohlberg's stages of moral development describe the progression of moral reasoning, which, while important, do not encompass the broad spectrum of identity development addressed by Erikson.
        - D) Freud's psychosexual stages concentrate on how personality develops through childhood, with a strong focus on psychosexual conflicts, not the broader psychosocial challenges outlined by Erikson.

Assessment and Intervention Planning

2. **Question**: A social worker is conducting an assessment for a client presenting with symptoms of depression. Which of the following is the MOST important for determining the severity of the client's depression?
    - **Correct Answer**: C) Duration and intensity of symptoms
        - **Explanation**: The duration and intensity of symptoms are critical for assessing the severity of depression, as they provide direct insight into how the disorder impacts the client's daily functioning and overall quality of life. Long-lasting symptoms and those that significantly interfere with personal, social, or occupational areas are indicative of more severe depression. This understanding guides the development of an effective, tailored intervention plan.
    - **Incorrect Choices**:

- A) Family history of mental illness can provide context but does not directly influence the current severity of the client's depression.
- B) The client's educational background might affect coping strategies but is less relevant to assessing symptom severity.
- D) Employment status may reflect some consequences of depression but does not directly determine its severity.

Direct and Indirect Practice

3. **Question**: In motivational interviewing, expressing empathy and supporting self-efficacy are essential components. Which of the following techniques best demonstrates these principles?
    - **Correct Answer**: C) Reflective listening
        - **Explanation**: Reflective listening is a core component of motivational interviewing that demonstrates both empathy and support for self-efficacy. By accurately reflecting back what the client has said, the social worker shows an understanding of the client's perspective and feelings, validating their experience. This technique fosters a supportive environment that encourages clients to express themselves openly and work towards change.
    - **Incorrect Choices**:
        - A) Advising the client without asking permission can undermine self-efficacy by implying the client cannot make their own decisions.
        - B) Arguing against the client's limitations may damage the therapeutic relationship and discourage open communication.
        - D) Establishing authority as an expert does not specifically convey empathy or support for the client's capacity to change, which are central to motivational interviewing.

Professional Relationships, Values, and Ethics

4. **Question**: A social worker discovers that a colleague has been falsifying client records. According to the NASW Code of Ethics, what is the FIRST action the social worker should take?
    - **Correct Answer**: B) Discuss the issue directly with the colleague
        - **Explanation**: The NASW Code of Ethics encourages addressing ethical issues among colleagues by first attempting to resolve the matter directly, if such action is likely to be effective and does not violate any confidentiality rights. This approach respects the dignity and autonomy of the colleague while seeking to correct the behavior. It allows for the possibility of misunderstanding or mistake and emphasizes the profession's commitment to ethical practice and accountability.
    - **Incorrect Choices**:
        - A) Reporting the colleague to the licensing board may be necessary if direct resolution is ineffective, but it is not the first step.
        - C) Ignoring the behavior contradicts the social worker's ethical obligation to uphold integrity and accountability within the profession.
        - D) Informing the supervisor or employer may become necessary if direct discussion with the colleague does not resolve the issue, but it should follow an attempt at direct resolution when appropriate.

These detailed explanations not only clarify why a particular answer is correct but also provide learning opportunities by discussing why the other options are not suitable, enhancing candidates' understanding and application of social work principles and ethics.

Practice Test Questions:

Welcome to the Practice Test section of your Licensed Master Social Worker (LMSW) Exam Prep Study Guide. This carefully curated collection of practice questions is designed to not only assess your knowledge and readiness for the LMSW examination but also to deepen your understanding of social work concepts, theories, and applications. Each question has been meticulously crafted to challenge your critical thinking and application skills, reflecting the depth and breadth of topics you'll encounter on the actual exam.

In this section, we have adopted a unique format where each question is immediately followed by the correct answer and a detailed explanation. This immediate feedback approach is rooted in educational psychology principles that underscore the importance of timely reinforcement in learning. By reviewing the rationale behind each correct answer right away, you'll be able to more effectively bridge gaps in your knowledge, reinforce your learning, and understand the application of various concepts in real-world scenarios.

We encourage you to approach these questions with an open mind and a critical eye. Read each question carefully, consider all possible answers, and then review the explanation provided, even for those questions you answer correctly. This process will not only prepare you for the types of questions you'll face on the exam but also enhance your overall comprehension and application of social work principles. Remember, the goal of this practice test section is not just to test your knowledge, but to enrich your understanding and prepare you comprehensively for your role as a Licensed Master Social Worker. Let's embark on this journey towards not just exam readiness, but towards becoming a more knowledgeable, skilled, and compassionate social worker.

1. A social worker evaluates a family where the youngest child, aged 5, shows significantly higher anxiety when separated from their parents compared to their siblings at the same age. This behavior is most closely aligned with which stage of Erik Erikson's psychosocial development theory?
a. Trust vs. Mistrust
b. Autonomy vs. Shame and Doubt
c. Initiative vs. Guilt
d. Industry vs. Inferiority

Answer: b. Autonomy vs. Shame and Doubt. Explanation: Erikson's stage of Autonomy vs. Shame and Doubt occurs between ages 2 and 4 and involves children learning to be self-sufficient in many activities, including toileting, feeding, and dressing. If a child in this stage is overly criticized or controlled, they may feel inadequate and lack self-esteem, leading to anxiety and dependence. The described behavior of the 5-year-old suggests difficulties navigating this stage, as the anxiety upon separation could reflect unresolved issues of autonomy and shame.

2. During a session, a 14-year-old client discusses their feelings of inferiority when comparing themselves to peers. According to Alfred Adler's Individual Psychology, which fundamental concept is most relevant to addressing the client's concerns?
a. Striving for superiority
b. Inferiority complex
c. Creative self

d. Social interest

Answer: b. Inferiority complex. Explanation: Adler's concept of the inferiority complex involves feelings of low self-esteem and doubts about oneself that arise from comparisons to others. In the therapy context, understanding this concept helps in addressing the client's feelings of inferiority, highlighting the importance of overcoming perceived deficiencies through social connection and personal development, rather than striving for superiority which is more about the motivation driving personal growth and success.

3. A social worker is planning a community program aimed at enhancing resilience among teenagers. Drawing from Urie Bronfenbrenner's Ecological Systems Theory, which of the following would be most effective?
a. Focusing exclusively on individual counseling sessions
b. Enhancing peer support networks within schools
c. Lobbying for statewide educational reform
d. Implementing strict parental controls on technology

Answer: b. Enhancing peer support networks within schools. Explanation: Bronfenbrenner's Ecological Systems Theory emphasizes the importance of various environmental systems in development, including the microsystem, which involves direct environments such as school. Enhancing peer support within schools targets this microsystem, promoting resilience by improving teenagers' immediate social environments and interactions, which is directly aligned with Bronfenbrenner's emphasis on the influence of close interpersonal relationships and settings on individual development.

4. A client in their late adulthood reflects on their life with a sense of fulfillment and accomplishment. According to Erik Erikson's stages of psychosocial development, this reflection is indicative of successful navigation of which stage?
a. Integrity vs. Despair
b. Generativity vs. Stagnation
c. Identity vs. Role Confusion
d. Intimacy vs. Isolation

Answer: a. Integrity vs. Despair. Explanation: Erikson's final stage, Integrity vs. Despair, occurs in late adulthood and involves reflecting on one's life. A sense of fulfillment and accomplishment suggests the individual has achieved integrity, having led a meaningful life. In contrast, those who look back with regret and feel they have unachieved goals enter a state of despair, feeling their life was wasted.

5. In applying Lev Vygotsky's theory of sociocultural development, a social worker should prioritize which aspect when working with a child who is struggling academically?
a. The child's performance on standardized intelligence tests
b. The zone of proximal development (ZPD) for the child
c. Strict behavioral management techniques
d. The child's innate learning capabilities

Answer: b. The zone of proximal development (ZPD) for the child. Explanation: Vygotsky's concept of the ZPD refers to the difference between what a learner can do without help and what they can achieve with guidance and encouragement from a skilled partner. This emphasizes the importance of social interaction in learning, suggesting that focusing on the ZPD allows the social worker to identify and utilize the child's potential for learning in a social context, thereby enhancing academic performance.

6. A social worker observes a child in the playground who is actively engaging with peers, initiating games, and confidently exploring new play equipment. According to Jean Piaget's stages of cognitive development, these behaviors most closely align with which stage?
a. Sensorimotor
b. Preoperational
c. Concrete operational
d. Formal operational

Answer: c. Concrete operational. Explanation: Piaget's Concrete Operational Stage, occurring roughly between the ages of 7 and 11, is marked by the development of logical thinking and the decrease of egocentrism. The child's active engagement and exploration suggest the ability to think logically about concrete events, understand the perspective of others (decreased egocentrism), and apply it to play, characteristic of this stage.

7. Social worker is evaluating the impact of recent factory closures on a small community. Which of the following is likely to be a direct effect of these closures on the community's social systems?
a) Increased participation in local governance and community organizations.
b) Decreased community cohesion due to the loss of shared employment experiences.
c) Improved environmental quality due to reduced industrial activity.
d) Enhanced economic diversification as residents seek new employment opportunities.

Answer: b) Decreased community cohesion due to the loss of shared employment experiences. Explanation: Factory closures in a small community can lead to significant economic strain, which in turn affects social relationships and community cohesion. The loss of shared employment experiences can weaken the social fabric, leading to isolation and reduced community support systems. While environmental quality might improve due to decreased pollution, and some residents may seek new opportunities, the immediate and most directly felt impact is often a decrease in community cohesion.

8. A social worker is assessing the needs of children in a neighborhood characterized by high levels of air pollution. What is an important consideration for developing interventions?
a) Implementing strict disciplinary actions to improve children's behavior.
b) Focusing solely on indoor pollution sources to improve air quality.
c) Addressing potential respiratory health issues that may impact children's overall well-being.
d) Prioritizing educational achievements over health concerns.

Answer: c) Addressing potential respiratory health issues that may impact children's overall well-being. Explanation: In environments with high levels of air pollution, children are at an increased risk of developing respiratory health issues, which can affect their physical health, academic performance, and general well-being. Interventions should prioritize health screenings and treatments for respiratory problems, along with advocating for cleaner air initiatives. This approach acknowledges the critical link between environmental factors and health outcomes.

9. In a community experiencing rapid urbanization, what should a social worker focus on to support families facing housing insecurity?
a) Encouraging families to move to less populated areas.
b) Advocating for sustainable development and affordable housing options.
c) Focusing solely on short-term emergency housing solutions.
d) Increasing reliance on private sector housing developments without subsidies.

Answer: b) Advocating for sustainable development and affordable housing options.
Explanation: Rapid urbanization often leads to housing insecurity, with affordable housing becoming scarce. Social workers should advocate for policies and programs that promote sustainable development and ensure the availability of affordable housing, addressing both immediate and long-term needs of families. This approach tackles the root causes of housing insecurity related to urbanization.

10. A rural community has recently experienced a natural disaster. What is an essential action for a social worker to take to support community resilience?
a) Discouraging community members from participating in recovery efforts.
b) Facilitating access to mental health support and resources for trauma recovery.
c) Focusing exclusively on physical infrastructure rebuilding.
d) Waiting for community members to request assistance before intervening.

Answer: b) Facilitating access to mental health support and resources for trauma recovery.
Explanation: After a natural disaster, addressing the psychological impact on affected individuals and communities is crucial for long-term recovery and resilience. Facilitating access to mental health support helps individuals process trauma, fosters community solidarity, and strengthens resilience. This proactive approach is essential for holistic recovery, beyond just physical rebuilding.

11. When working with a community that has limited access to clean water, what should be the priority of a social worker?
a) Encouraging the community to accept the situation as unchangeable.
b) Advocating for infrastructure improvements to ensure access to clean water.
c) Focusing on unrelated social programs to divert attention from water issues.
d) Advising the community to rely on bottled water for all needs indefinitely.

Answer: b) Advocating for infrastructure improvements to ensure access to clean water.
Explanation: Access to clean water is a fundamental human right and essential for health and well-being. A social worker should prioritize advocacy for infrastructure improvements and sustainable solutions to secure clean water access for the community. This approach addresses a basic need, highlighting the social worker's role in promoting social justice and human rights.

12. In a community affected by high unemployment rates, what intervention could a social worker propose to address the economic and social impacts?
a) Discouraging residents from seeking employment outside the community.
b) Developing job training programs in partnership with local businesses.
c) Ignoring economic factors and focusing only on individual counseling.
d) Promoting the idea that unemployment benefits should be reduced to encourage job seeking.

Answer: b) Developing job training programs in partnership with local businesses.
Explanation: Job training programs that align with the needs of local businesses can provide residents with relevant skills, improving employability and addressing both economic and social impacts of high unemployment. This solution fosters community collaboration and economic revitalization, reflecting a holistic approach to social work practice.

13. A community social worker is addressing the isolation of elderly residents. Which strategy would be most effective?
a) Limiting social interactions to reduce the risk of overstimulation.
b) Establishing a community garden project to encourage social engagement and physical activity.
c) Advising the elderly to use social media exclusively for interactions.
d) Recommending that family members minimize visits to encourage independence.

Answer: b) Establishing a community garden project to encourage social engagement and physical activity.
Explanation: Community garden projects provide a space for social interaction, physical activity, and engagement with nature, which can significantly reduce feelings of isolation among the elderly. This initiative promotes community bonding and improves mental and physical health, illustrating an innovative and holistic approach to addressing isolation.

14. In assessing the impact of a factory's emissions on a local community, what is an important environmental factor for a social worker to consider?
a) The aesthetic appeal of the factory's architecture.
b) The relationship between air quality and respiratory health issues in the community.
c) The impact of factory noise on local wildlife exclusively.
d) The benefits of factory tours for educational purposes.

Answer: b) The relationship between air quality and respiratory health issues in the community.
Explanation: The emissions from factories can significantly impact air quality, which in turn affects the respiratory health of the local population. A social worker assessing the factory's impact should prioritize understanding and addressing these health concerns, advocating for cleaner air initiatives to protect community health.

15. A social worker is developing a program to address food insecurity in a low-income urban neighborhood. What innovative approach could be integrated?
a) Discouraging community involvement in program planning.
b) Initiating a community-supported agriculture (CSA) program to provide fresh produce.
c) Limiting food assistance to non-perishable items to simplify distribution.

d) Focusing exclusively on short-term food drives rather than long-term solutions.

Answer: b) Initiating a community-supported agriculture (CSA) program to provide fresh produce.
Explanation: A CSA program involves community members subscribing to receive regular deliveries of produce from local farmers. This approach addresses food insecurity by ensuring access to fresh, nutritious food while supporting local agriculture. It offers a sustainable, community-centered solution, contrasting with short-term or less holistic approaches.

16. When addressing the effects of climate change on a coastal community's fishing industry, what role can a social worker play?
a) Insisting that climate change is beyond the community's control and discouraging action.
b) Facilitating discussions on diversifying income sources and sustainable fishing practices.
c) Focusing solely on immediate financial aid without considering long-term sustainability.
d) Encouraging reliance on government interventions without community input.

Answer: b) Facilitating discussions on diversifying income sources and sustainable fishing practices.
Explanation: Social workers can support communities affected by climate change by fostering resilience and adaptation. Facilitating discussions on diversification and sustainability helps the community explore new opportunities and practices that can mitigate the impact of climate change on their livelihoods, promoting long-term economic and environmental well-being.

17. When conducting a biopsychosocial assessment of a new client, which aspect is least likely to be relevant for understanding the client's current mental health status?
a) The client's current medication regimen and adherence.
b) The client's history of childhood trauma.
c) The client's educational background and achievements.
d) Recent changes in the client's employment status.

Answer: c) The client's educational background and achievements.
Explanation: While a client's educational background and achievements can provide context about their life experiences and resources, they are generally less directly relevant to assessing current mental health status compared to current medication regimen, history of trauma, and recent life changes such as employment status. Understanding medication adherence and past trauma can offer immediate insights into potential factors affecting mental health, while changes in employment status can indicate stressors or transitions impacting the client's well-being.

18. A social worker is gathering collateral data for a client struggling with substance use. Which source of information is likely to provide the most valuable insight into the client's patterns of substance use?
a) Financial records detailing the client's purchases.
b) Medical records from recent hospitalizations.
c) Observations and concerns from close family members.
d) Academic records from the client's schooling.

Answer: c) Observations and concerns from close family members.
Explanation: Close family members are often able to provide detailed observations and insights into the client's patterns of substance use, including changes in behavior, mood, social interactions, and possible triggers. While financial and medical records can offer objective data on expenditures related to substance use and medical complications arising from it, and academic records might show broader impacts on the client's life, the qualitative data from family observations can be crucial for a comprehensive understanding of the client's substance use.

19. In the assessment of a child with behavioral issues, what information would be most critical to determine the need for further evaluation or intervention?
a) The child's preference in leisure activities.
b) Parental discipline styles and consistency.
c) The child's performance on standardized academic tests.
d) The family's history of mental health issues.

Answer: b) Parental discipline styles and consistency.
Explanation: Understanding parental discipline styles and consistency is crucial in assessing a child with behavioral issues. This information can provide insights into possible environmental factors contributing to the child's behavior. While a family's history of mental health issues may also be relevant, and academic performance can signal distress, the immediate context of parental discipline approaches directly impacts the child's behavior and is essential for developing appropriate interventions.

20. A client presents with symptoms of depression. During the biopsychosocial assessment, which factor would be most important to explore for its potential impact on the client's symptoms?
a) The client's dietary habits and physical health.
b) The number of siblings in the client's family.
c) The client's favorite types of movies and books.
d) The client's proficiency in using technology.

Answer: a) The client's dietary habits and physical health.
Explanation: Dietary habits and physical health have a well-documented impact on symptoms of depression. Poor nutrition can exacerbate depressive symptoms, and physical health issues can both contribute to and worsen depression. While family size, entertainment preferences, and technology use might offer insights into the client's social and leisure activities, they are less directly connected to the client's mental health status than diet and physical health.

21. In evaluating a client for anxiety disorders, which aspect of their biopsychosocial history is least directly relevant?
a) The client's use of caffeine and other stimulants.
b) The client's recent job loss and financial stress.
c) The genres of music the client listens to regularly.
d) A family history of anxiety or other mental health disorders.

Answer: c) The genres of music the client listens to regularly.

Explanation: While the client's preferences in music can reflect aspects of their personality or coping mechanisms, they are generally less directly relevant to evaluating anxiety disorders compared to the use of stimulants, recent significant life stressors like job loss, and a family history of anxiety, all of which have a more established connection to the development or exacerbation of anxiety symptoms.

22. During the intake process with a new client reporting feelings of isolation and loneliness, what biopsychosocial factor would be crucial to assess?
a) The client's recent patterns of social media usage and its impact on their social interactions.
b) The client's favorite genres of literature and film.
c) The frequency of the client's travel for leisure.
d) The client's preferences for indoor versus outdoor activities.

Answer: a) The client's recent patterns of social media usage and its impact on their social interactions.
Explanation: In the context of reported feelings of isolation and loneliness, assessing the client's use of social media is critical. This is because excessive or specific patterns of social media use can significantly affect a person's real-world social interactions, perceptions of social connectedness, and feelings of loneliness. While the other options provide insights into the client's interests and lifestyle, they do not directly address the issue of social isolation in the way that understanding social media habits does.

23. For a client experiencing work-related stress, which component of their biopsychosocial history should be prioritized for immediate exploration?
a) The client's current workplace environment and stressors.
b) The client's high school GPA.
c) The client's vacation patterns over the last five years.
d) The client's history of pet ownership.

Answer: a) The client's current workplace environment and stressors.
Explanation: For a client presenting with work-related stress, understanding the specifics of their current workplace environment and identifiable stressors is paramount. This information directly informs the assessment of the client's stress levels and potential interventions. Other aspects like academic history, vacation patterns, and pet ownership, while potentially relevant to a broader biopsychosocial profile, are less immediately pertinent to addressing work-related stress.

24. In assessing a client who recently immigrated and is experiencing adjustment difficulties, which of the following should be considered most relevant?
a) The client's level of engagement with their cultural community in the new country.
b) The number of languages the client speaks.
c) The client's favorite sports and recreational activities.
d) The size of the client's hometown.

Answer: a) The client's level of engagement with their cultural community in the new country.
Explanation: For a client facing adjustment difficulties following immigration, their level of engagement with their cultural community in the new country can be a critical factor in their overall well-being and adjustment process. This engagement can provide a sense of belonging, support, and connection to

cultural roots, which are important for navigating and adapting to a new environment. The other options, while interesting, are less directly related to the immediate challenges of cultural adjustment and integration.

25. A client comes for assessment due to difficulty coping with a recent diagnosis of a chronic illness. In understanding the biopsychosocial impacts of the diagnosis, what information is critical to gather?
a) The client's understanding and perception of their illness.
b) The client's history of attendance at large social gatherings.
c) The client's favorite methods of relaxation prior to the diagnosis.
d) The client's clothing style and preferences.

Answer: a) The client's understanding and perception of their illness.
Explanation: The client's understanding and perception of their chronic illness are crucial in assessing its biopsychosocial impacts. These perceptions can influence their coping mechanisms, mental health, social interactions, and adherence to treatment. Understanding the client's perspective on their illness allows for a more tailored and effective support plan, addressing both psychological and social dimensions of coping with chronic illness. The other options, while part of a comprehensive biopsychosocial assessment, are less directly relevant to the immediate need to support coping with a new chronic illness diagnosis.

26. In a case where a teenager is showing signs of social withdrawal and academic decline, what biopsychosocial factor would be important to assess first?
a) Changes in the teenager's social relationships and peer group.
b) The teenager's choice of extracurricular activities.
c) The color scheme of the teenager's bedroom.
d) The teenager's dietary preferences and meal times.

Answer: a) Changes in the teenager's social relationships and peer group.
Explanation: In the context of social withdrawal and academic decline, assessing changes in social relationships and peer groups is critical. Peer influences are significant during adolescence, and shifts in these relationships can have profound impacts on social behavior and academic performance. Understanding the nature of these changes can provide insights into potential stressors or issues contributing to the teenager's current difficulties. While lifestyle factors like diet and extracurricular activities are relevant in a comprehensive assessment, immediate investigation into social dynamics is more directly pertinent to the presenting concerns.

27. In a first session with a client who reports feeling "down," what is the MOST critical step for a social worker to ensure an accurate assessment of the client's mental health?
a) Immediately prescribe antidepressants to address the symptoms.
b) Use open-ended questions to explore the client's feelings, behaviors, and life situation.
c) Suggest the client simply take some time off work to feel better.
d) Advise the client to engage in more social activities to improve mood.

Answer: b) Use open-ended questions to explore the client's feelings, behaviors, and life situation.

Explanation: The initial step in accurately assessing a client's mental health involves gathering comprehensive information about the client's feelings, behaviors, life situation, and history. Open-ended questions facilitate a deeper understanding of the client's experiences and symptoms, providing a foundation for accurate diagnosis and effective intervention planning. This approach is foundational in social work assessment, prioritizing client self-report and detailed exploration over immediate interventions or assumptions.

28. When conducting a biopsychosocial assessment, which of the following is NOT typically included?
a) A client's genetic history and any known hereditary conditions.
b) The client's current physical health status and medical history.
c) The client's financial records and spending habits.
d) Information on the client's social supports and relationships.

Answer: c) The client's financial records and spending habits.
Explanation: While a biopsychosocial assessment does consider a wide range of factors that affect a client's well-being, including biological, psychological, and social dimensions, detailed financial records and spending habits are not typically included unless directly relevant to the client's presenting problems or goals. The focus is on understanding the client's overall health, mental state, and social environment, not detailed financial behavior.

29. In evaluating a new client for potential mood disorders, what tool might a social worker use to complement the clinical interview?
a) The Beck Depression Inventory (BDI)
b) A Rorschach inkblot test
c) A Myers-Briggs Type Indicator (MBTI)
d) A polygraph test

Answer: a) The Beck Depression Inventory (BDI)
Explanation: The Beck Depression Inventory (BDI) is a widely used self-report tool that helps in assessing the presence and severity of depressive symptoms, making it a valuable complement to clinical interviews when evaluating for mood disorders. Unlike the other options listed, the BDI is specifically designed to quantify symptoms of depression, providing a structured approach to gather subjective information from the client.

30. What assessment technique is especially useful for understanding a child's world view and emotional state?
a) Structured employment history interview
b) Play therapy techniques
c) Financial audit
d) Medication compliance check

Answer: b) Play therapy techniques
Explanation: Play therapy techniques are particularly useful in assessing children, as they provide a non-threatening way for children to express their experiences, emotions, and world view. Through play,

children can reveal their inner feelings, thoughts, and perceptions, allowing social workers to gain insights into their emotional state and needs. This method is tailored to the developmental level of children, unlike the other options, which are more suited to adult assessments.

31. When assessing a client for anxiety disorders, why is it important to include a review of the client's current medications?
a) Some medications can induce anxiety-like symptoms or exacerbate existing anxiety.
b) All clients with anxiety disorders require medication adjustments.
c) Anxiety is always directly caused by medication non-compliance.
d) Medication reviews are legally required for all social work assessments.

Answer: a) Some medications can induce anxiety-like symptoms or exacerbate existing anxiety.
Explanation: Including a review of the client's current medications in an assessment for anxiety disorders is crucial because some medications can induce or worsen anxiety symptoms. Understanding the client's medication regimen helps in distinguishing between anxiety symptoms that are a direct result of medical conditions or side effects of medications and those stemming from psychological factors, ensuring accurate diagnosis and appropriate treatment planning.

32. For a social worker conducting a risk assessment for suicidality, which factor is generally considered MOST predictive of suicide risk?
a) Personality type
b) History of previous suicide attempts
c) Level of education
d) Income level

Answer: b) History of previous suicide attempts
Explanation: A history of previous suicide attempts is a significant risk factor and is considered the most predictive of future suicide risk during a risk assessment. This information is crucial for developing an appropriate safety plan and intervention. It highlights the importance of thorough risk assessments that include personal history to identify those at highest risk.

33. A social worker is using the DSM-5 for diagnostic purposes. Which of the following is a critical consideration when utilizing this manual?
a) The DSM-5 eliminates the need for clinical judgment in diagnosis.
b) Diagnoses should be made based solely on the number of symptoms present.
c) Cultural context should be considered when applying diagnostic criteria.
d) The DSM-5 is primarily used for billing purposes, not diagnosis.

Answer: c) Cultural context should be considered when applying diagnostic criteria.
Explanation: When using the DSM-5, it's important to consider the cultural context of the client, as cultural factors can influence the presentation and interpretation of symptoms. The DSM-5 includes guidelines for cultural formulation to ensure diagnoses are made within the appropriate cultural and social contexts, recognizing the role of cultural differences in mental health.

34. In assessing a client for potential substance use disorder, which of the following is an essential element to explore?
a) The client's favorite color, as it can indicate substance preference.
b) Patterns of use, including frequency, quantity, and context.
c) The client's political beliefs, as they often influence substance use.
d) Only the client's legal history related to substance use.

Answer: b) Patterns of use, including frequency, quantity, and context.
Explanation: Understanding the patterns of substance use, including how often the client uses the substance, the amount used, and the context in which use occurs, is critical in assessing for a substance use disorder. This information helps in determining the severity and impact of the substance use on the client's life, guiding appropriate intervention strategies.

35. What approach should a social worker take when using standardized assessment tools with clients from diverse cultural backgrounds?
a) Assume that all standardized tools are universally applicable without modification.
b) Modify standardized tools without permission to better fit the cultural context of the client.
c) Utilize standardized tools as is, disregarding any cultural discrepancies noted.
d) Apply standardized tools with cultural sensitivity and consider cultural factors in interpretation.

Answer: d) Apply standardized tools with cultural sensitivity and consider cultural factors in interpretation.
Explanation: When using standardized assessment tools with clients from diverse cultural backgrounds, it's important to apply these tools with cultural sensitivity and be mindful of how cultural factors might influence responses and interpretations. While standardized tools provide valuable data, recognizing and adjusting for cultural nuances ensures more accurate and meaningful assessment outcomes, respecting the client's unique cultural identity.

36. A social worker is assessing a family system's dynamics. Which assessment tool or approach is MOST effective for identifying patterns of interaction within a family?
a) Genogram
b) Financial ledger analysis
c) Single person IQ testing
d) Examination of individual members' dietary habits

Answer: a) Genogram
Explanation: A genogram is a graphic representation of a family tree that provides detailed information about relationships among family members, including patterns of interaction, conflicts, and bonds. It is an effective tool for visualizing family dynamics, generational patterns, and emotional relationships, making it invaluable in assessing and understanding family systems.

37. In developing an intervention plan for a client experiencing severe anxiety, which of the following should be prioritized?
a) Encouraging the client to avoid situations that trigger anxiety.
b) Teaching the client coping strategies for managing anxiety symptoms.

c) Recommending the client immediately start medication before trying other interventions.
d) Advising the client to simply "think positively" to reduce anxiety.

Answer: b) Teaching the client coping strategies for managing anxiety symptoms.
Explanation: Coping strategies empower the client to manage their anxiety symptoms effectively and provide them with tools to address anxiety as it arises. This approach is proactive and equips the client with skills that can improve their quality of life in the long term. Avoiding triggers can sometimes be helpful but doesn't address the underlying issue or help the client develop resilience. Immediate medication might be necessary in some cases but should not be the first line of action without considering non-pharmacological interventions. "Thinking positively" oversimplifies the complexity of anxiety disorders and is not a standalone solution.

38. A social worker is setting goals with a client who has recently been homeless and is now in transitional housing. What should be the initial focus of the goal-setting process?
a) Securing permanent housing
b) Addressing immediate health and safety concerns
c) Finding employment
d) Rebuilding family relationships

Answer: b) Addressing immediate health and safety concerns.
Explanation: The immediate health and safety concerns of a client transitioning from homelessness should be the initial focus to ensure stability and security, which are foundational before achieving other long-term goals. Addressing these concerns lays the groundwork for pursuing permanent housing, employment, and relational goals in a more sustainable and supported manner.

39. For a family struggling with communication issues, what intervention goal is most appropriate to enhance their interaction?
a) Decreasing the frequency of family meetings
b) Increasing the use of social media as a communication tool among family members
c) Encouraging the expression of thoughts and feelings in a structured setting
d) Promoting individual decision-making without family consultation

Answer: c) Encouraging the expression of thoughts and feelings in a structured setting.
Explanation: Encouraging open expression of thoughts and feelings within a structured setting can help improve understanding and empathy among family members, addressing the root of communication issues. This approach fosters a safe environment for all members to share, contributing to healthier communication patterns.

40. When planning interventions for a client with bipolar disorder, which goal is crucial for long-term stability?
a) Ceasing all medications to monitor natural mood fluctuations
b) Implementing a strict daily routine including sleep, meals, and exercise
c) Focusing solely on psychotherapy without considering medication management
d) Encouraging spontaneous activities to increase the client's adaptability

Answer: b) Implementing a strict daily routine including sleep, meals, and exercise.
Explanation: A consistent daily routine, especially regarding sleep, meals, and physical activity, is essential for managing bipolar disorder effectively. Regular schedules can help stabilize mood swings and contribute to overall wellness. Medication and psychotherapy are also important, but without a structured routine, their effectiveness can be compromised.

41. In addressing substance abuse within a family system, what goal should be set for the initial phase of intervention?
a) Immediately finding employment for the family member with substance abuse issues
b) Establishing boundaries and communication guidelines within the family
c) Focusing on past incidents of substance abuse to identify triggers
d) Planning a family vacation to relieve stress

Answer: b) Establishing boundaries and communication guidelines within the family.
Explanation: Establishing clear boundaries and effective communication guidelines is essential in creating a supportive environment for addressing substance abuse. It helps in managing expectations and interactions within the family, providing a stable foundation for further therapeutic interventions.

42. For a client experiencing social isolation due to chronic illness, which intervention goal is most appropriate?
a) Encouraging the client to ignore their limitations and engage in social activities as they did before their illness
b) Facilitating connections with support groups and communities for individuals with similar challenges
c) Advising the client to focus solely on medical treatment and ignore social interactions
d) Recommending relocation to a new city for a fresh start

Answer: b) Facilitating connections with support groups and communities for individuals with similar challenges.
Explanation: Connecting the client with support groups and communities offers a sense of belonging and understanding, which can significantly reduce feelings of isolation. It acknowledges the client's current limitations while promoting social interaction in a supportive environment.

43. When working with a teenager displaying aggressive behavior at school, what should be an immediate goal of the intervention plan?
a) Encouraging the teenager to suppress feelings of anger
b) Identifying triggers and alternative responses to anger
c) Recommending a change of school to avoid current triggers
d) Focusing exclusively on punishment for aggressive behavior

Answer: b) Identifying triggers and alternative responses to anger.
Explanation: Understanding what triggers the teenager's aggressive behavior and exploring alternative, healthier responses can address the root cause of the issue and promote long-term behavioral change. This approach helps the teenager develop coping mechanisms and emotional regulation skills.

44. In planning a community intervention for reducing stigma around mental health, which goal is most important?
a) Decreasing funding for mental health services to focus on self-help strategies
b) Increasing public awareness and education about mental health issues
c) Promoting isolation of individuals with mental health issues to reduce community stress
d) Encouraging families to manage mental health issues privately

Answer: b) Increasing public awareness and education about mental health issues.
Explanation: Increasing awareness and education about mental health can significantly reduce stigma, promoting a more supportive and understanding community environment. This facilitates open discussions about mental health, encourages individuals to seek help, and fosters a collective approach to addressing mental health concerns.

45. For a client dealing with grief after the loss of a spouse, what is a critical goal for the intervention?
a) Encouraging quick emotional recovery to resume daily activities
b) Identifying stages of grief and personal coping mechanisms
c) Avoiding discussions about the deceased to prevent sadness
d) Urging the client to start new relationships immediately

Answer: b) Identifying stages of grief and personal coping mechanisms.
Explanation: Recognizing the individual's stages of grief and identifying personal coping mechanisms allow for a tailored approach to navigating the grieving process. It supports the client in understanding their emotions and finding healthy ways to cope, respecting their unique experience of loss.

46. When working with an organization to improve employee well-being, what should be the primary focus of the intervention?
a) Increasing workload to boost productivity
b) Implementing comprehensive wellness programs that address physical, mental, and social health
c) Discouraging breaks during work to maintain focus
d) Isolating employees with poor performance

Answer: b) Implementing comprehensive wellness programs that address physical, mental, and social health.
Explanation: Wellness programs that encompass physical, mental, and social aspects of health can significantly improve employee well-being, leading to better engagement, satisfaction, and productivity. Focusing on holistic wellness rather than just workload or productivity respects the complex needs of employees and fosters a supportive workplace environment.

47. In the evaluation of a new intervention for reducing adolescent substance abuse within a community, which of the following would be considered a primary outcome measure?
a) The number of community events promoting healthy lifestyles.
b) The reported satisfaction of participants with the intervention activities.
c) Changes in rates of substance abuse among adolescents post-intervention.
d) The total cost of implementing the intervention across the community.

Answer: c) Changes in rates of substance abuse among adolescents post-intervention.
Explanation: In evidence-based practice, the primary outcome measure should directly reflect the intervention's target. For an intervention aimed at reducing adolescent substance abuse, the most direct measure of its effectiveness would be changes in the rates of substance abuse among adolescents post-intervention. This outcome directly assesses whether the intervention met its primary goal, unlike the other options, which measure secondary aspects or indirect outcomes.

48. A social worker is considering integrating a new therapeutic model for treating clients with PTSD. Which action aligns best with evidence-based practice principles before implementation?
a) Adopting the model based on a colleague's recommendation.
b) Reviewing published research studies on the model's effectiveness with similar populations.
c) Implementing the model on a trial-and-error basis to gauge client reaction.
d) Selecting the model based on its popularity in social media forums.

Answer: b) Reviewing published research studies on the model's effectiveness with similar populations.
Explanation: Evidence-based practice involves making clinical decisions based on the best available, current, and relevant research evidence. Before integrating a new therapeutic model, reviewing published research studies on its effectiveness with similar populations ensures that the intervention is grounded in scientific evidence and is likely to be beneficial for clients with PTSD. This approach is systematic and rigorous compared to the more anecdotal or trial-and-error methods.

49. When measuring the outcomes of a program designed to improve employment rates among veterans, which indicator would best reflect the program's success?
a) The number of veterans who attend the program's job fairs.
b) The increase in veterans' self-reported confidence in job interviews.
c) The percentage of program participants who secure employment within six months of completion.
d) Feedback from local employers on the quality of the program's workshops.

Answer: c) The percentage of program participants who secure employment within six months of completion.
Explanation: Outcome evaluation focuses on measuring the results of an intervention to determine its effectiveness. For a program aimed at improving employment rates among veterans, the most direct indicator of success is the percentage of participants who secure employment within a defined period post-completion. This measure directly assesses the program's primary objective, whereas the other options are more indicative of process measures or intermediate outcomes.

50. In a study evaluating the effectiveness of a new social skills training program for children with autism, which type of study design would provide the most robust evidence?
a) A case study of a single participant who completed the program.
b) An opinion survey of parents whose children participated in the program.
c) A randomized controlled trial comparing outcomes with a control group not receiving the intervention.
d) Anecdotal evidence from program instructors on participant improvements.

Answer: c) A randomized controlled trial comparing outcomes with a control group not receiving the intervention.
Explanation: A randomized controlled trial (RCT) is considered the gold standard for evaluating the effectiveness of interventions because it minimizes bias and allows for clear comparisons between the intervention group and a control group. This design provides the most robust evidence of causality between the intervention and the observed outcomes, making it superior to observational or anecdotal evidence for assessing the effectiveness of a social skills training program for children with autism.

51. To evaluate the long-term sustainability of a domestic violence prevention program, which metric would be MOST informative?
a) The initial cost of training facilitators for the program.
b) Participant satisfaction ratings immediately following the program.
c) The number of community partnerships formed as a result of the program.
d) Rates of domestic violence in the community five years after program implementation.

Answer: d) Rates of domestic violence in the community five years after program implementation.
Explanation: Long-term sustainability and effectiveness of a prevention program are best evaluated through outcome measures that reflect the program's ultimate goals. For a domestic violence prevention program, assessing the rates of domestic violence in the community years after implementation provides crucial information on the program's lasting impact, beyond immediate satisfaction or cost metrics.

52. In the process of selecting an evidence-based intervention for adolescent depression, what is a crucial step for ensuring the chosen intervention is appropriate for the specific client population?
a) Choosing the newest intervention available.
b) Ensuring the intervention has been successful in a different age demographic.
c) Confirming the intervention is endorsed by a celebrity or public figure.
d) Assessing the cultural and contextual relevance of the intervention's evidence base to the adolescent population.

Answer: d) Assessing the cultural and contextual relevance of the intervention's evidence base to the adolescent population.
Explanation: For an intervention to be effective, it must be culturally and contextually relevant to the target population. This involves ensuring that the evidence supporting the intervention's effectiveness is applicable to the specific characteristics, needs, and cultural background of the adolescents being treated. This step ensures the intervention is not only evidence-based in general but also likely to be effective for the specific client group in question.

53. A social worker is designing a program evaluation for a new homelessness intervention. What type of data collection method would BEST capture the qualitative impact of the program on participants' lives?
a) Financial audits of program costs.
b) Structured satisfaction surveys with closed-ended questions.
c) In-depth interviews with program participants.
d) Count of the number of participants who complete the program.

Answer: c) In-depth interviews with program participants.
Explanation: In-depth interviews allow for the collection of rich, qualitative data that can capture the nuanced impact of the program on participants' lives, including changes in feelings, perceptions, and personal experiences. This method is particularly suited to understanding the qualitative aspects of program outcomes, providing insights that quantitative methods alone cannot.

54. When implementing a new evidence-based practice, why is it important to engage in continuous outcome evaluation?
a) To ensure the practice does not become outdated over time.
b) To comply with federal regulations requiring annual reporting.
c) To continuously improve the practice based on real-world outcomes and feedback.
d) Solely to attract funding by demonstrating program success.

Answer: c) To continuously improve the practice based on real-world outcomes and feedback.
Explanation: Continuous outcome evaluation is crucial for identifying areas for improvement, assessing the ongoing effectiveness of the practice, and making adjustments based on feedback and outcomes. This iterative process ensures the intervention remains responsive to client needs and maximizes its impact over time, beyond mere compliance or funding concerns.

55. For a social worker evaluating the effectiveness of a peer support group for caregivers of individuals with Alzheimer's disease, which outcome measure is LEAST relevant?
a) Changes in caregivers' reported levels of stress and burden.
b) Caregivers' satisfaction with the support group format and timing.
c) Improvement in the physical health of the individuals with Alzheimer's.
d) Increased knowledge and coping strategies among caregivers.

Answer: c) Improvement in the physical health of the individuals with Alzheimer's.
Explanation: While the physical health of individuals with Alzheimer's is important, it is not a direct outcome measure for evaluating a peer support group aimed at caregivers. The focus of such a group is on the caregivers' well-being, knowledge, and coping strategies, making the physical health of the care recipients less relevant to the group's effectiveness evaluation.

56. A social work researcher is analyzing data from a program designed to improve academic outcomes for high school students at risk of dropping out. Which statistical method would be MOST appropriate for comparing pre- and post-intervention grade point averages (GPAs)?
a) Descriptive statistics to describe the GPAs.
b) A chi-square test to compare categorical variables.
c) A paired t-test to compare means before and after the intervention.
d) A correlation coefficient to determine the relationship between age and GPA.

Answer: c) A paired t-test to compare means before and after the intervention.
Explanation: A paired t-test is appropriate for comparing the means of two related groups (in this case, the same students' GPAs before and after the intervention). This method allows for the assessment of

whether the program had a statistically significant effect on students' academic outcomes, directly addressing the intervention's impact.

57. During a crisis intervention with a client who has just lost their job and is expressing suicidal thoughts, what is the FIRST step a social worker should take?
a) Provide the client with job listings to address the immediate cause of distress.
b) Assess the client's immediate risk of harm to themselves or others.
c) Encourage the client to consider the long-term view and recognize that job loss is temporary.
d) Immediately refer the client to a career counselor to help with job placement.

Answer: b) Assess the client's immediate risk of harm to themselves or others.
Explanation: The first and most critical step in crisis intervention, particularly when a client expresses suicidal thoughts, is to assess the immediate risk of harm. This assessment guides the urgency and nature of subsequent interventions, ensuring the safety of the client, which is the paramount concern in such situations. Addressing the job loss and other concerns comes after ensuring the client's immediate safety.

58. A family is brought to the emergency room after being involved in a severe car accident. As a social worker in the emergency department, what should be your INITIAL focus when interacting with the family?
a) Discussing the long-term psychological impact of the accident.
b) Providing information on legal recourse against the at-fault driver.
c) Assessing the family's immediate emotional and support needs.
d) Recommending long-term therapy options for post-traumatic stress disorder.

Answer: c) Assessing the family's immediate emotional and support needs.
Explanation: In the immediate aftermath of a traumatic event like a severe car accident, the initial focus should be on assessing and addressing the family's immediate emotional and support needs. This approach helps to stabilize the situation and provides a foundation for further interventions, such as long-term psychological support or legal assistance.

59. A client calls a crisis hotline expressing feelings of isolation and depression due to the COVID-19 pandemic. What is the MOST appropriate response from the hotline worker?
a) Suggesting the client simply turn off the news to avoid negative feelings.
b) Acknowledging the client's feelings and exploring coping strategies.
c) Advising the client to ignore their feelings as they are common during pandemics.
d) Immediately directing the client to seek psychiatric medication.

Answer: b) Acknowledging the client's feelings and exploring coping strategies.
Explanation: The most appropriate response involves acknowledging the client's feelings of isolation and depression as valid, and then collaboratively exploring coping strategies. This approach validates the client's experience, supports emotional processing, and empowers the client by focusing on actionable steps they can take to manage their feelings.

60. When working with a community that has experienced a natural disaster, which intervention strategy would be MOST effective for promoting community resilience?
a) Encouraging the community to rely solely on external disaster relief efforts.
b) Focusing on individual therapy for all community members.
c) Organizing community support groups and rebuilding efforts.
d) Advising the community to quickly forget the event and move on.

Answer: c) Organizing community support groups and rebuilding efforts.
Explanation: Organizing community support groups and collaborative rebuilding efforts are effective strategies for promoting community resilience. These interventions foster a sense of community, mutual support, and collective efficacy, which are critical for recovery and resilience in the aftermath of a natural disaster.

61. In the case of a client experiencing a panic attack during a session, what should a social worker do FIRST?
a) Begin an in-depth psychoanalytic assessment.
b) Teach the client advanced relaxation techniques that require weeks of practice.
c) Help the client focus on slow breathing and grounding techniques.
d) Leave the client alone to avoid overwhelming them.

Answer: c) Help the client focus on slow breathing and grounding techniques.
Explanation: The first and immediate response to a client experiencing a panic attack is to help them focus on slow breathing and grounding techniques. These strategies can quickly help reduce the intensity of the panic attack and bring the client back to a calmer state, providing immediate relief and stabilization.

62. A social worker is called to a school after a student reports witnessing domestic violence at home. What is the FIRST action the social worker should take?
a) Informing the student's friends to provide peer support.
b) Conducting a safety assessment to determine if the student is in immediate danger.
c) Advising the student on the importance of family unity.
d) Planning a school assembly to discuss the impacts of domestic violence.

Answer: b) Conducting a safety assessment to determine if the student is in immediate danger.
Explanation: The first and most critical action is to conduct a safety assessment to determine if the student is in immediate danger. Ensuring the student's safety is the paramount concern, guiding further actions and interventions.

63. After a significant community trauma, what strategy should a social worker prioritize to support community healing?
a) Encouraging community members to avoid discussing the trauma.
b) Implementing individual counseling sessions for all community members.
c) Facilitating community debriefing sessions to process the event collectively.
d) Recommending that the community quickly rebuild physical structures without addressing emotional needs.

Answer: c) Facilitating community debriefing sessions to process the event collectively.
Explanation: Facilitating community debriefing sessions allows community members to collectively process the trauma, share experiences, and offer mutual support. This collective processing is crucial for emotional healing and rebuilding a sense of community, fostering resilience and recovery.

64. In an initial response to a crisis call from a person reporting feeling overwhelmed by financial stress, what should the social worker's PRIMARY focus be?
a) Offering immediate solutions to all of the person's financial problems.
b) Validating the person's feelings and exploring immediate coping mechanisms.
c) Recommending that the person consider declaring bankruptcy.
d) Suggesting the person avoid thinking about their financial issues.

Answer: b) Validating the person's feelings and exploring immediate coping mechanisms.
Explanation: The primary focus should be on validating the person's feelings of being overwhelmed and exploring immediate coping mechanisms. This approach acknowledges the person's current emotional state and provides support for managing intense feelings, laying the groundwork for addressing the financial stress more concretely in follow-up interventions.

65. For a social worker assisting a child who has recently witnessed a violent crime, what is the MOST important factor to consider in the intervention plan?
a) Ensuring the child understands the legal implications of the crime.
b) Focusing on immediate, age-appropriate psychological support and stabilization.
c) Encouraging the child to forget the incident and move on as quickly as possible.
d) Involving the child in criminal justice proceedings to ensure justice is served.

Answer: b) Focusing on immediate, age-appropriate psychological support and stabilization.
Explanation: The most important factor is providing immediate, age-appropriate psychological support and stabilization to help the child cope with the trauma of witnessing a violent crime. Ensuring the child's emotional and psychological well-being is the first step in a trauma-informed approach to care, which is critical for the child's recovery and long-term resilience.

66. When responding to an emergency call from a person expressing thoughts of self-harm, what is the critical FIRST step for the social worker?
a) Scheduling an appointment for therapy in the next few weeks.
b) Assessing the immediate risk of self-harm and ensuring the person's safety.
c) Recommending relaxation techniques to distract from these thoughts.
d) Encouraging the person to spend time with friends to improve their mood.

Answer: b) Assessing the immediate risk of self-harm and ensuring the person's safety.
Explanation: The critical first step is to assess the immediate risk of self-harm to ensure the person's safety. This involves determining the level of risk and the need for emergency interventions to protect the individual. Immediate risk assessment is crucial for effectively managing the situation and preventing harm.

67. In a community experiencing a surge in youth violence, a social worker is tasked with designing an intervention. Which approach is most likely to be effective?
a) Implementing a curfew for all community members under the age of 18.
b) Developing a community-based peer mentoring and leadership program for youth.
c) Increasing police patrols and surveillance in areas where youth tend to gather.
d) Advising local schools to suspend students involved in any form of violence immediately.

Answer: b) Developing a community-based peer mentoring and leadership program for youth.
Explanation: A peer mentoring and leadership program addresses the issue at its roots by providing positive role models, fostering a sense of belonging, and empowering youth to contribute positively to their community. This intervention not only aims to reduce violence but also builds life skills and resilience among participants. The other options may only address the symptoms of youth violence without tackling underlying causes, potentially alienating youth further and not contributing to long-term solutions.

68. When working with a client who has recently been diagnosed with HIV, which intervention should a social worker prioritize to support the client's mental health?
a) Encouraging the client to keep the diagnosis a secret to avoid stigma.
b) Providing information on local support groups and counseling services for people living with HIV.
c) Suggesting immediate changes to the client's lifestyle to prevent spreading the virus.
d) Focusing solely on the medical aspects of HIV and avoiding discussion of emotional impacts.

Answer: b) Providing information on local support groups and counseling services for people living with HIV.
Explanation: Access to support groups and counseling services offers the client a network of support and a safe space to explore their feelings, concerns, and the impact of their diagnosis. This approach addresses the emotional and psychological aspects of living with HIV, promoting resilience and mental health. The other options either isolate the client, ignore the importance of emotional well-being, or are overly simplistic in addressing the complex needs of someone newly diagnosed with HIV.

69. For a family struggling with effective communication and frequent conflicts, which technique would be most beneficial to introduce in therapy sessions?
a) Encouraging family members to express grievances without interruption or feedback.
b) Teaching and practicing active listening and validation techniques.
c) Recommending that family members avoid discussing contentious topics.
d) Focusing solely on individual therapy for each family member rather than family therapy.

Answer: b) Teaching and practicing active listening and validation techniques.
Explanation: Active listening and validation are crucial skills in improving communication and reducing conflict within families. These techniques help family members feel heard and understood, which can decrease defensiveness and open pathways to resolving conflicts. Avoiding difficult topics or focusing only on individual issues may leave the underlying family dynamics unaddressed.

70. In addressing workplace burnout within a nonprofit organization, which intervention should a social worker recommend?
a) Increasing the workload for employees to improve productivity.
b) Implementing regular team-building activities and providing mental health days.
c) Advising the management to ignore signs of burnout as they are temporary.
d) Recommending the termination of employees showing signs of burnout.

Answer: b) Implementing regular team-building activities and providing mental health days.
Explanation: Team-building activities can enhance cohesion and morale, while mental health days offer employees time to recharge, both of which are effective strategies in addressing and preventing burnout. Increasing workloads or ignoring signs of burnout can exacerbate the problem, and terminating employees does not address the systemic issue.

71. For an individual experiencing homelessness and seeking employment, which of the following interventions would be most immediately helpful?
a) Advising the individual to apply for high-paying jobs to ensure financial stability.
b) Assisting in creating a resume and providing interview clothing and transportation assistance.
c) Recommending that the individual focus solely on finding housing before seeking employment.
d) Encouraging the individual to relocate to a different city with more job opportunities.

Answer: b) Assisting in creating a resume and providing interview clothing and transportation assistance.
Explanation: Practical assistance with job-seeking tasks, such as resume writing and access to appropriate interview attire and transportation, addresses immediate barriers to employment for individuals experiencing homelessness. This targeted support can significantly impact their ability to secure employment and improve their situation. The other options do not provide direct, actionable support in the job search process.

72. In developing a community intervention for an area with high rates of diabetes, which approach would be most effective?
a) Distributing pamphlets on diabetes to all community members.
b) Organizing comprehensive diabetes education programs and free screenings.
c) Advising community members to avoid all sugars and carbohydrates.
d) Implementing a policy that bans fast food restaurants in the community.

Answer: b) Organizing comprehensive diabetes education programs and free screenings.
Explanation: Education and screenings directly address the lack of awareness and undiagnosed cases, empowering individuals with knowledge and early detection. This approach fosters a proactive community health strategy, unlike the other options, which are less comprehensive or feasible.

73. When working with a child displaying aggressive behavior, what strategy should be prioritized to modify their behavior?
a) Punishing the child every time they display aggression.
b) Identifying triggers and teaching alternative, positive behaviors.
c) Ignoring the behavior in hopes it will disappear on its own.

d) Encouraging the child to watch less television as a solution.

Answer: b) Identifying triggers and teaching alternative, positive behaviors.
Explanation: Understanding what prompts the child's aggressive behavior and teaching them healthier ways to express their feelings or needs can lead to lasting behavioral change. This approach addresses the root cause and provides the child with tools for better self-regulation.

74. For an elderly client experiencing loneliness after the loss of a spouse, which intervention would be most appropriate?
a) Suggesting the client immediately start dating again.
b) Connecting the client with local social activities and bereavement groups.
c) Telling the client that loneliness is a normal part of aging.
d) Encouraging the client to adopt a pet without assessing their capability to care for one.

Answer: b) Connecting the client with local social activities and bereavement groups.
Explanation: Social activities and bereavement groups offer opportunities for connection and shared understanding, addressing the loneliness and grief the client is experiencing. This approach promotes social support and coping in a healthy and structured way.

75. In planning an intervention for a community affected by a natural disaster, which focus is essential for promoting resilience and recovery?
a) Advising the community to forget the event and move forward.
b) Establishing a centralized support system for mental health and resource distribution.
c) Recommending that individuals deal with their trauma privately.
d) Delaying any form of intervention to let the community independently recover.

Answer: b) Establishing a centralized support system for mental health and resource distribution.
Explanation: A centralized support system ensures accessible mental health services and fair distribution of resources, crucial for the community's resilience and recovery. This approach facilitates coordinated care and support, addressing both immediate needs and longer-term recovery efforts.

76. For a client reluctant to engage in social activities due to anxiety, which goal-setting strategy is most appropriate?
a) Forcing the client to attend large social gatherings to overcome their fear.
b) Setting small, achievable goals for social interaction that gradually increase in challenge.
c) Telling the client that their anxiety is irrational and they should ignore it.
d) Recommending the client only engage in online social interactions.

Answer: b) Setting small, achievable goals for social interaction that gradually increase in challenge.
Explanation: Gradual exposure through small, manageable goals can help the client build confidence and reduce anxiety in social situations. This tailored approach respects the client's current state and promotes gradual improvement, unlike the other options, which could exacerbate anxiety or avoid addressing the issue directly.

77. When facilitating a support group for parents of children with ADHD, what should be the primary focus to promote effective parenting strategies?
a) Encouraging parents to use strict discipline to manage their child's behavior.
b) Sharing evidence-based management techniques and fostering a supportive community.
c) Advising parents to seek medication solutions only.
d) Suggesting parents keep their children's ADHD diagnosis private to avoid stigma.

Answer: b) Sharing evidence-based management techniques and fostering a supportive community.
Explanation: Providing parents with evidence-based strategies and creating a supportive community environment can empower them with knowledge and support. This approach enhances their ability to manage their child's ADHD effectively and promotes resilience within the family, contrasting with the less constructive or singular solutions offered in the other options.

78. In developing a comprehensive case management plan for a client with chronic mental health issues, what is the FIRST step a social worker should take?
a) Immediately find a residential treatment facility for the client.
b) Assess the client's needs, strengths, resources, and preferences.
c) Prescribe medication to stabilize the client's symptoms.
d) Isolate the client from potentially stressful social situations.

Answer: b) Assess the client's needs, strengths, resources, and preferences.
Explanation: The first and most critical step in developing a case management plan is conducting a thorough assessment of the client's needs, strengths, resources, and preferences. This comprehensive assessment provides a foundation for all subsequent planning and intervention, ensuring that the case management plan is tailored to the individual client's unique situation and goals. This approach is holistic and client-centered, unlike the other options which either jump to solutions or do not involve the client in the planning process.

79. A social worker is coordinating services for an elderly client who wishes to remain living independently at home but requires assistance with daily activities. Which service option should be prioritized?
a) Immediate placement in a long-term care facility.
b) Enrollment in a meal delivery service and hiring a home health aide.
c) Recommendation for the client to move in with family members.
d) Advising the client to perform all activities unassisted to maintain independence.

Answer: b) Enrollment in a meal delivery service and hiring a home health aide.
Explanation: The priority should be to support the client's wish to remain living independently while ensuring their needs are met safely. Enrolling the client in a meal delivery service and hiring a home health aide addresses both nutritional needs and assistance with daily activities, directly supporting the client's goal of independent living. This option respects the client's preferences and promotes autonomy, unlike the other options that do not prioritize the client's expressed wishes or might compromise safety.

80. When coordinating services for a child with special educational needs, what is a KEY consideration for the social worker?

a) Focusing solely on the child's immediate academic performance.
b) Ensuring that services encompass both educational and social development needs.
c) Limiting the involvement of the child's family to avoid overwhelming them.
d) Recommending the child be educated separately from their peers.

Answer: b) Ensuring that services encompass both educational and social development needs.
Explanation: When working with a child with special educational needs, it is crucial to ensure that coordinated services address both the child's educational requirements and their broader social development needs. A holistic approach that includes support for academic learning, social skills, and emotional well-being is key to fostering the child's overall development. This consideration ensures that interventions are comprehensive, supporting the child in various life aspects, unlike the other options that take a more narrow or exclusionary approach.

81. For a client struggling with substance abuse and legal issues, what is the most important aspect of case management?
a) Advising the client to plead guilty to expedite the legal process.
b) Coordinating a multidisciplinary approach that includes legal assistance, substance abuse treatment, and social support.
c) Focusing exclusively on resolving the legal issues before addressing substance abuse.
d) Encouraging the client to handle legal matters independently to promote responsibility.

Answer: b) Coordinating a multidisciplinary approach that includes legal assistance, substance abuse treatment, and social support.
Explanation: The most effective case management approach for a client with both substance abuse issues and legal problems is a multidisciplinary one that addresses all facets of the client's needs. This includes coordinating legal assistance to navigate the legal system, substance abuse treatment to address the underlying issues, and social support to provide a comprehensive support network. This holistic approach ensures that the client receives coordinated care that addresses both the immediate legal concerns and the root causes of substance abuse, unlike the other options that either focus on one aspect or place undue burden on the client.

82. When managing cases for clients with multiple health care needs, why is it crucial to establish open communication between all service providers?
a) To ensure that the social worker maintains control over all decisions.
b) To prevent clients from manipulating service outcomes.
c) To facilitate coordinated care and avoid service duplication.
d) Because it is a legal requirement in all health care cases.

Answer: c) To facilitate coordinated care and avoid service duplication.
Explanation: Establishing open communication between all service providers involved in a client's care is essential for facilitating coordinated care and avoiding duplication of services. This ensures that each provider is aware of the interventions being made by others, leading to a more seamless, efficient, and effective care plan. Coordinated care is client-centered, focusing on the holistic needs of the client rather

than fragmented or duplicated efforts, unlike the other options that misinterpret the purpose of provider communication.

83. In a case where a family is facing homelessness due to eviction, what should be the social worker's IMMEDIATE action in coordinating services?
a) Recommending the family immediately purchase a new home.
b) Connecting the family with emergency housing services to prevent homelessness.
c) Advising the family to solve the problem on their own to build resilience.
d) Waiting to see if the family's situation improves before taking action.

Answer: b) Connecting the family with emergency housing services to prevent homelessness.
Explanation: The immediate action should be to connect the family with emergency housing services to prevent homelessness and provide stability in a crisis. This intervention addresses the urgent need for shelter, providing a basis from which the family can address other issues such as long-term housing, financial stability, and other related needs. This direct and proactive approach is crucial in crisis situations, unlike the other options that are either unrealistic, neglectful, or counterproductive.

84. For clients transitioning out of homelessness, what is a critical component of successful case management?
a) Ensuring the client never discusses their past experiences of homelessness.
b) Providing comprehensive support that includes housing, employment, and mental health services.
c) Recommending the client move to a different city to start fresh.
d) Focusing solely on obtaining housing without regard for other needs.

Answer: b) Providing comprehensive support that includes housing, employment, and mental health services.
Explanation: Successful case management for clients transitioning out of homelessness involves providing comprehensive support that addresses not just immediate housing needs but also employment assistance and mental health services. This holistic approach ensures that clients have support in all critical areas of their lives, facilitating a sustainable transition out of homelessness. This method recognizes the interconnectedness of these needs, unlike the other options that suggest a more narrow or avoidance-based approach.

85. When a social worker is coordinating care for an older adult with dementia, what factor is paramount in the selection of services?
a) The services' ability to guarantee a cure for dementia.
b) The cost-effectiveness of the services above all other considerations.
c) The alignment of services with the client's and family's goals and preferences.
d) The convenience of the service location for the social worker.

Answer: c) The alignment of services with the client's and family's goals and preferences.
Explanation: In coordinating care for an older adult with dementia, it is paramount that the services align with the client's and family's goals and preferences. This person-centered approach ensures that the care plan respects the client's dignity, values, and wishes, facilitating the most appropriate and effective

support. This focus prioritizes the client's well-being and quality of life over other considerations such as cost, convenience, or the unrealistic expectation of a cure for dementia.

86. In managing a case for a teenager with a history of truancy and substance abuse, what is an essential strategy for the social worker?
a) Immediately removing the teenager from their home environment.
b) Focusing exclusively on punitive measures to correct behavior.
c) Coordinating a support network that includes educational, legal, and therapeutic services.
d) Isolating the teenager from peers to prevent negative influences.

Answer: c) Coordinating a support network that includes educational, legal, and therapeutic services.
Explanation: An essential strategy in managing a case involving a teenager with truancy and substance abuse issues is to coordinate a comprehensive support network. This network should include educational support to address truancy, legal guidance to navigate any judicial concerns, and therapeutic services to tackle substance abuse and underlying issues. This integrated approach offers the teenager multifaceted support, addressing the root causes of the behavior rather than simply imposing punitive measures or isolation, which do not address the underlying problems.

87. For a client with a physical disability seeking employment, what role does a social worker play in coordinating services?
a) Discouraging the client from seeking employment due to their disability.
b) Connecting the client with vocational rehabilitation services and accessible employment opportunities.
c) Recommending the client focus solely on disability benefits rather than employment.
d) Ensuring the client only applies for jobs that do not require accommodations.

Answer: b) Connecting the client with vocational rehabilitation services and accessible employment opportunities.
Explanation: The social worker plays a critical role in empowering the client with a physical disability by connecting them with vocational rehabilitation services and accessible employment opportunities. This approach supports the client's right to work and pursue career goals, facilitating access to resources that can help overcome barriers to employment. It underscores the social worker's role in advocating for inclusion and accessibility, contrary to discouraging employment or focusing solely on disability benefits.

88. In a community facing significant health disparities, which advocacy strategy would be most effective in promoting social justice in healthcare access?
a) Organizing community members to demand luxury health facilities.
b) Lobbying for policies that ensure healthcare access for all, regardless of income.
c) Encouraging individuals to use alternative medicine exclusively.
d) Advising the community to avoid seeking healthcare to protest disparities.

Answer: b) Lobbying for policies that ensure healthcare access for all, regardless of income.
Explanation: Lobbying for inclusive healthcare policies addresses the root cause of health disparities by advocating for systemic change that benefits all community members, especially those disadvantaged by

income. This approach focuses on long-term solutions that promote equity and access, unlike the other options, which do not effectively address the systemic nature of healthcare disparities.

89. When working with a client who is a refugee facing discrimination, which initial action by a social worker best represents advocacy for social justice?
a) Instructing the client to ignore discrimination and focus on assimilation.
b) Providing the client with resources and support to navigate and challenge discrimination.
c) Suggesting the client relocate to a less discriminatory environment.
d) Recommending the client only interact with others from their own cultural background.

Answer: b) Providing the client with resources and support to navigate and challenge discrimination.
Explanation: Offering resources and support empowers the client to address and challenge discrimination directly, fostering resilience and self-advocacy. This approach aligns with social work's commitment to social justice by actively addressing barriers and supporting clients in advocating for their rights and well-being.

90. For a social worker advocating for affordable housing in a city with a high homelessness rate, which strategy would be most impactful?
a) Encouraging homeless individuals to purchase homes.
b) Organizing a media campaign to highlight the effects of homelessness on the community.
c) Suggesting homeless individuals relocate to areas with cheaper living costs.
d) Lobbying for the construction of more luxury condos to increase overall housing stock.

Answer: b) Organizing a media campaign to highlight the effects of homelessness on the community.
Explanation: A media campaign raises public awareness about homelessness, creating pressure on policymakers to address affordable housing. This strategy leverages public opinion to advocate for systemic change, unlike the other options, which do not directly address the issue of affordable housing or misinterpret the systemic nature of homelessness.

91. In addressing racial disparities in school disciplinary actions, which intervention should a social worker prioritize?
a) Implementing stricter disciplinary policies to ensure uniform application.
b) Training school staff on implicit bias and promoting restorative justice practices.
c) Advising minority students to accept disciplinary actions without protest.
d) Encouraging schools to eliminate all forms of disciplinary action.

Answer: b) Training school staff on implicit bias and promoting restorative justice practices.
Explanation: Training on implicit bias and restorative justice addresses the root causes of disparities by promoting fairness and understanding, leading to more equitable treatment of all students. This approach seeks to change systemic issues within school discipline practices, unlike the other options, which do not address the underlying causes of disparities.

92. For a social worker advocating for LGBTQ+ rights in a conservative community, which approach would likely be most effective in promoting understanding and tolerance?

a) Organizing confrontational protests against those with opposing views.
b) Facilitating workshops that educate the community about LGBTQ+ issues and rights.
c) Recommending that LGBTQ+ individuals hide their identity to avoid conflict.
d) Ignoring instances of discrimination to avoid escalating tensions.

Answer: b) Facilitating workshops that educate the community about LGBTQ+ issues and rights.
Explanation: Education through workshops can foster understanding, challenge misconceptions, and promote tolerance in a non-confrontational way. This strategy aims to build bridges and encourage dialogue, which is more likely to lead to lasting change in attitudes and behaviors toward LGBTQ+ individuals.

93. When a social worker identifies a pattern of elder abuse within a nursing home, what should be the first step in advocacy?
a) Advising the elderly to fight back against their abusers.
b) Immediately going to the media to expose the abuse.
c) Reporting the abuse to the appropriate authorities and following up on the investigation.
d) Suggesting that all residents move out of the facility.

Answer: c) Reporting the abuse to the appropriate authorities and following up on the investigation.
Explanation: Reporting to and cooperating with the authorities ensures that the issue is formally addressed through the proper legal channels, providing a foundation for systemic change and accountability. This response prioritizes the safety and rights of the elders, unlike the other options, which could potentially exacerbate the situation or fail to address the abuse adequately.

94. In advocating for individuals with disabilities, which action by a social worker supports the principle of social inclusion?
a) Promoting policies that segregate individuals with disabilities for their protection.
b) Encouraging businesses to comply with accessibility standards voluntarily.
c) Lobbying for legislation that mandates equal opportunities in employment and education.
d) Advising individuals with disabilities to adapt to the existing structures without demanding changes.

Answer: c) Lobbying for legislation that mandates equal opportunities in employment and education.
Explanation: Advocating for laws that ensure equal opportunities addresses systemic barriers and promotes social inclusion, ensuring that individuals with disabilities have the same access and rights as everyone else. This approach targets the root of exclusionary practices, unlike the other options, which could reinforce segregation or passivity in the face of discrimination.

95. In a scenario where a community's access to clean water is compromised, what action embodies environmental justice advocacy?
a) Encouraging community members to purchase bottled water indefinitely.
b) Organizing a community-led initiative to test water quality and demand action from local authorities.
c) Telling the community that water quality is not a significant issue.
d) Recommending that the community focuses on other issues instead.

Answer: b) Organizing a community-led initiative to test water quality and demand action from local authorities.
Explanation: Empowering the community to document and challenge water quality issues directly addresses environmental injustice and advocates for systemic solutions. This collaborative approach holds authorities accountable and prioritizes the community's health and rights, unlike the other options, which disregard the significance of the issue or bypass systemic change.

96. When a social worker sees an increase in anti-immigrant sentiment affecting client well-being, which advocacy approach is appropriate?
a) Encouraging clients to avoid public attention and keep a low profile.
b) Creating a public awareness campaign that celebrates diversity and the contributions of immigrants.
c) Telling clients that changing public opinion is impossible.
d) Advising clients to only associate with others from their cultural background.

Answer: b) Creating a public awareness campaign that celebrates diversity and the contributions of immigrants.
Explanation: A public awareness campaign challenges negative stereotypes and promotes a more inclusive view of immigrants, directly addressing the root of the sentiment and fostering a more supportive environment. This approach educates the broader community, advocating for a shift in perception and improved well-being for immigrants.

97. For a social worker assisting a low-income neighborhood facing food insecurity, which strategy would best address the issue sustainably?
a) Advising residents to eat less to conserve food.
b) Supporting the development of community gardens and local food co-ops.
c) Ignoring the issue as it is considered a natural outcome of economic disparities.
d) Blaming the residents for their food choices.

Answer: b) Supporting the development of community gardens and local food co-ops.
Explanation: Promoting community gardens and food co-ops empowers residents by providing sustainable, local solutions to food insecurity. This approach fosters community engagement, resilience, and self-sufficiency, addressing both immediate needs and long-term food sustainability, unlike the other options, which do not offer constructive or sustainable solutions.

98. In cognitive-behavioral therapy (CBT), what is the primary focus when working with a client experiencing anxiety?
a) Exploring the client's past relationships to find the root cause of the anxiety.
b) Identifying and challenging negative thought patterns that contribute to anxiety.
c) Providing unconditional positive regard to boost the client's self-esteem.
d) Encouraging the expression of repressed emotions through art therapy.

Answer: b) Identifying and challenging negative thought patterns that contribute to anxiety.
Explanation: CBT focuses on identifying, challenging, and changing unhelpful cognitive distortions (negative thought patterns) and behaviors, teaching the individual new, more positive ways of thinking. In

the case of anxiety, CBT aims to help clients understand how their thoughts contribute to anxious feelings and how to alter these thought patterns to reduce anxiety, making it a direct and effective approach for managing symptoms.

99. A social worker utilizes motivational interviewing with a client who is ambivalent about quitting smoking. What is the key technique employed in motivational interviewing?
a) Direct confrontation about the dangers of smoking.
b) Developing discrepancy between the client's current behaviors and their goals.
c) Assigning homework to track the number of cigarettes smoked each day.
d) Advising the client on the best strategies to quit smoking based on expert opinions.

Answer: b) Developing discrepancy between the client's current behaviors and their goals.
Explanation: Motivational interviewing is a client-centered counseling style for eliciting behavior change by helping clients explore and resolve ambivalence. The key technique is developing a discrepancy between the client's current behavior (smoking) and their broader life goals or values, such as health or longevity, which can motivate the client to consider change more seriously. This method avoids direct confrontation or unsolicited advice, which can often lead to resistance.

100. When applying the principles of solution-focused brief therapy (SFBT) in a session, what would a social worker be MOST likely to ask?
a) "Can you talk about your childhood relationship with your parents?"
b) "What do you think is the root cause of your current distress?"
c) "If you woke up tomorrow and your problem was solved, what would be different?"
d) "How does your behavior affect the dynamics of your family?"

Answer: c) "If you woke up tomorrow and your problem was solved, what would be different?"
Explanation: SFBT focuses on desired future outcomes rather than past problems or the root cause of distress. This question, known as the "miracle question," helps clients envision the changes they would like to see in their lives, thereby identifying goals and potential steps toward achieving them. This future-oriented, goal-focused approach is a hallmark of SFBT, emphasizing solutions rather than problems.

101. A therapist is using dialectical behavior therapy (DBT) with a client who has borderline personality disorder (BPD). Which element is central to DBT?
a) The interpretation of dreams as a pathway to understanding unconscious conflicts.
b) The use of aversion therapy to decrease harmful behaviors.
c) Teaching coping skills for managing intense emotions and improving relationships.
d) Revisiting childhood experiences to resolve emotional pain.

Answer: c) Teaching coping skills for managing intense emotions and improving relationships.
Explanation: DBT is a form of cognitive-behavioral therapy that emphasizes the development of coping skills to manage intense emotions and enhance interpersonal relationships. It is particularly effective for individuals with BPD, as it teaches skills in mindfulness, emotion regulation, distress tolerance, and interpersonal effectiveness. This focus on skill-building is designed to help clients lead more manageable and fulfilling lives.

102. In applying psychodynamic therapy, what is the therapist MOST likely to focus on during sessions?
a) Teaching the client assertiveness training techniques.
b) Exploring unconscious processes that influence the client's current behavior.
c) Setting specific, measurable goals for therapy.
d) Practicing mindfulness meditation.

Answer: b) Exploring unconscious processes that influence the client's current behavior.
Explanation: Psychodynamic therapy focuses on the psychological roots of emotional suffering. It emphasizes understanding the influence of the past on present behavior, with a particular focus on unconscious processes. Therapists work with clients to uncover these unconscious thoughts and feelings, which are believed to contribute to current problems, through techniques like free association and dream analysis.

103. A client is experiencing low self-esteem and social anxiety. The social worker decides to use a humanistic approach to therapy. Which technique is LEAST likely to be used in this approach?
a) Encouraging the client to explore their self-perception and personal values.
b) Providing unconditional positive regard to foster a non-judgmental therapy environment.
c) Implementing a token economy system to reinforce positive social interactions.
d) Emphasizing the client's capacity for self-healing and personal growth.

Answer: c) Implementing a token economy system to reinforce positive social interactions.
Explanation: Humanistic therapy focuses on helping individuals develop a stronger, healthier sense of self, and to access and understand their feelings to gain a sense of meaning in life. Techniques like providing unconditional positive regard and emphasizing self-healing are common. A token economy system, which is a behaviorist method used to reinforce desired behaviors through rewards, is not aligned with the principles of humanistic therapy, which prioritize internal experience over external reinforcements.

104. In narrative therapy, a social worker asks a client to "externalize" their problem. What does this mean?
a) The client is asked to physically remove the problem from their life.
b) The client is encouraged to blame external factors for their issues.
c) The client is guided to talk about the problem as if it is separate from themselves.
d) The client is instructed to write down their problems and throw the paper away.

Answer: c) The client is guided to talk about the problem as if it is separate from themselves.
Explanation: Externalization is a technique in narrative therapy where clients are encouraged to talk about their problems as separate entities from themselves. This allows individuals to view their issues more objectively, reduces personal blame, and enhances their ability to address and resolve these issues. It shifts the perspective from being identified by the problem to having a problem, thereby fostering a sense of empowerment and agency.

105. In treating a client with severe depression, a social worker combines medication management with psychotherapy. This approach is known as:
a) Transference-focused therapy.

b) Integrated therapy.
c) Psychoanalysis.
d) Monotherapy.

Answer: b) Integrated therapy.
Explanation: Integrated therapy refers to the combination of medication management (often by a psychiatrist or other medical professional) and psychotherapy to treat mental health disorders. This holistic approach is particularly effective for severe depression, as it addresses both biological and psychological aspects of the disorder, enhancing the overall effectiveness of treatment. Monotherapy refers to the use of either medication or psychotherapy alone, not in combination.

106. A therapist working with a group of teenagers uses Gestalt therapy techniques to enhance self-awareness and present moment experience. Which activity might be included in this therapy?
a) Role-playing to enact past traumatic events.
b) Completing homework assignments to track negative thoughts.
c) The empty chair technique to explore conflicting feelings.
d) Systematic desensitization to reduce phobias.

Answer: c) The empty chair technique to explore conflicting feelings.
Explanation: The empty chair technique is a Gestalt therapy method used to help clients explore conflicting feelings or thoughts. The client engages in a dialogue with an imaginary person or aspect of themselves seated in an empty chair. This technique facilitates self-awareness and emotional processing by encouraging clients to express thoughts and emotions, fostering insight into their internal experiences and behavior patterns in the present moment.

107. A couple is experiencing communication difficulties and seeks therapy. The social worker decides to use the Gottman Method. What aspect of their relationship will this therapy MOST directly address?
a) Uncovering unconscious desires and motivations from childhood.
b) Learning communication and conflict resolution skills based on empirical data.
c) Reenacting traumatic events to release repressed emotions.
d) Changing the individual personality traits that are incompatible with the relationship.

Answer: b) Learning communication and conflict resolution skills based on empirical data.
Explanation: The Gottman Method is an evidence-based form of couples therapy that focuses on disarming conflicting verbal communication, increasing intimacy, respect, and affection, removing barriers that create a feeling of stagnancy in conflicting situations, and creating a heightened sense of empathy and understanding within the context of the relationship. It emphasizes the development of practical skills in communication and conflict resolution, based on years of empirical research on marital stability and divorce prediction, rather than focusing on individual psychodynamics or reenacting past traumas.

108. The Settlement House Movement, a cornerstone in the development of social work in the United States, aimed primarily to:
a) Provide legal services exclusively to the poor.
b) Offer medical care to underserved rural communities.

c) Address social and structural inequalities through community-based services.
d) Promote religious education and values.

Answer: c) Address social and structural inequalities through community-based services.
Explanation: The Settlement House Movement, pioneered by figures like Jane Addams, focused on addressing the root causes of poverty and inequality by providing a range of community-based services such as education, healthcare, and employment assistance. This movement laid foundational principles for modern social work by emphasizing direct community involvement and support, unlike the other options which are more narrowly focused or unrelated to the movement's core objectives.

109. The concept of "person-in-environment" (PIE) that is central to social work practice highlights the importance of:
a) Focusing treatment exclusively on the individual's psychological state.
b) Understanding individuals within the context of their social and environmental conditions.
c) Encouraging clients to change their environment to suit their personal goals.
d) Analyzing the global political climate's impact on individual behavior.

Answer: b) Understanding individuals within the context of their social and environmental conditions.
Explanation: The "person-in-environment" (PIE) concept is a fundamental principle in social work that emphasizes the need to understand and address the complex interactions between a person and their various environmental systems (social, physical, economic). This approach recognizes that an individual's issues cannot be fully understood or addressed without considering the broader social and environmental context.

110. The National Association of Social Workers (NASW) was established to:
a) Provide a platform for social workers to share research exclusively.
b) Serve as the sole licensing body for social workers in the United States.
c) Unify the profession under a common set of ethical standards and advocacy goals.
d) Focus on the development of social work education programs.

Answer: c) Unify the profession under a common set of ethical standards and advocacy goals.
Explanation: The NASW was founded to unify social work practitioners under a shared set of ethical standards and to advocate for issues pertinent to the profession and its clientele. While NASW is involved in research dissemination, education, and licensing standards, its primary mission is to serve as a professional organization that supports and advocates for the interests of social workers and their clients.

112. The Social Security Act of 1935, a critical piece of legislation in the history of social welfare in the United States, was significant because it:
a) Privatized all social services.
b) Introduced unemployment insurance, old-age benefits, and aid to dependent children.
c) Made social work an exclusively government-operated profession.
d) Outlawed private charity organizations.

Answer: b) Introduced unemployment insurance, old-age benefits, and aid to dependent children.
Explanation: The Social Security Act of 1935 marked a pivotal moment in social welfare, establishing foundational components of the modern welfare state in the United States, including unemployment insurance, Social Security for the elderly, and aid for dependent children. This legislation significantly impacted social work practice by institutionalizing support for vulnerable populations, contrary to the other options which misrepresent the Act's scope and intentions.

113. Jane Addams, often considered the mother of social work, is best known for:
a) Her development of the first academic degree in social work.
b) Establishing Hull House, a settlement house in Chicago.
c) Implementing the first child labor laws in the United States.
d) Founding the American Psychological Association.

Answer: b) Establishing Hull House, a settlement house in Chicago.
Explanation: Jane Addams co-founded Hull House, a settlement house in Chicago that provided a variety of essential services to the immigrant and poor populations. Hull House became a model for social work practice focused on community engagement and social reform, highlighting Addams' role in the history of social work far beyond the other options listed.

114. The ecological systems theory, integral to social work practice, was popularized by:
a) Sigmund Freud
b) Urie Bronfenbrenner
c) Karl Marx
d) Abraham Maslow

Answer: b) Urie Bronfenbrenner
Explanation: Urie Bronfenbrenner developed the ecological systems theory, which emphasizes the multiple environmental layers influencing an individual's development and well-being. This theory aligns with social work's person-in-environment perspective by highlighting the complex interactions between individuals and their various social systems.

115. The professional value of "social justice" in social work is primarily concerned with:
a) Ensuring that social workers receive competitive salaries.
b) Promoting fairness and equity in access to resources and opportunities among all people.
c) Focusing exclusively on legal representation for the underprivileged.
d) Encouraging social workers to participate in political elections.

Answer: b) Promoting fairness and equity in access to resources and opportunities among all people.
Explanation: The value of social justice in social work is centered on challenging social injustices and working towards a more equitable society. This includes efforts to address disparities and barriers faced by vulnerable populations, ensuring equal access to resources, opportunities, and rights.

116. The self-determination principle in social work practice means:
a) Social workers deciding what is best for their clients without input.

b) Clients having the freedom to make their own choices and control their own lives.
c) Government agencies determining the needs of the population.
d) Families making decisions on behalf of all their members.

Answer: b) Clients having the freedom to make their own choices and control their own lives.
Explanation: The principle of self-determination respects individuals' rights to make their own decisions and to control their own lives, as far as this does not harm others. This principle is fundamental in social work, emphasizing the importance of autonomy and empowering clients in the decision-making process.

117. The Code of Ethics for social workers emphasizes the importance of:
a) Competence, which means social workers should:
b) Practicing within their areas of expertise and continually updating their skills.
c) Limiting services to only financially lucrative areas.
d) Avoiding work with diverse populations to minimize ethical dilemmas.
e) Providing services based on social status.

Answer: a) Competence, which means social workers should:
Explanation: Practicing within their areas of expertise and continually updating their skills to provide the best possible service to clients. The NASW Code of Ethics outlines competence as a core value, emphasizing the need for social workers to maintain professional growth and development to enhance their ability to help others effectively.

118. In the early 20th century, the Charity Organization Society (COS) model focused on:
a) Direct financial assistance with no strings attached.
b) Individual casework and moral guidance to alleviate poverty.
c) Government takeover of all charity work.
d) Disbanding private charity organizations in favor of public institutions.

Answer: b) Individual casework and moral guidance to alleviate poverty.
Explanation: The COS model was predicated on the idea that poverty could be alleviated through individual casework, providing moral guidance and coordinating charitable efforts to avoid duplication of services. This approach emphasized personal responsibility and the moral uplift of the poor, contrasting with direct financial assistance or broader structural reforms suggested in the other options.
A social worker is offered a gift of significant value from a client as a thank-you for the services provided.

119. According to the NASW Code of Ethics, how should the social worker respond?
a) Accept the gift to avoid offending the client.
b) Politely decline the gift, explaining the ethical standards regarding gifts.
c) Accept the gift but report it to their supervisor to avoid personal bias.
d) Suggest the client donate the gift to a charity of the social worker's choice.

Answer: b) Politely decline the gift, explaining the ethical standards regarding gifts.

Explanation: The NASW Code of Ethics advises social workers to avoid accepting gifts of significant value from clients to maintain professional boundaries and avoid conflicts of interest or the appearance of a quid pro quo relationship. Politely declining the gift and providing an explanation based on ethical standards helps educate the client on professional boundaries while preserving the integrity of the therapeutic relationship.

120. When a social worker discovers confidential information that indicates a client may be a danger to themselves or others, what is the MOST appropriate course of action?
a) Immediately terminate services with the client.
b) Discuss the concern with the client and consider the need to break confidentiality for safety.
c) Share the information with all stakeholders for collective decision-making.
d) Ignore the information unless the client acts on the threat.

Answer: b) Discuss the concern with the client and consider the need to break confidentiality for safety.
Explanation: When a social worker believes a client poses a danger to themselves or others, ethical standards require considering the duty to warn or protect those at risk. This often involves discussing the concern with the client while evaluating the necessity and legal requirements to breach confidentiality for safety reasons. This approach seeks to balance the client's confidentiality with the responsibility to prevent harm.

121. A social worker conducting group therapy learns that two members are engaging in a romantic relationship outside the group. What ethical consideration is MOST pressing in this situation?
a) Encouraging the relationship if it seems beneficial to both parties.
b) Addressing the potential impact on group dynamics and maintaining professional boundaries.
c) Ignoring the relationship as long as it does not disrupt group sessions.
d) Advising other group members to form similar relationships to enhance therapeutic outcomes.

Answer: b) Addressing the potential impact on group dynamics and maintaining professional boundaries.
Explanation: The social worker's primary ethical concern should be how the romantic relationship affects group dynamics and the importance of maintaining professional boundaries within the therapeutic setting. Addressing these issues directly, either with the individuals involved or with the group as a whole, helps maintain the integrity of the therapeutic environment and ensures that all members continue to benefit from participation.

122. During a home visit, a social worker notices that a client's living conditions are unsafe for their children. According to ethical standards, what should be the social worker's FIRST step?
a) Immediately remove the children from the home.
b) Work with the client to improve the living conditions and ensure child safety.
c) Report the client to the authorities without discussing it with them.
d) Suggest that the client move to a new residence.

Answer: b) Work with the client to improve the living conditions and ensure child safety.
Explanation: The first step should be to work collaboratively with the client to address and improve the unsafe living conditions, with a focus on ensuring the safety and well-being of the children. This approach

respects the client's autonomy and dignity while fulfilling the social worker's ethical responsibility to protect vulnerable individuals. Immediate removal of the children or reporting to authorities may be necessary if the situation does not improve or if there is immediate danger, but it should not be the first step without attempting intervention.

123. A social worker receives a friend request on a social media platform from a former client. How should the social worker respond to maintain ethical boundaries?
a) Accept the friend request to support the former client's social network.
b) Decline the friend request and explain the ethical considerations to the former client.
c) Ignore the request without any further action.
d) Accept the request but limit the former client's access to personal posts.

Answer: b) Decline the friend request and explain the ethical considerations to the former client.
Explanation: To maintain professional boundaries and adhere to ethical standards, the social worker should decline the friend request. Explaining the reason for this decision to the former client helps to educate them on the importance of maintaining clear boundaries between professional and personal relationships, even after the formal relationship has ended.

124. A social worker begins to feel attracted to their client. What is the most appropriate course of action?
a) Discuss these feelings with the client to maintain transparency.
b) Seek supervision and guidance on managing these feelings while maintaining professional boundaries.
c) Ignore the feelings, assuming they will dissipate over time.
d) Pursue a relationship, believing it could be therapeutic.

Answer: b) Seek supervision and guidance on managing these feelings while maintaining professional boundaries.
Explanation: Experiencing personal feelings toward a client can challenge professional boundaries. The most ethical and professional response is to seek supervision to address and manage these feelings appropriately, ensuring that the client's well-being remains the priority and that professional boundaries are maintained. Engaging in a personal relationship with a client violates ethical standards and can harm the client.

125. A client offers a social worker a gift as a token of appreciation. Which response aligns with ethical guidelines?
a) Accepting the gift to avoid offending the client.
b) Politely declining the gift, explaining the policy on gifts to maintain professional boundaries.
c) Asking the client to donate the gift to charity instead.
d) Accepting the gift but reporting it to a supervisor.

Answer: b) Politely declining the gift, explaining the policy on gifts to maintain professional boundaries.
Explanation: While the gesture may be well-intentioned, accepting gifts can blur the lines of the professional relationship. Politely declining the gift and providing an explanation based on policy or ethical guidelines helps maintain clear professional boundaries and the integrity of the therapeutic relationship.

126. A social worker is invited to a former client's graduation ceremony. How should the social worker respond?
a) Attend the ceremony to show support for the client's achievements.
b) Politely decline the invitation, citing the need to maintain professional boundaries post-termination.
c) Accept the invitation but maintain a professional distance during the event.
d) Ask a colleague to attend in their place to avoid boundary issues.

Answer: b) Politely decline the invitation, citing the need to maintain professional boundaries post-termination.
Explanation: While attending might seem supportive, it's essential to maintain professional boundaries even after the formal client-social worker relationship has ended. Politely declining helps preserve these boundaries and the integrity of the professional relationship.

127. During a home visit, a client expresses romantic feelings for the social worker. What is the social worker's best response?
a) Exploring these feelings as part of the therapeutic process.
b) Clearly stating that the professional relationship does not allow for romantic involvement.
c) Accepting the feelings as a compliment and continuing with the session.
d) Ending the session immediately without addressing the client's feelings.

Answer: b) Clearly stating that the professional relationship does not allow for romantic involvement.
Explanation: It's crucial for social workers to address any expressions of romantic feelings by reaffirming the professional nature of the relationship and setting clear boundaries. This ensures the focus remains on the client's needs and maintains the integrity of the therapeutic environment.

128. A social worker is treating a client who is a close friend of a family member. What should the social worker do to maintain ethical practice?
a) Continue treatment, as the social worker believes they can remain objective.
b) Discuss the situation with the client and consider a referral to another professional if necessary.
c) Keep the sessions strictly confidential and avoid discussing them with family.
d) Use the connection to gather more background information about the client.

Answer: b) Discuss the situation with the client and consider a referral to another professional if necessary.
Explanation: When personal connections overlap with professional roles, it's essential to address potential conflicts of interest. Discussing the situation openly with the client and considering a referral helps maintain ethical standards and protects the client's best interests.

129. A social worker on the ethics committee receives a report about a colleague potentially violating client confidentiality. What is the first step?
a) Confront the colleague directly and demand an explanation.
b) Review the evidence and follow the organization's protocol for investigating such reports.
c) Dismiss the report if the colleague is known to be generally ethical.
d) Immediately report the colleague to the licensing board without further investigation.

Answer: b) Review the evidence and follow the organization's protocol for investigating such reports.
Explanation: Upon receiving a report of potential unethical behavior, the correct approach is to review the available evidence and follow established protocols for investigation. This ensures a fair and systematic process, maintaining the integrity of the profession and the welfare of clients.

130. A social worker is asked by a friend for advice on a personal issue. The friend is not a client. What should the social worker do?
a) Provide advice as requested, as the friend is not a client.
b) Refer the friend to another social worker or professional for help.
c) Offer to treat the friend as a client starting immediately.
d) Use social work techniques in a casual setting to help the friend.

Answer: b) Refer the friend to another social worker or professional for help.
Explanation: While it may seem helpful to offer advice, it's important to recognize the distinction between personal and professional relationships. Referring the friend to another professional helps maintain this boundary and ensures the friend receives appropriate support.

131. A social worker discovers that their new client is a neighbor. To maintain professionalism, the social worker should:
a) Immediately terminate the therapeutic relationship to avoid dual relationships.
b) Discuss the potential for boundary issues with the client and consider a referral if appropriate.
c) Continue with the sessions but avoid discussing anything related to the neighborhood.
d) Move to a different neighborhood to avoid any dual relationship with the client.

Answer: b) Discuss the potential for boundary issues with the client and consider a referral if appropriate.
Explanation: The discovery of a pre-existing relationship with a client requires careful consideration of potential boundary issues. Discussing these openly with the client and considering a referral to another professional if necessary is the best approach to maintaining ethical standards.

132. When a client offers to do repair work on a social worker's home as a form of payment, the social worker should:
a) Accept, if the value of the work is equivalent to the session fees.
b) Decline and discuss acceptable forms of payment as per agency policy.
c) Accept but ensure that a formal contract is in place.
d) Suggest a barter system for future sessions as well.

Answer: b) Decline and discuss acceptable forms of payment as per agency policy.
Explanation: Accepting services as payment can create conflicts of interest and boundary issues. Declining the offer and clarifying acceptable payment methods maintain professional boundaries and the integrity of the therapeutic relationship.

133. A social worker's client requests to connect on social media. The appropriate response is to:
a) Accept the request to review the client's online activities.
b) Politely decline and discuss the importance of maintaining professional boundaries.

c) Accept the request but not interact with the client's posts.
d) Create a professional account for such connections to keep them separate.

Answer: b) Politely decline and discuss the importance of maintaining professional boundaries.
Explanation: Connecting with clients on social media can blur the lines between professional and personal relationships. Politely declining such requests and explaining the rationale helps preserve the integrity of the therapeutic relationship and professional boundaries.

134. A social worker seeks to expand their expertise in trauma-informed care. Which of the following activities would BEST fulfill this goal while also meeting continuing education requirements?
a) Reading popular self-help books on trauma recovery.
b) Attending an accredited workshop on trauma-informed care practices.
c) Watching unrelated documentary films to gain a broader perspective on human experiences.
d) Participating in non-educational community events to network with other professionals.

Answer: b) Attending an accredited workshop on trauma-informed care practices.
Explanation: Attending an accredited workshop specifically focused on trauma-informed care practices is the most direct and effective way to expand a social worker's expertise in this area while also fulfilling continuing education requirements. Accredited workshops are designed to provide current, research-based knowledge and skills relevant to professional practice, ensuring that the social worker remains competent and effective in their role.

135. A licensed social worker wants to stay updated with the latest research and developments in social work practice. What is the MOST effective strategy for achieving this?
a) Limiting reading to social work materials published over ten years ago to build a strong foundational knowledge.
b) Subscribing to leading social work journals and participating in relevant webinars and conferences.
c) Relying solely on informal discussions with colleagues for new information.
d) Focusing exclusively on gaining practical experience and avoiding theoretical updates.

Answer: b) Subscribing to leading social work journals and participating in relevant webinars and conferences.
Explanation: Staying updated with the latest research and developments in social work is critical for professional growth and effectiveness. Subscribing to leading social work journals and participating in relevant webinars and conferences are effective strategies for achieving this. These activities provide access to current research findings, theories, and evidence-based practices, contributing to ongoing professional development and ensuring that social workers can provide the best possible service to their clients.

136. In planning for professional development, a social worker is interested in developing leadership skills within their agency. Which of the following actions would MOST directly facilitate this goal?
a) Focusing solely on daily tasks and avoiding additional responsibilities.
b) Seeking mentorship from an experienced leader within the agency.
c) Declining opportunities for project management or team leadership to avoid overcommitment.

d) Isolating professional development efforts to non-leadership-related online courses.

Answer: b) Seeking mentorship from an experienced leader within the agency.
Explanation: Seeking mentorship from an experienced leader within the agency is a direct and effective strategy for a social worker interested in developing leadership skills. Mentorship provides opportunities for personalized learning, guidance, and feedback from someone with proven leadership abilities and experience. This approach not only helps in acquiring leadership skills but also offers insights into navigating the organizational culture and advancing professionally within the agency.

137. A social worker is considering taking a continuing education course online. What factor is MOST important to ensure that the course contributes meaningfully to their professional development?
a) The course is offered at a convenient time.
b) The course is approved by a recognized social work accreditation body.
c) The course promises easy completion with minimal effort.
d) The course content is unrelated to the social worker's current field of practice.

Answer: b) The course is approved by a recognized social work accreditation body.
Explanation: The most important factor in choosing a continuing education course is that it is approved by a recognized social work accreditation body. This ensures that the course meets established standards for educational content, relevance to practice, and contributes to the professional development of the social worker. Accreditation signifies that the course is designed to enhance professional skills and knowledge in a meaningful way, which is essential for maintaining competence and fulfilling licensure renewal requirements.

138. To fulfill licensure renewal requirements, a social worker must complete 30 hours of continuing education every two years. If the social worker completes 40 hours in two years, how should they approach the excess hours?
a) Carry over the excess 10 hours to the next renewal period, if allowed by the licensing board.
b) Disregard the extra hours as they do not contribute to professional development.
c) Stop engaging in professional development activities once the required hours are met.
d) Only count the hours related to their specific area of practice, discarding unrelated hours.

Answer: a) Carry over the excess 10 hours to the next renewal period, if allowed by the licensing board.
Explanation: If a social worker completes more continuing education hours than required and the licensing board allows for carryover of excess hours to the next renewal period, this would be the most efficient and beneficial approach. It allows the social worker to apply their extra effort toward future requirements, acknowledging their dedication to ongoing professional development. However, it's important to verify this option with the specific licensing board's policies as practices can vary.

139. A social worker is evaluating different professional development opportunities. Which criterion is LEAST important in making this decision?
a) The opportunity's relevance to the social worker's current client population and practice area.
b) The cost of the professional development opportunity.
c) The prestige of the organization offering the opportunity.

d) The potential for the opportunity to expand the social worker's skills and knowledge base.

Answer: c) The prestige of the organization offering the opportunity.
Explanation: While the prestige of the organization offering professional development opportunities may have some merit, it is the least important criterion compared to the relevance to the social worker's practice, the cost, and the potential to expand skills and knowledge. The primary focus should be on the applicability and benefit of the content to the social worker's professional growth and the needs of their clients, rather than the status of the organization providing the training.

140. In considering participation in a new research project, what ethical consideration should a social worker prioritize?
a) The potential for the research to significantly increase the social worker's income.
b) Ensuring that the research is designed to contribute to the knowledge base of social work and benefit client populations.
c) Choosing research topics that are personally interesting over those that are relevant to social work practice.
d) Focusing on research that supports the social worker's personal beliefs, regardless of its relevance to broader social issues.

Answer: b) Ensuring that the research is designed to contribute to the knowledge base of social work and benefit client populations.
Explanation: The primary ethical consideration for a social worker considering participation in research is ensuring that the research aims to contribute to the knowledge base of social work and has the potential to benefit client populations. This aligns with the social work profession's commitment to advancing practice, education, and research for the betterment of society and the individuals served. The focus should always be on ethical, relevant, and impactful research rather than personal gain or interests.

141. When a newly licensed social worker is looking to develop a specialty in substance abuse counseling, which of the following would be the MOST effective approach?
a) Limiting learning to on-the-job training in substance abuse counseling settings.
b) Attending a variety of unrelated workshops for general knowledge.
c) Pursuing specialized training and certification in substance abuse counseling.
d) Focusing exclusively on self-study through books on substance abuse.

Answer: c) Pursuing specialized training and certification in substance abuse counseling.
Explanation: Pursuing specialized training and certification in substance abuse counseling is the most effective approach for a newly licensed social worker looking to develop a specialty in this area. Specialized training programs provide comprehensive, focused education on theories, techniques, and best practices specific to substance abuse counseling, equipping the social worker with the necessary skills and knowledge. Certification additionally validates the social worker's expertise, enhancing their credibility and opportunities in this specialty area.

142. To maintain a high standard of practice, a social worker decides to engage in peer supervision with colleagues. What is the PRIMARY benefit of this type of professional development?

a) It provides a formal evaluation for promotion within an agency.
b) It offers an opportunity to receive feedback and learn from the experiences of peers.
c) It replaces the need for continuing education credits for licensure renewal.
d) It focuses solely on administrative skills rather than clinical practice.

Answer: b) It offers an opportunity to receive feedback and learn from the experiences of peers.
Explanation: The primary benefit of engaging in peer supervision is the opportunity to receive constructive feedback and learn from the experiences and perspectives of peers. This collaborative form of professional development fosters a supportive learning environment where social workers can discuss challenges, share strategies, and enhance their practice through mutual exchange of knowledge. Peer supervision complements formal education and training by providing real-world insights and ongoing learning opportunities, rather than serving as a formal evaluation tool or replacing continuing education requirements.

143. When a new social worker encounters a complex case involving suspected child abuse, the FIRST step they should take is:
a) Immediately report the suspicion to child protective services without further assessment.
b) Consult with a supervisor to review the situation and decide on the appropriate action.
c) Discuss their suspicions with the child's family to gather more information.
d) Ignore the suspicion until more concrete evidence is observed.

Answer: b) Consult with a supervisor to review the situation and decide on the appropriate action.
Explanation: Consulting with a supervisor allows the social worker to benefit from the supervisor's experience and knowledge, ensuring that any action taken is informed, ethical, and in line with legal obligations. Immediate reporting or discussing suspicions with the family before a thorough assessment could jeopardize the child's safety or the investigation's integrity. Ignoring the suspicion is not ethically or legally defensible.

144. In the context of use of supervision, a social worker feeling overwhelmed by the emotional toll of their caseload should:
a) Take a leave of absence until they feel ready to return.
b) Discuss their feelings and seek support and guidance during supervision.
c) Manage their feelings independently to maintain professionalism.
d) Transfer challenging cases to colleagues without consultation.

Answer: b) Discuss their feelings and seek support and guidance during supervision.
Explanation: Supervision provides a safe and supportive environment for social workers to explore professional challenges, including emotional distress. Discussing these issues with a supervisor can lead to strategies for managing the emotional impact of the work, professional growth, and preventing burnout. Other options may avoid addressing the root issue or impede the social worker's development.

145. A social worker is unsure about the ethical implications of a decision in their practice. The BEST course of action is to:
a) Make the decision based on personal judgment and experience.

b) Seek advice from peers informally over lunch.
c) Consult with their supervisor to explore the ethical dimensions of the decision.
d) Postpone the decision indefinitely until it becomes clearer.

Answer: c) Consult with their supervisor to explore the ethical dimensions of the decision.
Explanation: Consulting with a supervisor provides an opportunity to explore the ethical considerations in a structured, informed manner, leveraging the supervisor's experience and understanding of professional ethics. This approach ensures that decisions are not only legally compliant but also ethically sound. Relying solely on personal judgment or informal peer advice might not fully address the complexities of ethical dilemmas in social work practice.

146. A social worker realizes they have developed a dual relationship with a client who has become a close personal friend. They should:
a) Continue the friendship and professional relationship, as the client seems to benefit from both.
b) Terminate the professional relationship and refer the client to another social worker.
c) Discuss the situation with the client and mutually decide how to proceed.
d) Bring up the issue in supervision to determine the most ethical course of action.

Answer: d) Bring up the issue in supervision to determine the most ethical course of action.
Explanation: Dual relationships can compromise the integrity of the therapeutic relationship and pose ethical dilemmas. Discussing the situation in supervision allows the social worker to navigate these complexities with professional guidance, ensuring actions taken are ethical and in the best interest of the client. Termination and referral may be necessary, but this decision should be informed by ethical guidelines and supervisory input.

147. When a social worker feels that their personal values are in conflict with their professional duties, they should FIRST:
a) Resign from their position.
b) Ignore their personal values and continue with their duties.
c) Attempt to change the client's situation to align with their own values.
d) Discuss the conflict in supervision to seek guidance on managing personal and professional boundaries.

Answer: d) Discuss the conflict in supervision to seek guidance on managing personal and professional boundaries.
Explanation: Supervision provides a platform to explore and resolve conflicts between personal values and professional responsibilities. This discussion can lead to strategies for managing personal biases and ensuring that professional actions remain client-centered and ethically sound, rather than allowing personal values to unduly influence practice.

148. In supervisory sessions, the PRIMARY focus for discussing cases should be:
a) Sharing detailed accounts of each session with clients for the supervisor's entertainment.
b) Seeking validation for the social worker's feelings about clients.
c) Developing the social worker's skills and ensuring the quality of client care.
d) Comparing clients' progress to that of others to establish benchmarks.

Answer: c) Developing the social worker's skills and ensuring the quality of client care.
Explanation: Supervision aims to enhance professional competence, support ethical practice, and ensure client care's quality and effectiveness. Discussions should focus on skill development, ethical decision-making, and strategies for addressing client needs, rather than on validation, entertainment, or comparison with other clients.

149. A social worker is considering starting a private practice. In supervision, they should explore:
a) How to minimize time spent with clients to increase profitability.
b) Ethical marketing strategies and maintaining professional standards in private practice.
c) Ways to avoid dealing with insurance companies.
d) Strategies for selecting only high-paying clients.

Answer: b) Ethical marketing strategies and maintaining professional standards in private practice.
Explanation: Transitioning to private practice requires careful consideration of ethical practices, including marketing, client rights, and professional standards. Supervision can offer valuable insights into navigating these aspects ethically and effectively, focusing on quality care rather than profit maximization or selective client practices.

150. A social worker receives a subpoena for client records. They should FIRST:
a) Immediately comply and send all requested documents.
b) Destroy records that could potentially harm the client if disclosed.
c) Consult with their supervisor and possibly legal counsel to respond appropriately.
d) Inform the client and allow them to decide which records to release.

Answer: c) Consult with their supervisor and possibly legal counsel to respond appropriately.
Explanation: Responding to legal requests for client records requires careful consideration of ethical, legal, and professional obligations. Consulting with a supervisor and legal counsel ensures that the social worker navigates these requests appropriately, balancing legal compliance with client confidentiality and rights.

151. When a social worker identifies a potential gap in service provision within their agency, they should:
a) Ignore it, assuming someone else will address the issue.
b) Discuss the observation and potential solutions in supervision.
c) Start an independent service to fill the gap without consulting the agency.
d) Complain to colleagues about the agency's shortcomings.

Answer: b) Discuss the observation and potential solutions in supervision.
Explanation: Identifying service gaps and discussing them in supervision allows for collaborative problem-solving and strategic planning to enhance service provision. This proactive approach contributes to agency improvement and better client care, unlike the other options, which do not constructively address the issue.

152. The Temporary Assistance for Needy Families (TANF) program is designed to help families in need achieve self-sufficiency. Which of the following is NOT a primary focus of TANF?
a) Providing financial assistance to families.

b) Encouraging the formation and maintenance of two-parent families.
c) Mandating that beneficiaries find employment within two weeks of receiving benefits.
d) Preventing and reducing the incidence of out-of-wedlock pregnancies.

Answer: c) Mandating that beneficiaries find employment within two weeks of receiving benefits.
Explanation: The Temporary Assistance for Needy Families (TANF) program has several key objectives, including providing financial assistance to families, encouraging the formation and maintenance of two-parent families, and preventing and reducing out-of-wedlock pregnancies. However, there is no requirement that beneficiaries must find employment within two weeks of receiving benefits. While TANF does include work requirements, the specifics of these requirements allow for more flexibility than a strict two-week timeframe to find employment, focusing instead on promoting job preparation and work as a means to achieving self-sufficiency over time.

153. In the context of social welfare policy, what does the term "means-tested" refer to?
a) Programs available to all citizens regardless of income.
b) Programs that require recipients to pass a skills test.
c) Programs whose eligibility depends upon the individual's or family's income and assets.
d) Programs funded solely through charitable donations.

Answer: c) Programs whose eligibility depends upon the individual's or family's income and assets.
Explanation: Means-tested programs are those social welfare programs whose eligibility criteria include the income and assets of an individual or family. This means that to qualify for the program, applicants must demonstrate that their financial resources fall below certain thresholds, thereby targeting assistance to those most in need. Unlike universal programs that are available to all citizens regardless of income, means-tested programs specifically aim to provide support to lower-income individuals and families.

154. A social worker is advocating for increased funding for affordable housing initiatives. Which social welfare policy principle BEST supports this advocacy?
a) Reducing government intervention in the housing market.
b) Ensuring that all citizens have access to basic human needs.
c) Encouraging private sector solutions to housing shortages.
d) Limiting public spending on social welfare programs.

Answer: b) Ensuring that all citizens have access to basic human needs.
Explanation: The advocacy for increased funding for affordable housing initiatives is best supported by the social welfare policy principle that all citizens should have access to basic human needs, which include safe and affordable housing. This principle underlines the importance of government and societal action to ensure that individuals and families have access to essential services and supports, including housing, as a foundation for health, safety, and well-being. Unlike the other options, this principle emphasizes the role of public policy in addressing and meeting the basic needs of the population.

155. What role does the Social Security Act of 1935 play in the United States' social welfare system?
a) It established the first national health insurance program for all Americans.
b) It introduced unemployment insurance, old-age insurance, and welfare programs.

c) It created the TANF program to replace all previous welfare initiatives.
d) It exclusively funded educational programs for low-income families.

Answer: b) It introduced unemployment insurance, old-age insurance, and welfare programs.
Explanation: The Social Security Act of 1935 was a landmark piece of legislation in the United States that introduced several key components of the social welfare system, including unemployment insurance, old-age insurance (which later evolved into Social Security retirement benefits), and welfare programs for the needy, aged, and disabled. This Act laid the foundation for the modern social welfare system in the U.S., aiming to provide a safety net for various populations at risk of economic insecurity. It did not establish a national health insurance program or exclusively fund educational programs, nor did it create the TANF program, which was established much later.

156. When assessing the impact of the Affordable Care Act (ACA) on healthcare access, which population group has seen significant increases in coverage?
a) Only individuals over the age of 65.
b) High-income individuals and families.
c) Individuals with pre-existing conditions and young adults.
d) Non-citizens exclusively.

Answer: c) Individuals with pre-existing conditions and young adults.
Explanation: The Affordable Care Act (ACA), also known as Obamacare, significantly increased healthcare coverage for various population groups, particularly individuals with pre-existing conditions and young adults. One of the key provisions of the ACA prohibits insurance companies from denying coverage based on pre-existing conditions. Additionally, the ACA allows young adults to stay on their parents' health insurance plans until the age of 26. These measures have contributed to increased access to healthcare for these groups, unlike the other options listed, which misrepresent the scope and intent of the ACA.

157. When developing a new community program aimed at reducing youth violence, what is the FIRST step a social worker should take?
a) Launch the program immediately to address the urgent need.
b) Conduct a needs assessment to identify the specific issues and resources within the community.
c) Secure funding without specifying program goals.
d) Design promotional materials to raise awareness about the program.

Answer: b) Conduct a needs assessment to identify the specific issues and resources within the community.
Explanation: Conducting a needs assessment is crucial as it helps in understanding the community's specific issues, needs, and resources related to youth violence. This initial step ensures that the program is tailored to address the community's unique context and has a stronger foundation for effectiveness and sustainability, compared to jumping straight into implementation or focusing on funding and promotion without a clear understanding of the community's needs.

158. In evaluating the effectiveness of a program designed to improve mental health access for rural populations, which indicator would be MOST important?

a) The number of promotional materials distributed in the community.
b) The increase in the number of individuals accessing mental health services.
c) The overall budget spent on the program.
d) The number of staff hired for the program.

Answer: b) The increase in the number of individuals accessing mental health services.
Explanation: The most direct indicator of a program's success in improving mental health access is the increase in the number of individuals actually accessing those services. This outcome directly reflects the program's primary goal, unlike budgetary, staffing, or promotional metrics, which do not directly measure effectiveness in meeting the program's objectives.

159. When implementing a new program to address homelessness, why is it critical to involve stakeholders in the planning process?
a) Stakeholders can provide financial support for the program.
b) Involvement of stakeholders ensures legal compliance.
c) Stakeholders offer diverse perspectives that can enhance the program's relevance and acceptance.
d) Stakeholders are responsible for program evaluation.

Answer: c) Stakeholders offer diverse perspectives that can enhance the program's relevance and acceptance.
Explanation: Involving stakeholders, such as community members, service users, and local organizations, in the planning process is critical because their diverse perspectives and insights can significantly enhance the program's design, relevance, and community acceptance. While financial support, legal compliance, and evaluation are important, the primary value of stakeholder involvement lies in the richness of perspectives they bring, ensuring the program is well-adapted to meet community needs.

160. For a program aimed at reducing drug use among teenagers, which method would be most effective for evaluating long-term success?
a) Pre- and post-surveys of drug use attitudes among participants.
b) Counting the number of workshops conducted.
c) Assessments of participant satisfaction immediately following the program.
d) Longitudinal tracking of participants' drug use behavior changes over time.

Answer: d) Longitudinal tracking of participants' drug use behavior changes over time.
Explanation: Longitudinal tracking provides data on the sustainability of behavior changes, which is crucial for evaluating the long-term success of a program aimed at reducing drug use. While pre- and post-surveys, workshop counts, and satisfaction assessments can offer valuable insights, tracking actual behavior changes over an extended period gives the clearest picture of the program's effectiveness in achieving its primary goal.

161. When designing a program to assist unemployed individuals in gaining employment, what factor is essential to consider for program sustainability?
a) The program’s name and logo design.
b) Short-term funding opportunities only.

c) Partnerships with local businesses and educational institutions.
d) The number of staff members involved in the program.

Answer: c) Partnerships with local businesses and educational institutions.
Explanation: Forming partnerships with local businesses and educational institutions is essential for program sustainability as it ensures ongoing support, resources, and opportunities for participants. These partnerships can provide a pathway to employment for participants and contribute to the program's long-term viability, unlike the other options, which do not directly impact sustainability.

162. In assessing a program designed to improve literacy rates among adults, which outcome measure is MOST critical?
a) The number of books purchased for the program.
b) Participant feedback on the program's enjoyability.
c) Improvement in participants' reading levels.
d) Attendance rates at program sessions.

Answer: c) Improvement in participants' reading levels.
Explanation: The most direct outcome measure of a literacy improvement program is the improvement in participants' reading levels, as this directly reflects the program's effectiveness in achieving its primary goal. While feedback, attendance, and resources are important for program implementation and evaluation, they do not measure outcome success as directly as changes in reading levels.

163. For a program focused on reducing domestic violence, which strategy is essential for effective program evaluation?
a) Relying solely on self-reported data from participants.
b) Using a combination of qualitative and quantitative data sources.
c) Conducting evaluations only at the end of the program.
d) Comparing the program's budget with those of similar programs.

Answer: b) Using a combination of qualitative and quantitative data sources.
Explanation: A comprehensive evaluation of a domestic violence reduction program requires both qualitative and quantitative data to fully understand the program's impact. Quantitative data can measure changes in incidence rates, while qualitative data can provide deeper insights into participant experiences and program effectiveness. This approach offers a more complete evaluation than any single data source or financial comparisons.

164. In developing a community health program, what is the MOST effective way to ensure the program meets the community's needs?
a) Implementing a standardized program used in similar communities.
b) Conducting community forums and surveys to gather input from community members.
c) Basing the program solely on the latest health research.
d) Copying the program structure of a successful international health program.

Answer: b) Conducting community forums and surveys to gather input from community members.
Explanation: Directly engaging with the community through forums and surveys ensures that the program is tailored to meet the specific needs, preferences, and circumstances of the community it serves. While research and models from other programs can provide valuable insights, community input is essential for relevance and effectiveness.

165. When evaluating the effectiveness of a new social work intervention program, which factor is crucial to consider?
a) The theoretical foundation of the program alone.
b) The program's popularity on social media.
c) The cost-effectiveness of the program compared to its outcomes.
d) The number of participants who completed the program.

Answer: c) The cost-effectiveness of the program compared to its outcomes.
Explanation: While theoretical foundations, participant completion rates, and social media presence can inform aspects of a program's design and reach, the crucial factor in evaluating effectiveness is the cost-effectiveness of the program. This involves assessing the program's outcomes in relation to its costs, ensuring that resources are being used efficiently to achieve the desired impact.
166. A social work program aimed at increasing access to affordable housing is being developed. Which stakeholder's input is MOST valuable during the planning phase?
a) A local celebrity to promote the program.
b) Potential program participants facing housing instability.
c) A software company offering to build a program website.
d) An international NGO with no local branches.

Answer: b) Potential program participants facing housing instability.
Explanation: Engaging potential program participants in the planning phase ensures that their needs, experiences, and perspectives directly inform the program design, making it more likely to effectively address the issue of housing instability. While other stakeholders may offer valuable support or resources, the input from those directly affected by the issue is most critical for creating a relevant and impactful program.

167. Human resources management in social service settings The implementation of the Affordable Care Act (ACA) primarily aimed to:
a) Reduce the defense budget to allocate more funds to healthcare.
b) Increase access to health insurance for Americans, including those with pre-existing conditions.
c) Privatize all healthcare services to increase competition.
d) Decrease funding for public health programs.

Answer: b) Increase access to health insurance for Americans, including those with pre-existing conditions.
Explanation: The ACA, or Obamacare, was designed to increase healthcare access by expanding Medicaid coverage, providing health insurance marketplace subsidies, and ensuring that people with pre-existing conditions could not be denied coverage. This policy significantly impacted social work practice by

broadening client access to healthcare services, unlike the other options, which do not accurately reflect the ACA's objectives.

168. The introduction of HIPAA regulations affected social work practice by:
a) Limiting social workers' ability to communicate with healthcare providers.
b) Increasing the need for social workers to be trained in privacy and confidentiality practices.
c) Discouraging the use of electronic records in healthcare settings.
d) Reducing the emphasis on client confidentiality in social work education.

Answer: b) Increasing the need for social workers to be trained in privacy and confidentiality practices.
Explanation: HIPAA, the Health Insurance Portability and Accountability Act, emphasizes the protection of patient health information, requiring social workers and other healthcare professionals to ensure the confidentiality and security of client data. This has necessitated increased training and awareness around privacy practices in social work, contrary to the other options, which misinterpret HIPAA's impact.

169. When analyzing the impact of "No Child Left Behind" legislation on client systems, a social worker might note:
a) A decrease in standardized testing within public schools.
b) Increased accountability measures for schools, potentially leading to teaching to the test.
c) A significant increase in federal funding for all educational programs.
d) The elimination of the achievement gap in education.

Answer: b) Increased accountability measures for schools, potentially leading to teaching to the test.
Explanation: "No Child Left Behind" emphasized standardized testing as a measure of accountability for schools, which critics argue has led to a focus on "teaching to the test" at the expense of broader educational objectives. This shift has implications for clients within the education system, unlike the other options, which inaccurately describe the legislation's effects.

170. The passage of the Fair Housing Act is an example of a policy designed to:
a) Reduce federal oversight in housing.
b) Ensure equal access to rental housing and homeownership opportunities, irrespective of race, religion, or national origin.
c) Increase the construction of luxury housing developments.
d) Decrease public housing availability for low-income families.

Answer: b) Ensure equal access to rental housing and homeownership opportunities, irrespective of race, religion, or national origin.
Explanation: The Fair Housing Act was enacted to eliminate discrimination in housing based on race, color, religion, sex, disability, familial status, or national origin, promoting equal housing opportunities for all. This law directly impacts social work practice by addressing systemic barriers to housing, unlike the other options, which do not reflect the law's purpose or effects.

171. The adoption of evidence-based practice in social work was primarily influenced by:
a) The desire to decrease the cost of social services.

b) The movement towards more personalized client care.
c) The need for social work interventions to be grounded in scientific research and proven effectiveness.
d) The goal of eliminating all traditional practices in social work.

Answer: c) The need for social work interventions to be grounded in scientific research and proven effectiveness.
Explanation: Evidence-based practice in social work emphasizes the use of interventions that have been empirically tested and proven effective, ensuring that clients receive the most effective care. This approach supports informed decision-making and quality improvement in practice, unlike the other options, which mischaracterize the motivation behind evidence-based practice.

172. The implementation of welfare reform policies in the 1990s, particularly the Personal Responsibility and Work Opportunity Reconciliation Act (PRWORA), was intended to:
a) Expand the availability of welfare benefits to all low-income individuals.
b) Encourage dependency on government assistance programs.
c) Shift welfare programs from federal to state control and emphasize work as a condition for receiving aid.
d) Increase the federal government's role in providing direct assistance.

Answer: c) Shift welfare programs from federal to state control and emphasize work as a condition for receiving aid.
Explanation: PRWORA represented a significant shift in welfare policy, aiming to reduce dependency on government aid by instituting work requirements and transferring the administration of welfare programs to the states through block grants. This policy change directly impacted social work practice, particularly in how services are provided to individuals and families in need, unlike the other options that misrepresent the law's intentions and effects.
173. The expansion of Medicaid under the Affordable Care Act impacted social work practice by:
a) Decreasing the number of clients eligible for Medicaid.
b) Making it more difficult for social workers to refer clients to healthcare services.
c) Increasing access to healthcare services for low-income individuals and families.
d) Eliminating the need for social workers in healthcare settings.

Answer: c) Increasing access to healthcare services for low-income individuals and families.
Explanation: The expansion of Medicaid eligibility under the ACA significantly increased access to healthcare for millions of low-income Americans, affecting social work practice by broadening the scope of clients eligible for services and enhancing the ability to connect clients with necessary healthcare resources, unlike the other options, which inaccurately describe the ACA's impact on Medicaid and social work practice.

174. The development of child labor laws in the United States can be seen as a response to:
a) The increasing need for skilled labor in factories.
b) Advocacy by social workers and others concerned with the welfare and rights of children.
c) A desire to increase the employment rates of adults.
d) Efforts to standardize education systems across states.

Answer: b) Advocacy by social workers and others concerned with the welfare and rights of children.
Explanation: Child labor laws were significantly influenced by social reformers, including social workers, who advocated for the protection of children from exploitation and harmful work conditions. This advocacy was rooted in concerns for children's rights, health, and access to education, rather than the other factors mentioned, which do not directly relate to the impetus for these laws.

175. The Social Security Act of 1935, a cornerstone of the New Deal, significantly impacted social work practice by:
a) Limiting social workers' roles to only providing direct relief assistance.
b) Introducing unemployment insurance, old-age benefits, and aid to dependent children.
c) Encouraging private charities to take over the role of public assistance.
d) Decreasing the federal government's involvement in social welfare programs.

Answer: b) Introducing unemployment insurance, old-age benefits, and aid to dependent children.
Explanation: The Social Security Act established several key programs that form the basis of America's social safety net, directly influencing social work practice by expanding the range of services and supports available to vulnerable populations. This act marked a significant increase in federal involvement in social welfare, contrary to the other options, which misrepresent the act's provisions and effects on social work.

176. Which leadership theory emphasizes the importance of leaders being able to adapt their style to the maturity of the team members they are leading?
a) Trait theory
b) Situational leadership theory
c) Transformational leadership theory
d) Laissez-faire leadership theory

Answer: b) Situational leadership theory.
Explanation: Situational leadership theory, developed by Paul Hersey and Ken Blanchard, posits that effective leadership is dependent on the leader's ability to adapt their style according to the situation and the maturity level of their followers. This theory suggests that there is no single "best" style of leadership; instead, leaders should adjust their approach based on the readiness, competence, and motivation of their team members, making it a versatile and dynamic leadership model.

177. In transformational leadership, what is the primary focus of leaders when interacting with their followers?
a) Ensuring that tasks are completed efficiently with minimal supervision
b) Encouraging followers to transcend their own self-interests for the sake of the team or organization
c) Maintaining a strict hierarchy and clear division between leaders and followers
d) Delegating as many tasks as possible to increase followers' responsibility

Answer: b) Encouraging followers to transcend their own self-interests for the sake of the team or organization.
Explanation: Transformational leadership focuses on inspiring and motivating followers to exceed their own interests and limitations for the greater good of the team or organization. Transformational leaders

work to elevate followers' level of awareness about the importance of their tasks and the importance of their contribution, fostering an environment of trust, loyalty, and commitment. This style is characterized by the leader's ability to inspire change through vision, communication, and by setting an example.

178. What does the Servant Leadership theory primarily emphasize?
a) The leader's role as serving the needs of their followers
b) The importance of leaders making all key decisions
c) That leadership is an innate trait and cannot be learned
d) The prioritization of the leader's vision over the needs of the employees

Answer: a) The leader's role as serving the needs of their followers.
Explanation: Servant Leadership, a term coined by Robert K. Greenleaf, focuses on the leader's primary role as serving the needs of their followers. It is a leadership philosophy where the main goal of the leader is to serve others by focusing on their followers' needs, development, and well-being, as a priority over the leader's own interests. This approach promotes a more democratic, inclusive, and ethical environment in organizations.

179. Which leadership practice involves creating a shared vision and guiding change through inspiration?
a) Transactional leadership
b) Autocratic leadership
c) Transformational leadership
d) Bureaucratic leadership

Answer: c) Transformational leadership.
Explanation: Transformational leadership is centered on the ability of the leader to inspire and motivate followers to achieve more than what is usually expected of them, through the creation of a compelling vision of the future. Transformational leaders are characterized by their capacity to initiate change by inspiring followers to transcend their own interests for the good of the group or organization, encouraging innovation, and challenging the status quo.

180. How does emotional intelligence contribute to effective leadership?
a) By ensuring leaders adhere strictly to organizational policies
b) By enabling leaders to ignore their own and others' emotions for task efficiency
c) By enhancing leaders' ability to understand and manage their own emotions and those of others
d) By promoting a distant and formal relationship between leaders and followers

Answer: c) By enhancing leaders' ability to understand and manage their own emotions and those of others.
Explanation: Emotional intelligence plays a critical role in effective leadership as it encompasses the leader's ability to be aware of, control, and express their own emotions, and to handle interpersonal relationships judiciously and empathetically. This understanding and management of emotions aid leaders in navigating complex social situations and in making informed, sensitive decisions that respect and consider the feelings of others, thereby fostering positive relationships and a supportive work environment.

181. Which leadership style is characterized by decision-making without input from team members, focusing on efficiency and control?
a) Democratic leadership
b) Laissez-faire leadership
c) Autocratic leadership
d) Participative leadership

Answer: c) Autocratic leadership.
Explanation: Autocratic leadership is characterized by individual control over all decisions and little input from team members. Autocratic leaders typically make choices based on their ideas and judgments and rarely accept advice from followers. This leadership style focuses on efficiency and control, often leading to quicker decision-making but can result in decreased employee satisfaction and creativity due to the lack of involvement and autonomy.

182. In the context of leadership theories, which theory suggests that leaders are born with certain traits that predispose them to be leaders?
a) Behavioral theory
b) Contingency theory
c) Trait theory
d) Skills theory

Answer: c) Trait theory.
Explanation: Trait theory of leadership suggests that certain individuals have specific qualities or traits that make them better suited to leadership roles. These traits, such as intelligence, assertiveness, adaptability, and sociability, are often considered innate and contribute to an individual's ability to lead effectively. This theory posits that leaders are "born, not made," emphasizing the natural attributes that predispose individuals to be leaders.

183. What leadership theory or approach emphasizes the leader's role in clarifying the path to goal achievement and increasing followers' satisfaction by providing rewards?
a) Path-Goal theory
b) Equity theory
c) Expectancy theory
d) Goal-setting theory

Answer: a) Path-Goal theory.
Explanation: Path-Goal theory of leadership focuses on how leaders motivate their followers to achieve set goals and perform at their best. According to this theory, leaders clarify the path to help their followers achieve work goals, remove obstacles, and provide or increase rewards along the path to goal attainment. The theory posits that leadership behavior is effective when employees view it as a source of satisfaction or as paving the way to future satisfaction.

184. Which practice is MOST aligned with the principles of ethical leadership in social work?

a) Using power and authority to influence decisions without consulting stakeholders
b) Prioritizing the well-being of clients and communities in decision-making processes
c) Making decisions based solely on financial considerations
d) Ignoring ethical dilemmas to avoid conflict

Answer: b) Prioritizing the well-being of clients and communities in decision-making processes.
Explanation: Ethical leadership in social work is fundamentally concerned with prioritizing the well-being of clients and communities above all else in decision-making processes. This practice involves considering the impact of decisions on those served and ensuring that actions taken are in the best interests of clients and promote social justice. Ethical leaders in social work are committed to values such as integrity, dignity, and respect for all individuals, guiding their actions and decisions with these principles at the forefront.

185. In the context of organizational theory, the concept of "systems thinking" is best described as:
a) A focus on individual employee performance as the determinant of organizational success.
b) An approach that views the organization as a complex entity made up of interrelated and interdependent elements.
c) A strategy that prioritizes the organization's hierarchy over its process and functions.
d) The analysis of an organization as a closed system, unaffected by external environments.

Answer: b) An approach that views the organization as a complex entity made up of interrelated and interdependent elements.
Explanation: Systems thinking is a holistic approach to analysis that focuses on the way that a system's constituent parts interrelate and how systems work over time and within the context of larger systems. This perspective is crucial in organizational theory and management, as it helps to understand how different components of an organization influence one another and the organization's overall performance, unlike the other options that offer a more narrow or incorrect view of organizational dynamics.

186. When applying the contingency theory of leadership to social work management, a leader must:
a) Stick to one leadership style, regardless of the situation.
b) Adapt their leadership style to the specific circumstances and needs of the organization or situation.
c) Focus solely on the outcomes and ignore the processes leading to those outcomes.
d) Prioritize administrative tasks over the needs and inputs of team members.

Answer: b) Adapt their leadership style to the specific circumstances and needs of the organization or situation.
Explanation: The contingency theory of leadership suggests that there is no single best way to lead a team or organization. Instead, the most effective leadership style depends on the specifics of the situation, including the task, the people involved, and the environment. This adaptability is crucial in social work management, where diverse challenges and dynamic environments are common.

187. A social work organization is considering implementing a flat organizational structure. This would mean:
a) Increasing the number of hierarchical levels to ensure greater control.

b) Removing or reducing levels of middle management to promote more direct communication and collaboration.
c) Centralizing decision-making authority with top management exclusively.
d) Outsourcing most decision-making processes to external consultants.

Answer: b) Removing or reducing levels of middle management to promote more direct communication and collaboration.
Explanation: A flat organizational structure is characterized by fewer hierarchical levels, with the aim of fostering an environment of open communication and collaboration. This structure can lead to greater employee involvement in decision-making processes and faster response times to organizational challenges, unlike the other options which describe more traditional or externalized management models.

188. In managing a non-profit social work agency, the theory of transformational leadership focuses on:
a) Maintaining the status quo and focusing on administrative efficiency.
b) Motivating employees through rewards and punishments based on performance.
c) Inspiring and empowering employees to achieve exceptional outcomes.
d) Delegating all leadership responsibilities to a select group of employees.

Answer: c) Inspiring and empowering employees to achieve exceptional outcomes.
Explanation: Transformational leadership is a style that seeks to inspire and motivate employees to exceed their own expectations and capabilities, fostering an environment of commitment and engagement towards achieving the organization's goals. This approach is particularly effective in the non-profit sector, where passion and dedication to the mission can significantly impact organizational success.

189. An effective organizational culture in a social work setting is most likely characterized by:
a) Strict adherence to top-down decision-making.
b) High levels of competitiveness among staff members.
c) Openness, mutual respect, and a shared commitment to client well-being.
d) Isolation of departments to increase specialization.

Answer: c) Openness, mutual respect, and a shared commitment to client well-being.
Explanation: In social work settings, an effective organizational culture is one that promotes openness, mutual respect among staff, and a shared dedication to the well-being of clients. This type of culture supports collaborative problem-solving, innovation, and ethical practice, which are crucial for delivering high-quality social services.

190. To improve client services, a social work agency implements a Total Quality Management (TQM) approach. This primarily involves:
a) Focusing on reducing the costs of services.
b) Enhancing services through continuous feedback and systemic changes.
c) Increasing the quantity of clients served over the quality of service.
d) Centralizing decision-making to improve service efficiency.

Answer: b) Enhancing services through continuous feedback and systemic changes.
Explanation: TQM is a management approach focused on continuous improvement of organizational processes and outcomes, including the quality of services provided to clients. It involves systematic collection of feedback, involvement of all employees, and making changes to improve service quality and client satisfaction, rather than focusing solely on cost reduction or service quantity.

191. In the context of social work, "burnout" is best managed through organizational strategies that include:
a) Increasing workloads gradually to build resilience.
b) Implementing comprehensive wellness and support programs for staff.
c) Discouraging staff from taking personal time off to avoid disruptions in client services.
d) Isolating staff complaints about stress to individual cases rather than addressing systemic issues.

Answer: b) Implementing comprehensive wellness and support programs for staff.
Explanation: Addressing burnout in social work requires organizational commitment to staff well-being, including the implementation of wellness programs, support systems, and measures that promote work-life balance. These strategies help mitigate the effects of stress and prevent burnout by providing resources and support, rather than increasing workloads or minimizing the significance of staff concerns.

192. A social work agency is considering adopting a participative management style. This would mean:
a) Allowing clients to make all decisions regarding their care plans without social worker input.
b) Involving employees at all levels in decision-making processes affecting their work and client services.
c) Limiting decision-making to a select group of senior staff members.
d) Outsourcing management decisions to an external consulting firm.

Answer: b) Involving employees at all levels in decision-making processes affecting their work and client services.
Explanation: Participative management, also known as democratic management, emphasizes the involvement of employees in decision-making processes. This approach can enhance employee satisfaction, foster a sense of ownership, and improve the quality of decisions by incorporating diverse perspectives, particularly relevant in social work settings where frontline insights can significantly impact service effectiveness.

193. When a social work organization adopts an evidence-based practice model, it emphasizes:
a) The exclusive use of traditional practices that have been used for decades.
b) Making decisions based on intuition and individual experience.
c) The integration of best current research evidence with clinical expertise and client values.
d) A strict adherence to administrative procedures over client outcomes.

Answer: c) The integration of best current research evidence with clinical expertise and client values.
Explanation: An evidence-based practice model in social work focuses on the conscientious, explicit, and judicious use of current best evidence in making decisions about the care of individual clients. This approach combines research evidence, clinical expertise, and client preferences and values to provide high-quality services tailored to meet individual client needs.

194. In managing a diverse team within a social service agency, what is a key strategy for promoting inclusivity?
a) Assigning tasks based solely on seniority to avoid conflict.
b) Developing policies that strictly limit cultural expressions in the workplace to maintain professionalism.
c) Implementing regular diversity training workshops and encouraging open dialogue about differences.
d) Encouraging team members to resolve any issues of discrimination or bias privately without involving management.

Answer: c) Implementing regular diversity training workshops and encouraging open dialogue about differences.
Explanation: Promoting inclusivity within a diverse team involves creating an environment where all members feel valued and understood. Implementing regular diversity training workshops and encouraging open dialogue about differences helps to educate employees about diversity and inclusion, fosters understanding and respect among team members, and addresses any biases or misconceptions. This approach supports a positive and inclusive workplace culture, unlike the other options that either avoid addressing diversity directly or could exacerbate exclusion.

195. What is the primary purpose of conducting performance appraisals in social service settings?
a) To determine the basis for terminating underperforming employees.
b) To identify employees' development needs and set goals for future performance.
c) To focus solely on past mistakes and assign blame.
d) To establish a justification for not providing salary increases or promotions.

Answer: b) To identify employees' development needs and set goals for future performance.
Explanation: The primary purpose of conducting performance appraisals in social service settings is to assess employees' work performance, identify areas for development, and establish goals for future performance. This process is designed to be constructive, providing feedback that helps employees grow and improve in their roles. It serves as an opportunity for open communication between employees and management about expectations, achievements, and areas needing improvement, rather than focusing on punitive measures or financial constraints.

196. When recruiting for a new position in a social service agency, which factor is MOST crucial to consider for ensuring the best fit between the candidate and the role?
a) The candidate's ability to negotiate a higher salary.
b) The social prestige and connections the candidate brings to the agency.
c) The candidate's qualifications, experience, and alignment with the agency's values.
d) The candidate's personal relationship with the hiring manager.

Answer: c) The candidate's qualifications, experience, and alignment with the agency's values.
Explanation: In recruiting for a new position, the most crucial factor to consider is the candidate's qualifications, experience, and how well they align with the agency's mission, values, and the specific requirements of the role. This ensures that the selected candidate is capable of performing the job duties effectively and is committed to the agency's goals and client population. A focus on qualifications and value alignment promotes a productive and harmonious workplace, enhancing service delivery.

197. How can a social service agency best support the professional development of its employees?
a) By offering competitive salaries higher than any other agency in the area.
b) Limiting access to professional development opportunities to senior staff only.
c) Providing access to ongoing training, education opportunities, and career advancement paths.
d) Encouraging self-study outside of work hours without organizational support.

Answer: c) Providing access to ongoing training, education opportunities, and career advancement paths.
Explanation: The best way to support the professional development of employees in a social service agency is by providing access to ongoing training and education opportunities, as well as clear paths for career advancement within the organization. This approach helps employees enhance their skills, stay updated on best practices in social work, and remain motivated and engaged in their work by seeing opportunities for growth and progression. Offering competitive salaries may help attract talent, but it does not substitute for professional development support.

198. In addressing employee burnout in a high-stress social work environment, what strategy should management prioritize?
a) Increasing the workload to improve time management skills.
b) Ignoring signs of burnout as a normal part of the job.
c) Implementing regular wellness checks and providing access to mental health resources.
d) Discouraging time off as it may increase work for others.

Answer: c) Implementing regular wellness checks and providing access to mental health resources.
Explanation: To address employee burnout, especially in high-stress environments like social work, management should prioritize the well-being of their staff by implementing regular wellness checks and providing access to mental health resources, such as counseling services or stress management programs. This proactive approach acknowledges the challenges of the work, supports employees in managing stress, and helps prevent burnout by ensuring that employees have the resources they need to maintain their mental health.

199. What role does effective communication play in human resources management within social service agencies?
a) It is only important for managers, not for entry-level staff.
b) It helps in preventing any form of feedback to ensure employees remain focused on their tasks.
c) It facilitates clear understanding of roles, expectations, and feedback among all staff members.
d) It is used solely for disciplinary purposes and to communicate policy changes.

Answer: c) It facilitates clear understanding of roles, expectations, and feedback among all staff members.
Explanation: Effective communication is crucial in human resources management as it ensures that all staff members, regardless of their level, have a clear understanding of their roles, the expectations set for them, and receive timely feedback on their performance. Good communication also fosters a positive work environment, encourages collaboration, and helps in resolving conflicts, making it essential for the smooth operation of social service agencies.

200. When managing conflicts within a social service team, what is the MOST effective approach?

a) Encouraging team members to avoid discussing conflicts to maintain peace.
b) Addressing conflicts directly through mediation and collaborative problem-solving.
c) Allowing conflicts to resolve naturally without any intervention.
d) Focusing solely on the opinions of senior team members to reach a resolution.

Answer: b) Addressing conflicts directly through mediation and collaborative problem-solving.
Explanation: The most effective approach to managing conflicts within a team is to address them directly through mediation and collaborative problem-solving. This involves facilitating open and respectful communication among team members to understand different perspectives and working together to find a mutually satisfactory solution. This approach recognizes the value of each team member's input and fosters a positive and supportive team environment.

201. In developing a new employee orientation program for a social service agency, what component is ESSENTIAL to include?
a) Instructions on how to avoid all social interactions at work.
b) Information on the agency's history, mission, services, and client population.
c) A detailed analysis of the agency's financial status.
d) An extensive list of all employees' personal hobbies and interests.

Answer: b) Information on the agency's history, mission, services, and client population.
Explanation: An essential component of a new employee orientation program is comprehensive information about the agency's history, mission, values, services provided, and the client population served. This foundational knowledge helps new employees understand the context of their work, align with the agency's goals, and fosters a sense of belonging and purpose from the start. It is critical for ensuring that employees are well-informed and motivated to contribute effectively to the agency's objectives.

202. To enhance teamwork and collaboration within a social service agency, what initiative could HR implement?
a) Discouraging employees from sharing their ideas or suggestions.
b) Creating competitive environments where only the top performers are recognized.
c) Establishing cross-functional teams for project work to encourage diverse perspectives.
d) Segregating departments to reduce the possibility of conflict.

Answer: c) Establishing cross-functional teams for project work to encourage diverse perspectives.
Explanation: Implementing cross-functional teams for project work is an effective initiative to enhance teamwork and collaboration within a social service agency. This approach brings together employees from different specialties or departments to work on projects, encouraging the sharing of diverse perspectives, skills, and expertise. It fosters a culture of collaboration, learning, and mutual respect, as team members work towards a common goal, contrasting with strategies that emphasize competition or segregation.

203. In a social service program aimed at reducing homelessness, which method of evaluation focuses on the program's processes, including how services are delivered?
a) Outcome evaluation

b) Formative evaluation
c) Summative evaluation
d) Cost-benefit analysis

Answer: b) Formative evaluation.
Explanation: Formative evaluation is concerned with the processes of a program, including how services are delivered, the quality and quantity of services provided, and the efficiency of the program operations. It is typically conducted during the development or early implementation stages of a program to improve or fine-tune its delivery, rather than assessing the program's overall effectiveness or outcomes.

204. Which approach in quality improvement involves team members from different departments working together to solve program issues?
a) Cross-sectional analysis
b) Interdisciplinary team approach
c) Singular department focus
d) Top-down management directive

Answer: b) Interdisciplinary team approach.
Explanation: An interdisciplinary team approach involves members from various departments or disciplines working together to address and solve issues within a program. This approach leverages the diverse skills, knowledge, and perspectives of team members, fostering collaborative problem-solving and innovative solutions to improve program quality and effectiveness.

205. When conducting a program evaluation for a family counseling service, what type of data collection method is best suited to understand the clients' personal experiences and satisfaction with the service?
a) Financial audits
b) Quantitative surveys
c) In-depth interviews
d) Administrative data analysis

Answer: c) In-depth interviews.
Explanation: In-depth interviews are qualitative data collection methods that allow for a deep understanding of the clients' personal experiences, perceptions, and satisfaction with the family counseling service. This method facilitates detailed responses and insights into how clients perceive the impact of the service on their lives, providing valuable information for program evaluation and improvement.

206. In quality improvement efforts for a child welfare program, which indicator would be considered a "lagging indicator"?
a) Number of staff training sessions conducted each quarter
b) Client satisfaction ratings collected immediately after services are provided
c) Decrease in the recurrence of child maltreatment cases within a year of service
d) Increase in program enrollment numbers each month

Answer: c) Decrease in the recurrence of child maltreatment cases within a year of service.
Explanation: A lagging indicator refers to an outcome or result that can only be measured after the fact, providing information on the program's effectiveness over time. In the context of a child welfare program, a decrease in the recurrence of child maltreatment cases within a year of service is a lagging indicator, as it reflects the long-term impact and effectiveness of the program's interventions.

207. What is the primary purpose of conducting a cost-benefit analysis in social service programs?
a) To determine the emotional impact of the program on clients
b) To identify the most popular services among clients
c) To assess the financial efficiency of the program by comparing costs to benefits
d) To calculate the exact number of clients served

Answer: c) To assess the financial efficiency of the program by comparing costs to benefits.
Explanation: The primary purpose of conducting a cost-benefit analysis in social service programs is to assess the financial efficiency and effectiveness of the program by comparing the costs of running the program to the monetary value of the benefits it produces. This analysis helps in determining whether the program provides good value for the resources invested and informs decisions on program continuation, expansion, or modification.

208. In implementing a new quality improvement initiative within a social service agency, what step should be taken FIRST?
a) Celebrating the anticipated success of the initiative
b) Identifying specific, measurable objectives for the initiative
c) Allocating all available resources to the initiative immediately
d) Disregarding any potential resistance from staff

Answer: b) Identifying specific, measurable objectives for the initiative.
Explanation: The first step in implementing a new quality improvement initiative is to identify specific, measurable objectives for what the initiative aims to achieve. Setting clear, measurable objectives provides a foundation for planning, executing, and evaluating the initiative, ensuring that all efforts are aligned towards achieving these goals and facilitating the tracking of progress over time.

209. How can social service programs use client feedback for continuous quality improvement?
a) By using feedback solely for promotional materials
b) By disregarding negative feedback to maintain staff morale
c) By integrating feedback into program evaluation and development processes
d) By only considering feedback from high-profile clients

Answer: c) By integrating feedback into program evaluation and development processes.
Explanation: Social service programs can use client feedback for continuous quality improvement by systematically integrating this feedback into their program evaluation and development processes. This involves regularly collecting, analyzing, and responding to feedback from clients about their experiences and satisfaction with services. Utilizing client feedback in this way helps programs to identify areas for

improvement, make informed decisions about program modifications, and enhance service quality and client satisfaction over time.

210. When evaluating the effectiveness of a new intervention aimed at improving employment outcomes for young adults, what is an example of an "outcome measure"?
a) The number of participants enrolled in the intervention
b) The participants' employment rates six months after completing the intervention
c) The cost of implementing the intervention per participant
d) The qualifications of the staff delivering the intervention

Answer: b) The participants' employment rates six months after completing the intervention.
Explanation: An "outcome measure" assesses the results or impacts of an intervention, reflecting the changes or benefits experienced by participants. In the context of evaluating an employment intervention for young adults, the participants' employment rates six months after completing the intervention serve as an outcome measure, indicating the effectiveness of the intervention in achieving its intended goal of improving employment outcomes.

211. In preparing a budget for a new community mental health program, which factor should be prioritized to ensure the program's sustainability?
a) Estimating high for all expenses to ensure a surplus.
b) Identifying and securing multiple sources of funding.
c) Focusing solely on government grants, regardless of restrictions.
d) Allocating the majority of funds to promotional activities.

Answer: b) Identifying and securing multiple sources of funding.
Explanation: For a community mental health program to be sustainable, it's crucial to have a diversified funding strategy. Relying on multiple sources of funding, including grants, donations, and other revenues, can help ensure financial stability and resilience against changes in funding landscapes. This approach is more sustainable compared to the other options, which may either be unrealistic, limit the program's financial base, or misallocate vital resources.

212. When analyzing the cost-effectiveness of a new social service intervention, a social worker should:
a) Compare the program's costs against its measurable outcomes.
b) Choose the intervention with the lowest implementation cost.
c) Base the decision solely on client feedback.
d) Focus on the intervention's popularity in the community.

Answer: a) Compare the program's costs against its measurable outcomes.
Explanation: Cost-effectiveness analysis involves comparing the relative costs and outcomes (effects) of two or more courses of action. In social services, this means assessing how financial resources are utilized to achieve measurable program outcomes, ensuring that funds are spent on interventions that provide significant value to clients and communities, unlike the other options that overlook the importance of outcomes or base decisions on less relevant factors.

213. A non-profit organization's board of directors is reviewing a proposed budget that includes a significant increase in administrative costs. What should be a key consideration in their decision?
a) The impact of increased administrative costs on overall program effectiveness.
b) The necessity to match the administrative costs of similar organizations.
c) Automatically approving the increase to accommodate staff requests.
d) Cutting direct service funding to support the increase in administrative costs.

Answer: a) The impact of increased administrative costs on overall program effectiveness.
Explanation: When evaluating changes in the budget, particularly increases in administrative costs, the board should consider how these changes impact the organization's ability to deliver effective programs. The primary focus should be on maintaining or enhancing program effectiveness and ensuring that administrative costs do not disproportionately divert resources from direct services, unlike the other options that do not prioritize organizational impact or propose less responsible financial management strategies.

214. In planning for a new social work initiative, the concept of "zero-based budgeting" involves:
a) Starting the budgeting process from a "zero base" and justifying every expense, rather than starting from the previous year's budget levels.
b) Ensuring the budget balances to zero by the end of the fiscal year.
c) Cutting all expenses by a fixed percentage to reach a zero-sum budget.
d) Allocating all available funds to program expenses, leaving no reserves.

Answer: a) Starting the budgeting process from a "zero base" and justifying every expense, rather than starting from the previous year's budget levels.
Explanation: Zero-based budgeting is a method where all expenses must be justified for each new period, starting from a zero base. This approach requires each function within an organization to be analyzed for its needs and costs, ensuring that allocated funds are essential and efficiently used. It differs from traditional budgeting, which might simply adjust previous allocations, allowing for more deliberate and justified allocation of resources.

215. A social work agency is forecasting its financial needs for the upcoming year. The most accurate method to predict future funding requirements would be to:
a) Base predictions solely on the funding received in the previous year.
b) Use a combination of historical financial data and anticipated changes in service demand.
c) Assume a fixed percentage increase in funding needs across all programs.
d) Wait for government announcements about funding before making any predictions.

Answer: b) Use a combination of historical financial data and anticipated changes in service demand.
Explanation: An accurate forecast of financial needs involves analyzing past financial performance while considering expected changes in program demands and costs. This comprehensive approach allows for a more precise prediction of future funding requirements, helping to ensure that the agency can continue to meet its service commitments effectively.

216. When considering the implementation of a sliding fee scale for services, a social work organization should FIRST:
a) Determine the minimum payment required to cover basic service costs.
b) Set a standard discount rate that applies to all clients equally.
c) Consult with clients to understand what they can afford to pay.
d) Eliminate all fees to ensure services are accessible to everyone.

Answer: a) Determine the minimum payment required to cover basic service costs.
Explanation: Implementing a sliding fee scale involves determining the lowest payment that can be accepted to cover the essential costs of providing services. This ensures the organization can maintain financial viability while offering more accessible pricing to clients with varying ability to pay, unlike the other options, which do not first consider the financial sustainability of the service model.

217. A social work department is reviewing its budget due to an unexpected reduction in funding. The most responsible initial action would be to:
a) Reduce staff salaries across the board to save costs.
b) Re-evaluate program priorities and explore alternative funding sources.
c) Immediately terminate all non-essential programs without review.
d) Borrow funds to cover the deficit without making budget adjustments.

Answer: b) Re-evaluate program priorities and explore alternative funding sources.
Explanation: Facing a reduction in funding, the most responsible approach is to carefully review and prioritize programs based on current needs and effectiveness, while also seeking alternative funding sources to sustain operations. This strategic response allows the organization to adapt to financial challenges without resorting to drastic measures that could compromise service quality or financial stability.

218. For a social work agency, the process of "financial auditing" is important because it:
a) Provides a detailed record of employee personal expenses.
b) Offers an in-depth analysis of client satisfaction with services.
c) Ensures the organization's financial statements are accurate and comply with legal standards.
d) Guarantees increased funding from all sources for the next fiscal year.

Answer: c) Ensures the organization's financial statements are accurate and comply with legal standards.
Explanation: Financial auditing involves an independent evaluation of an organization's financial statements to ensure accuracy and compliance with accounting standards and legal requirements. This process helps maintain transparency and accountability, fostering trust among stakeholders, funders, and regulatory bodies.

219. In managing a grant-funded project, the principle of "fiscal responsibility" requires the project manager to:
a) Spend the entire grant as quickly as possible to ensure renewal.
b) Allocate funds based on the project's proposed budget and objectives, monitoring expenses closely.
c) Redirect surplus funds to other unrelated projects within the organization.

d) Use the grant to cover general organizational deficits rather than the specified project activities.

Answer: b) Allocate funds based on the project's proposed budget and objectives, monitoring expenses closely.
Explanation: Fiscal responsibility in grant management involves carefully allocating and monitoring funds according to the project's approved budget and objectives. This ensures that resources are used effectively to achieve the project goals and comply with the grant's terms, unlike the other options, which represent mismanagement of grant funds.

220. Which research method is best suited for exploring the lived experiences of clients with chronic illness in a detailed and in-depth manner?
a) Experimental research
b) Quantitative survey research
c) Qualitative case study research
d) Cross-sectional study

Answer: c) Qualitative case study research.
Explanation: Qualitative case study research is designed to explore complex phenomena within their contexts, making it ideal for understanding the nuanced and personal experiences of clients with chronic illness. This method allows for an in-depth exploration of individuals' perceptions, feelings, and experiences, providing rich, detailed insights that quantitative methods may not capture.

221. A social worker wants to measure the effect of a new group counseling technique on reducing anxiety levels among teenagers. Which research design would be most appropriate?
a) Ethnography
b) Randomized controlled trial (RCT)
c) Phenomenological study
d) Narrative analysis

Answer: b) Randomized controlled trial (RCT).
Explanation: A randomized controlled trial (RCT) is the gold standard for determining the causality of an intervention, such as a new group counseling technique, on an outcome like anxiety levels. By randomly assigning participants to either the intervention or a control group, RCTs can more accurately assess the effectiveness of the counseling technique.

222. When conducting a research study on the outcomes of a community-based mental health program, which data collection method is best suited for quantifying the level of improvement in participants' mental health status?
a) Open-ended interviews
b) Participant observation
c) Standardized mental health assessments
d) Focus groups

Answer: c) Standardized mental health assessments.
Explanation: Standardized mental health assessments are specifically designed to quantitatively measure aspects of mental health, such as symptom severity or quality of life, providing objective data that can be used to evaluate the effectiveness of the program. These assessments allow for the collection of consistent, comparable data across participants.

223. In studying the relationship between social support and recovery time from surgery, a researcher decides to use existing medical records to collect data. This approach is known as:
a) Experimental research
b) Longitudinal study
c) Secondary data analysis
d) Action research

Answer: c) Secondary data analysis.
Explanation: Secondary data analysis involves using existing data collected for another purpose to answer a new research question. In this case, the researcher is analyzing medical records, a form of secondary data, to study the relationship between social support and recovery time, which can provide insights without the need for new data collection.

224. A qualitative study exploring the challenges faced by single parents during the COVID-19 pandemic would likely employ which of the following data collection methods?
a) Structured questionnaires
b) Biological measurements
c) In-depth interviews
d) Statistical analysis

Answer: c) In-depth interviews.
Explanation: In-depth interviews are a qualitative data collection method that allows for a deep exploration of individuals' experiences, perceptions, and feelings. This method is well-suited for understanding the complex challenges faced by single parents during the pandemic in a detailed and nuanced way.

225. To determine the average number of hours social workers spend on administrative tasks per week, the most appropriate research method would be:
a) Qualitative content analysis
b) Quantitative survey research
c) Grounded theory methodology
d) Discourse analysis

Answer: b) Quantitative survey research.
Explanation: Quantitative survey research is ideal for collecting numerical data from a large group of respondents, making it suitable for calculating averages, such as the hours spent on administrative tasks by social workers. This method allows for the collection of specific, quantifiable information across a sample that can be generalized to the broader population of social workers.

226. A study aiming to compare the job satisfaction levels of social workers in urban versus rural settings would benefit most from which research design?
a) Case-control study
b) Correlational study
c) Cross-sectional study
d) Ethnographic study

Answer: c) Cross-sectional study.
Explanation: A cross-sectional study design, which observes a specific population at a single point in time, is well-suited for comparing different groups—such as social workers in urban versus rural settings—on specific outcomes like job satisfaction. This design allows for the collection of data from both groups simultaneously to make comparative analyses.

227. To explore how policies on homelessness are implemented across different cities and their impact on homeless populations, a researcher should utilize:
a) Comparative case studies
b) Experimental methods
c) Psychometric testing
d) Biological markers

Answer: a) Comparative case studies.
Explanation: Comparative case studies allow for an in-depth examination of the implementation and impact of policies across different contexts, such as cities. This method facilitates a detailed comparison and understanding of variations in policy implementation and outcomes on homeless populations, providing insights into factors that contribute to policy effectiveness.

228. In assessing the reliability of a new scale measuring client satisfaction with social work services, a researcher should focus on:
a) The scale's ability to produce consistent results over time.
b) The scale's popularity among social workers.
c) Qualitative feedback from clients about the scale's relevance.
d) The cost of administering the scale.

Answer: a) The scale's ability to produce consistent results over time.
Explanation: Reliability in research refers to the consistency of a measure, and for a new client satisfaction scale, it is crucial to assess whether the scale can consistently produce the same results under the same conditions over time. This assessment ensures the scale's reliability before it is widely adopted for evaluating client satisfaction.

229. When analyzing qualitative data collected from focus groups discussing experiences with foster care, the most appropriate method to identify common themes would be:
a) Descriptive statistics
b) Thematic analysis
c) Linear regression
d) Factor analysis

Answer: b) Thematic analysis.
Explanation: Thematic analysis is a qualitative research method used for identifying, analyzing, and reporting patterns (themes) within data. It is particularly suitable for data from focus groups, as it allows the researcher to explore and interpret the diverse experiences and perspectives shared by participants about foster care, providing depth and context to the findings.

230. What is the primary purpose of conducting evaluation research in social service programs?
a) To fulfill grant requirements with minimal effort.
b) To compare the salaries of social workers across different programs.
c) To assess the effectiveness and impact of programs on target populations.
d) To focus on the personal achievements of the program staff.

Answer: c) To assess the effectiveness and impact of programs on target populations.
Explanation: The primary purpose of conducting evaluation research in social service programs is to assess the effectiveness and impact of these programs on their target populations. This involves examining program outcomes to determine whether the program objectives are being met and how the program is contributing to changes in the well-being of those it serves. Evaluation research provides essential data that can guide program improvements, funding decisions, and policy formulations, ensuring that programs are delivering value and making a meaningful difference in the lives of participants.

231. When applying findings from evaluation research to practice, what is a critical consideration for social workers?
a) Ignoring results that do not align with preconceived notions.
b) Applying findings universally, regardless of contextual differences.
c) Tailoring the application of findings to the specific context and needs of their service population.
d) Focusing solely on quantitative data and disregarding qualitative insights.

Answer: c) Tailoring the application of findings to the specific context and needs of their service population.
Explanation: A critical consideration when applying findings from evaluation research to practice is the need to tailor the application of these findings to the specific context and needs of the service population. This involves considering the unique characteristics, challenges, and resources of the population served as well as the environmental and organizational context. Effective application of research findings requires a thoughtful, context-sensitive approach that recognizes the diversity of social work settings and client needs, ensuring that interventions are relevant, appropriate, and effective.

232. In evaluation research, why is it important to use both qualitative and quantitative methods?
a) To ensure that the research process is more time-consuming and complex.
b) To satisfy all possible preferences of the program funders.
c) To provide a comprehensive understanding of program outcomes and processes.
d) To focus exclusively on statistical significance without context.

Answer: c) To provide a comprehensive understanding of program outcomes and processes.

Explanation: Using both qualitative and quantitative methods in evaluation research is important because it provides a more comprehensive understanding of program outcomes and processes. Quantitative methods can offer measurable data on the effectiveness of a program, while qualitative methods can provide deeper insights into how and why certain outcomes were achieved, participants' experiences, and the context in which the program operates. This mixed-methods approach enriches the evaluation by capturing both the breadth and depth of information needed to fully assess and understand program impacts.

233. What does the term "fidelity" refer to in the context of implementing evidence-based practices?
a) The financial profitability of a practice.
b) The degree to which the practice is implemented as originally designed.
c) The practice's popularity among social workers.
d) The legal protections associated with a practice.

Answer: b) The degree to which the practice is implemented as originally designed.
Explanation: In the context of implementing evidence-based practices, "fidelity" refers to the degree to which the practice is implemented as originally designed or intended. High fidelity implementation ensures that the practice is delivered in a way that is true to its original model, which is crucial for achieving the expected outcomes. Monitoring fidelity helps to ensure that any outcomes can be accurately attributed to the practice itself, rather than variations in implementation.

234. How can social workers effectively communicate the findings of evaluation research to non-expert stakeholders?
a) By using complex statistical jargon to highlight their expertise.
b) Through interactive presentations that simplify concepts and focus on key findings and implications.
c) By limiting the information to only the most positive outcomes.
d) Focusing solely on the methodology used in the research.

Answer: b) Through interactive presentations that simplify concepts and focus on key findings and implications.
Explanation: Social workers can effectively communicate the findings of evaluation research to non-expert stakeholders by using interactive presentations that simplify complex concepts and focus on the key findings and their implications. This approach involves breaking down information into understandable segments, using visual aids, and highlighting how the research findings impact the stakeholders' interests and concerns. It's important to convey the information in a way that is accessible and relevant to the audience, facilitating informed decision-making and engagement.

235. When a new intervention shows promise according to recent evaluation research, what step should social workers take before wide-scale implementation?
a) Assume that the intervention will be effective in all contexts and immediately implement it across all programs.
b) Conduct a pilot study in a controlled environment to test the intervention's effectiveness and feasibility.
c) Disregard the research findings and continue with existing practices.
d) Immediately publish the findings to claim credit for the intervention's success.

Answer: b) Conduct a pilot study in a controlled environment to test the intervention's effectiveness and feasibility.
Explanation: Before wide-scale implementation of a new intervention that shows promise, social workers should conduct a pilot study in a controlled environment. This step allows for the careful testing of the intervention's effectiveness and feasibility in a smaller, more manageable context. A pilot study can identify potential challenges, needed adjustments, and the intervention's impact, providing valuable insights that can inform successful scaling and implementation across broader settings.

236. In utilizing evaluation research findings, what ethical consideration is paramount for social workers?
a) Ensuring the findings are used to promote the social worker's personal brand.
b) Applying the findings in a way that respects the dignity and worth of every individual.
c) Using the findings exclusively to secure additional funding.
d) Prioritizing the application of findings for populations not included in the original research.

Answer: b) Applying the findings in a way that respects the dignity and worth of every individual.
Explanation: The paramount ethical consideration when utilizing evaluation research findings is to apply them in a way that respects the dignity and worth of every individual. This involves considering the implications of the findings for all stakeholders, especially the service population, and ensuring that the application of these findings contributes positively to their well-being and rights. Social workers must adhere to ethical principles that prioritize the interests and welfare of clients and communities in the application of research findings.

237. What strategy can social workers use to ensure the sustainability of a successful program evaluated through research?
a) Ceasing all evaluation activities once the desired outcomes are achieved.
b) Developing a detailed plan that includes strategies for funding, staffing, and ongoing evaluation.
c) Keeping successful program strategies confidential to prevent replication.
d) Relying solely on initial funding sources for indefinite program operation.

Answer: b) Developing a detailed plan that includes strategies for funding, staffing, and ongoing evaluation.
Explanation: To ensure the sustainability of a successful program, social workers should develop a detailed plan that addresses critical components such as securing diverse and long-term funding sources, maintaining adequate staffing, and implementing ongoing evaluation processes to monitor and adapt the program as needed. This comprehensive planning ensures that the program can continue to operate and serve the target population effectively over time, adapting to changes and challenges that may arise.

238. When integrating the findings of evaluation research into social work practice, what is a key factor in facilitating the adoption of new evidence-based interventions?
a) Limiting training opportunities to senior staff only.
b) Ensuring that staff receive adequate training and support in the new interventions.
c) Focusing on interventions that are only supported by anecdotal evidence.
d) Avoiding feedback from staff on the feasibility and practicality of new interventions.

Answer: b) Ensuring that staff receive adequate training and support in the new interventions.
Explanation: A key factor in facilitating the adoption of new evidence-based interventions into social work practice is ensuring that staff receive adequate training and support. This includes providing comprehensive education on the intervention, opportunities for practice and feedback, and ongoing support as staff integrate these new approaches into their work. Adequate training and support help staff to feel confident and competent in using new interventions, increasing the likelihood of successful implementation and positive outcomes for the service population.

239. When analyzing data from a survey on client satisfaction with social work services, which measure would give the most typical client response?
a) Mean
b) Median
c) Mode
d) Range

Answer: c) Mode
Explanation: The mode, which is the most frequently occurring value in a set of data, would provide the most typical response in a survey on client satisfaction. This measure is particularly useful in identifying the most common experience or opinion among clients, as opposed to the mean or median, which might be skewed by unusually high or low satisfaction ratings. The range, indicating the spread of responses, does not offer insight into typical responses.

240. To compare the effectiveness of two different interventions for reducing anxiety, a social worker should use which statistical test?
a) Chi-square test
b) T-test
c) ANOVA
d) Pearson correlation

Answer: b) T-test
Explanation: A t-test is used to compare the means of two groups to see if they are statistically different from each other. This test is suitable for evaluating the effectiveness of two interventions on a continuous outcome like anxiety levels, determining if there is a significant difference in outcomes between the two groups. ANOVA is used for comparing more than two groups, while the Chi-square test is for categorical variables, and Pearson correlation assesses the relationship between two continuous variables.

241. When a social worker wants to understand the relationship between age and feelings of loneliness among elderly clients, which statistical method is most appropriate?
a) Chi-square test
b) Pearson correlation
c) ANOVA
d) T-test

Answer: b) Pearson correlation

Explanation: The Pearson correlation coefficient is a statistical measure used to evaluate the strength and direction of the linear relationship between two continuous variables, in this case, age and feelings of loneliness. This method is ideal for examining whether a relationship exists between these two variables and how strong that relationship might be.

242. In assessing the impact of a community intervention program on reducing homelessness, a significant p-value ($p < 0.05$) in the data analysis suggests that:
a) There is no real difference, and the findings are due to chance.
b) The intervention had a significant impact on reducing homelessness.
c) The sample size was too small to determine effectiveness.
d) The intervention had no impact on homelessness.

Answer: b) The intervention had a significant impact on reducing homelessness.
Explanation: A significant p-value (typically $p < 0.05$) indicates that the observed results are unlikely to have occurred by chance alone, suggesting that the intervention had a statistically significant impact on reducing homelessness. This threshold is commonly used to decide whether to reject the null hypothesis, which posits no effect or no difference.

243. To determine if there is a significant difference in job satisfaction among social workers across various sectors (government, non-profit, private), which statistical test should be used?
a) Chi-square test
b) Pearson correlation
c) ANOVA (Analysis of Variance)
d) T-test

Answer: c) ANOVA (Analysis of Variance)
Explanation: ANOVA is used when comparing the means of three or more groups, making it suitable for assessing differences in job satisfaction across multiple sectors. It can help determine if any significant differences exist among the groups without specifying what those differences are. T-tests are limited to two groups, while Chi-square and Pearson correlation serve different statistical purposes.

244. In a study on factors influencing social work burnout, a social worker finds a correlation coefficient (r) of -0.45 between hours worked and job satisfaction. This means:
a) As hours worked increase, job satisfaction increases.
b) As hours worked increase, job satisfaction decreases.
c) There is no relationship between hours worked and job satisfaction.
d) The number of hours worked causes decreased job satisfaction.

Answer: b) As hours worked increase, job satisfaction decreases.
Explanation: A negative correlation coefficient (r) indicates an inverse relationship between the two variables, meaning that as one variable increases, the other decreases. In this case, a correlation of -0.45 suggests that an increase in hours worked is associated with a decrease in job satisfaction. This does not imply causation, only an association.

245. For a longitudinal study tracking the same individuals' mental health status over time, the most appropriate data analysis technique would be:
a) Cross-sectional analysis
b) Repeated measures ANOVA
c) Independent samples T-test
d) Chi-square test

Answer: b) Repeated measures ANOVA
Explanation: Repeated measures ANOVA is designed to compare means across more than two time points or conditions for the same participants. This makes it ideal for a longitudinal study where the same individuals' mental health status is assessed at multiple time points, allowing for an analysis of changes over time within subjects.

246. When planning a research study involving human participants, which principle is MOST crucial to ensure their protection?
a) Ensuring the results will have a significant impact on public policy.
b) Guaranteeing financial benefits for all participants.
c) Obtaining informed consent from all participants.
d) Promising anonymity to participants who achieve significant results.

Answer: c) Obtaining informed consent from all participants.
Explanation: Obtaining informed consent is a fundamental ethical principle in research involving human participants. It ensures that participants are fully informed about the nature of the study, including its purpose, procedures, risks, benefits, and their rights to withdraw at any time. This process respects participants' autonomy and their right to make an informed decision about their involvement in the research, which is crucial for their protection.

247. In a study assessing the effectiveness of a new therapeutic intervention for depression, what ethical consideration is paramount when selecting participants?
a) Choosing participants based solely on their socioeconomic status.
b) Ensuring participants are selected based on the severity of their symptoms alone.
c) Avoiding participants who have not previously received any form of therapy.
d) Ensuring the selection process is equitable and free from bias.

Answer: d) Ensuring the selection process is equitable and free from bias.
Explanation: Ensuring an equitable and bias-free selection process is paramount in research to respect the dignity and rights of all potential participants. This ethical consideration is essential to prevent discrimination and ensure that the benefits and burdens of research are fairly distributed among diverse groups. Equity in participant selection promotes the validity and generalizability of the research findings and upholds ethical standards.

248. When conducting research with vulnerable populations, such as children or individuals with cognitive impairments, what additional ethical safeguard is necessary?
a) Obtaining assent from the participants in addition to consent from their legal guardians.

b) Offering higher compensation to these groups compared to other participants.
c) Excluding vulnerable populations from studies involving any risk.
d) Publishing participants' names to acknowledge their contribution to the study.

Answer: a) Obtaining assent from the participants in addition to consent from their legal guardians.
Explanation: When conducting research with vulnerable populations, obtaining assent from the participants themselves, in addition to consent from their legal guardians, is an essential ethical safeguard. This process involves explaining the study to the participants in a way they can understand and seeking their agreement to participate, respecting their autonomy to the greatest extent possible. This measure ensures that both the participant and their guardian are informed and agree to the participation, providing an additional layer of protection for those who may not fully comprehend the implications of the research.

249. How should researchers address the potential for conflicts of interest in their studies?
a) By keeping any conflicts of interest confidential to avoid biasing the results.
b) Only disclosing conflicts of interest if the research findings are favorable.
c) Transparently disclosing any potential conflicts of interest to the participants and in the publication of results.
d) Ignoring conflicts of interest, as they do not impact the integrity of the research.

Answer: c) Transparently disclosing any potential conflicts of interest to the participants and in the publication of results.
Explanation: Transparent disclosure of any potential conflicts of interest is crucial in maintaining the integrity of research. Conflicts of interest can influence the research process and the interpretation of results, potentially biasing the study. By openly disclosing these conflicts to participants and in the publication of results, researchers uphold ethical standards, foster trust, and allow for an informed assessment of the research findings by the scientific community and the public.

250. What ethical principle guides the need for researchers to debrief participants after the conclusion of a study?
a) Beneficence - to maximize benefits and minimize harm.
b) Justice - to ensure equitable distribution of research benefits and burdens.
c) Respect for persons - to acknowledge participants' autonomy and contribution.
d) Nonmaleficence - to ensure that no harm comes to participants.

Answer: c) Respect for persons - to acknowledge participants' autonomy and contribution.
Explanation: Debriefing participants after the conclusion of a study is guided by the ethical principle of respect for persons. This process involves explaining the study's purposes, revealing any deceptions used, and providing participants with the opportunity to ask questions. Debriefing acknowledges the participants' valuable contributions to the research and respects their autonomy by offering them a complete understanding of the study in which they participated.

251. In research involving online surveys, what measure is essential to protect participants' privacy?
a) Limiting survey access to researchers only.

b) Ensuring the anonymity of responses or securing informed consent if responses will be identifiable.
c) Publishing all survey responses online to promote transparency.
d) Requiring participants to provide their social security numbers for verification.

Answer: b) Ensuring the anonymity of responses or securing informed consent if responses will be identifiable.
Explanation: When conducting online surveys, protecting participants' privacy is paramount. Ensuring the anonymity of survey responses helps protect participants' privacy. If responses need to be identifiable for the study's purpose, obtaining informed consent specifically acknowledging this aspect is crucial. This approach respects participants' rights to privacy and informed decision-making regarding their participation in the research.

252. What is the role of an Institutional Review Board (IRB) in research ethics?
a) To provide funding for research projects.
b) To review and approve the marketing strategies for research findings.
c) To ensure research proposals meet ethical standards for the protection of participants.
d) To assist in the recruitment of participants for research studies.

Answer: c) To ensure research proposals meet ethical standards for the protection of participants.
Explanation: The primary role of an Institutional Review Board (IRB) is to review research proposals to ensure that they meet established ethical standards for the protection of human participants. The IRB assesses aspects such as risk to participants, informed consent procedures, and measures to protect participants' privacy and confidentiality. This review process is essential in safeguarding the rights and welfare of participants and maintaining the integrity of the research process.

253. A 32-year-old client presents with a three-month history of persistent sadness, loss of interest in almost all activities, significant weight loss, and insomnia. Which of the following diagnoses is most consistent with these symptoms?
a) Bipolar Disorder
b) Major Depressive Disorder
c) Generalized Anxiety Disorder
d) Schizophrenia

Answer: b) Major Depressive Disorder.
Explanation: The symptoms described are consistent with Major Depressive Disorder, characterized by a pervasive low mood, lack of interest in activities, significant weight change, and sleep disturbances lasting for at least two weeks according to DSM-5 criteria. Bipolar Disorder involves episodes of mania or hypomania, Generalized Anxiety Disorder is primarily focused on excessive worry, and Schizophrenia involves symptoms like hallucinations and delusions, which are not mentioned.

254. A client diagnosed with Borderline Personality Disorder (BPD) is most likely to exhibit which of the following behaviors?
a) A consistent pattern of disregard for the rights of others.
b) Persistent difficulty with impulse control and frequent job changes.

c) Intense fear of abandonment and unstable personal relationships.
d) Hallucinations and disorganized speech.

Answer: c) Intense fear of abandonment and unstable personal relationships.
Explanation: Individuals with Borderline Personality Disorder commonly exhibit an intense fear of abandonment, unstable personal relationships, emotional instability, and impulsive behavior. These characteristics distinguish BPD from other disorders, such as Antisocial Personality Disorder (characterized by a disregard for others), or Schizophrenia (which may include hallucinations and disorganized speech).

255. When assessing a child for Attention-Deficit/Hyperactivity Disorder (ADHD), it is important to consider:
a) Symptoms must be present in multiple settings, such as at home and in school.
b) The primary symptom must be the presence of hallucinations.
c) Symptoms typically emerge for the first time in adolescence.
d) The disorder is diagnosed more frequently in girls than in boys.

Answer: a) Symptoms must be present in multiple settings, such as at home and in school.
Explanation: For an ADHD diagnosis, symptoms must be observed in more than one setting (e.g., both at home and school), demonstrating that the symptoms significantly impair social, academic, or occupational functioning. Hallucinations are not a criterion for ADHD, symptoms often first appear in early childhood, and ADHD is more commonly diagnosed in boys than in girls.

256. A 45-year-old individual who exhibits excessive worry about multiple life circumstances for more than six months may be best diagnosed with:
a) Panic Disorder
b) Obsessive-Compulsive Disorder (OCD)
c) Generalized Anxiety Disorder (GAD)
d) Post-Traumatic Stress Disorder (PTSD)

Answer: c) Generalized Anxiety Disorder (GAD).
Explanation: Generalized Anxiety Disorder is characterized by persistent and excessive worry about various domains, including work, health, and daily life activities, lasting for six months or more. This distinguishes GAD from Panic Disorder (sudden episodes of intense fear), OCD (presence of obsessions and/or compulsions), and PTSD (anxiety following a traumatic event).

257. In treating clients with Schizophrenia, social workers should be aware that:
a) Cognitive Behavioral Therapy (CBT) is contraindicated.
b) Medication management is often necessary but should be combined with psychosocial interventions.
c) The disorder is typically diagnosed based solely on client self-report.
d) Symptoms of schizophrenia usually resolve on their own without treatment.

Answer: b) Medication management is often necessary but should be combined with psychosocial interventions.

Explanation: Schizophrenia treatment commonly includes antipsychotic medications to manage symptoms like hallucinations and delusions. However, combining medication with psychosocial interventions, such as CBT, can help address the broader impacts on the client's life. Schizophrenia diagnosis involves more than self-report, considering observed behavior and other diagnostic criteria, and symptoms usually do not resolve without treatment.

258. A social worker designing a program for clients with Post-Traumatic Stress Disorder (PTSD) should prioritize:
a) Activities that encourage avoidance of trauma reminders.
b) Therapeutic interventions that help clients process traumatic events and manage symptoms.
c) A focus on medication treatment only, without psychotherapy.
d) Group sessions exclusively focused on sharing traumatic experiences.

Answer: b) Therapeutic interventions that help clients process traumatic events and manage symptoms.
Explanation: Effective PTSD programs typically include therapeutic interventions that assist clients in processing trauma, learning coping strategies to manage symptoms, and reducing avoidance behaviors. While medication can be helpful, psychotherapy is a crucial component of treatment. Sharing traumatic experiences in group therapy can be beneficial but should be approached with care to avoid re-traumatization.

259. When evaluating the effectiveness of a new treatment program for Major Depressive Disorder, the most relevant outcome measure would be:
a) Increase in clients' social media activity.
b) Improvement in clients' self-reported mood and functioning.
c) Clients' adherence to societal norms.
d) Reduction in clients' income levels due to participation in the program.

Answer: b) Improvement in clients' self-reported mood and functioning.
Explanation: The primary goal of depression treatment programs is to improve mood and overall functioning, making clients' self-reported experiences of these changes the most relevant outcome measure. While social media activity or adherence to societal norms might change as a result of improved mood, they are not direct measures of treatment effectiveness. A reduction in income is not a desired outcome of treatment.

260. For clients with Obsessive-Compulsive Disorder (OCD), social workers should be knowledgeable about the efficacy of:
a) Exposure and Response Prevention (ERP) therapy.
b) Avoidance of situations that trigger compulsions.
c) Increased reliance on compulsive behaviors to reduce anxiety.
d) Use of stimulant medications as the first line of treatment.

Answer: a) Exposure and Response Prevention (ERP) therapy.
Explanation: ERP, a type of cognitive-behavioral therapy, is considered one of the most effective treatments for OCD. It involves exposing clients to thoughts, images, and situations that trigger anxiety

and teaching them to refrain from the compulsive behaviors typically employed to reduce this anxiety. Avoidance of triggers and increased reliance on compulsive behaviors are counterproductive, and stimulant medications are not the first line of treatment for OCD.

261. A client who experiences periods of extreme mood elevation followed by episodes of severe depression may be best diagnosed with:
a) Bipolar I Disorder
b) Cyclothymic Disorder
c) Major Depressive Disorder
d) Persistent Depressive Disorder (Dysthymia)

Answer: a) Bipolar I Disorder
Explanation: Bipolar I Disorder is characterized by manic episodes lasting at least 7 days or by manic symptoms that are so severe that immediate hospital care is needed. These episodes are typically followed by depressive episodes lasting at least 2 weeks. The presence of manic episodes distinguishes Bipolar I Disorder from Cyclothymic Disorder (milder highs and lows), Major Depressive Disorder (absence of manic episodes), and Persistent Depressive Disorder (chronic depression without mania).

262. What is the primary goal of motivational interviewing in treating individuals with substance use disorders?
a) To persuade clients to choose abstinence through directive advice.
b) To explore and resolve ambivalence about change in substance use behavior.
c) To provide detailed information about the dangers of substance use.
d) To implement strict consequences for continued substance use.

Answer: b) To explore and resolve ambivalence about change in substance use behavior.
Explanation: Motivational interviewing is a client-centered, directive method for enhancing intrinsic motivation to change by exploring and resolving ambivalence. It focuses on engaging clients in a conversation about change in a non-confrontational manner, helping them to voice their reasons for change and resolve their mixed feelings about substance use, thereby increasing their readiness to change their behavior.

263. In the context of substance use treatment, what does the term "harm reduction" refer to?
a) A strategy that aims to completely eliminate substance use among individuals.
b) Policies and programs designed to minimize the negative health, social, and legal impacts associated with substance use without necessarily requiring cessation of use.
c) A legal approach that imposes strict penalties on individuals who use substances to deter use.
d) An educational program that focuses solely on the dangers of substance use to prevent initiation.

Answer: b) Policies and programs designed to minimize the negative health, social, and legal impacts associated with substance use without necessarily requiring cessation of use.
Explanation: Harm reduction refers to strategies, policies, and programs that aim to reduce the negative consequences associated with drug use. It acknowledges that while not all individuals are ready or able to stop substance use, there are ways to make substance use safer to prevent harm to the individual and

society. This approach can include needle exchange programs, medication-assisted treatment, and providing information on safer drug use practices.

264. Which therapeutic approach emphasizes the importance of family systems and dynamics in the treatment of substance use disorders?
a) Cognitive-behavioral therapy
b) Psychodynamic therapy
c) Family therapy
d) Solution-focused brief therapy

Answer: c) Family therapy.
Explanation: Family therapy is a therapeutic approach that focuses on treating substance use disorders within the context of family systems and dynamics. It recognizes that family relationships and interactions can significantly impact an individual's substance use and recovery. Family therapy aims to address these dynamics, improve communication and support within the family, and engage family members in the treatment process to foster a supportive environment for change.

265. What role does the concept of "readiness to change" play in the treatment of addictive behaviors?
a) It determines the severity of the substance use disorder.
b) It identifies the appropriate medication for treatment.
c) It assesses where an individual is in their willingness to change their substance use behavior.
d) It measures the individual's moral strength and character.

Answer: c) It assesses where an individual is in their willingness to change their substance use behavior.
Explanation: The concept of "readiness to change" is central to understanding and treating addictive behaviors. It refers to the Transtheoretical Model of Change, which posits that individuals move through stages of readiness—precontemplation, contemplation, preparation, action, and maintenance—when changing addictive behaviors. Assessing an individual's stage of readiness allows clinicians to tailor interventions to match the individual's current motivational level, thereby enhancing the effectiveness of treatment.

266. Which substance use disorder treatment model focuses on achieving complete abstinence as its primary goal?
a) The harm reduction model
b) The 12-step facilitation model
c) The motivational enhancement model
d) The contingency management model

Answer: b) The 12-step facilitation model.
Explanation: The 12-step facilitation model, which includes programs such as Alcoholics Anonymous and Narcotics Anonymous, focuses on achieving complete abstinence from substances as its primary goal. It is a group-based intervention that encourages individuals to follow a set of guiding principles (the 12 steps) in the recovery process, which includes admitting powerlessness over the addiction, seeking help from a higher power, and making amends for harm caused by substance use.

267. In evaluating the effectiveness of a new outpatient treatment program for alcohol use disorder, which outcome measure would be MOST relevant?
a) The number of participants who complete the program.
b) The change in participants' quality of life post-treatment.
c) The program's cost-effectiveness compared to inpatient treatment.
d) The participants' blood alcohol content at the beginning of the program.

Answer: b) The change in participants' quality of life post-treatment.
Explanation: While all the listed measures can provide valuable information, the change in participants' quality of life post-treatment is the most relevant outcome measure when evaluating the effectiveness of a treatment program for alcohol use disorder. This measure reflects the holistic impact of the program on participants' well-being, including improvements in health, social functioning, and overall life satisfaction, which are critical goals of substance use disorder treatment.

268. How does the biopsychosocial model inform the treatment of substance use disorders?
a) By focusing treatment exclusively on biological factors, such as genetics.
b) By considering only the psychological aspects of addiction, ignoring social and biological factors.
c) By integrating biological, psychological, and social factors to provide comprehensive treatment.
d) By attributing substance use disorders solely to individuals' choices and behaviors.

Answer: c) By integrating biological, psychological, and social factors to provide comprehensive treatment.
Explanation: The biopsychosocial model informs the treatment of substance use disorders by recognizing that addiction is influenced by a combination of biological (e.g., genetics, brain chemistry), psychological (e.g., mental health disorders, coping mechanisms), and social (e.g., family dynamics, social support) factors. This comprehensive approach to understanding and treating addiction allows for more personalized and effective interventions that address the multiple dimensions influencing substance use and recovery.

269. What is the significance of "dual diagnosis" in the context of substance use treatment?
a) It refers to individuals who are diagnosed with more than one substance use disorder.
b) It indicates a diagnosis of a substance use disorder and a co-occurring mental health disorder.
c) It denotes patients who have been diagnosed by two different clinicians.
d) It signifies individuals who deny having a substance use disorder or mental health issue.

Answer: b) It indicates a diagnosis of a substance use disorder and a co-occurring mental health disorder.
Explanation: "Dual diagnosis" is significant in the context of substance use treatment because it refers to individuals who have been diagnosed with both a substance use disorder and a co-occurring mental health disorder, such as depression, anxiety, or bipolar disorder. This recognition is crucial for providing integrated treatment that addresses both conditions simultaneously, as treating one condition without addressing the other can hinder recovery and exacerbate both disorders.

270. In assessing a family for potential child neglect, which indicator should a social worker consider most critical?
a) The family's socioeconomic status.

b) Evidence of the child being left alone in situations inappropriate for their age.
c) The cleanliness of the family's home.
d) The child's performance in school.

Answer: b) Evidence of the child being left alone in situations inappropriate for their age.
Explanation: While socioeconomic status, home cleanliness, and school performance can be factors in assessing a family's situation, the most direct indicator of potential neglect is evidence of a child being left alone or unsupervised in situations that are inappropriate for their age and development. This situation directly impacts the child's safety and well-being and is a key consideration in child welfare assessments.

271. A social worker is developing a safety plan with a family experiencing domestic violence. What is the PRIMARY goal of this plan?
a) To mediate the relationship between the perpetrator and the victim.
b) To ensure the immediate safety of all family members, particularly the children.
c) To document instances of domestic violence for legal proceedings.
d) To encourage the family to resolve their differences and stay together.

Answer: b) To ensure the immediate safety of all family members, particularly the children.
Explanation: The primary goal of a safety plan in situations of domestic violence is to ensure the immediate safety of all vulnerable family members. This involves identifying safe places, planning how to leave in an emergency, and connecting with supportive resources. While documentation and mediation may be components of broader interventions, the immediate safety of those at risk, especially children, is the most critical focus.

272. In the context of foster care, the concept of "permanency planning" refers to:
a) Finding a temporary placement for a child in need.
b) Ensuring that foster care placements are not disrupted.
c) Developing a long-term plan for a child's living situation, aiming for stability and continuity.
d) Assessing foster parents' ability to provide care on a short-term basis.

Answer: c) Developing a long-term plan for a child's living situation, aiming for stability and continuity.
Explanation: Permanency planning in child welfare focuses on creating a stable, long-term living situation for children who cannot safely return to their parents. Options may include reunification with the family (when safe), adoption, guardianship, or another planned permanent living arrangement. This approach seeks to avoid the instability of temporary placements and ensure that every child has a lasting home where they can thrive.

273. A social worker observes that a child becomes extremely withdrawn and anxious when their parent arrives to pick them up from a community center. The social worker should FIRST:
a) Discuss these observations with the child in a safe and supportive environment.
b) Immediately confront the parent about the child's behavior.
c) Ignore the behavior as it is not occurring within the family home.
d) Report the parent for suspected child abuse without further assessment.

Answer: a) Discuss these observations with the child in a safe and supportive environment.
Explanation: Observing changes in a child's behavior can be an important indicator of potential issues. The first step should be to talk with the child in a setting where they feel safe and supported to understand their perspective and gather more information. Immediate confrontation or reporting without further assessment may not be appropriate or helpful in understanding the situation fully.

274. When implementing a program aimed at preventing child abuse within a community, which approach is MOST effective?
a) Focusing exclusively on punitive measures for perpetrators after abuse has occurred.
b) Providing education and support to families at risk before abuse occurs.
c) Limiting intervention efforts to school settings.
d) Only involving law enforcement in prevention efforts.

Answer: b) Providing education and support to families at risk before abuse occurs.
Explanation: Preventive approaches that offer education, resources, and support to families at risk can be highly effective in preventing child abuse. By addressing potential issues before they escalate into abuse, social workers can help families develop healthier coping strategies and strengthen protective factors, unlike the more reactive or limited strategies listed in the other options.

275. A 10-year-old child in foster care expresses a desire to be adopted by their foster family. What principle should guide the social worker's response to this situation?
a) The best interest of the child, taking into account their wishes and the stability of the foster home.
b) The preference of the biological parents regardless of the child's wishes.
c) The financial ability of the foster family to provide for the child.
d) The length of time the child has already spent in foster care.

Answer: a) The best interest of the child, taking into account their wishes and the stability of the foster home.
Explanation: In matters of adoption, especially from foster care, the guiding principle should always be the best interest of the child. This includes considering the child's wishes, the stability and safety of the prospective adoptive home, and the potential for providing a loving and permanent family. While other factors like biological parents' preferences, financial stability, and time in foster care are considered, they are secondary to what is best for the child's overall well-being and future.

276. To assess the impact of a school-based program designed to educate students about child rights and protection, a social worker should look for changes in:
a) The number of extracurricular activities students participate in.
b) Students' understanding and awareness of their rights and how to seek help.
c) The overall grade point averages of students in the school.
d) The frequency of parent-teacher meetings.

Answer: b) Students' understanding and awareness of their rights and how to seek help.
Explanation: The primary goal of a program focused on child rights and protection education is to increase students' knowledge and awareness of their rights and the available mechanisms for protection and

assistance. Assessing changes in students' understanding and awareness before and after the program implementation would be the most direct measure of its impact, unlike the other options, which do not directly relate to the program's objectives.

277. In a case where a child discloses experiencing abuse at home, the social worker's IMMEDIATE next step should be to:
a) Advise the child to avoid the abuser until a long-term solution is found.
b) Ensure the child's safety by following legal and organizational protocols for reporting abuse.
c) Wait to see if the child makes any further disclosures before taking action.
d) Discuss the disclosure with the child's family to get their perspective.

Answer: b) Ensure the child's safety by following legal and organizational protocols for reporting abuse.
Explanation: When a child discloses abuse, the social worker's immediate responsibility is to ensure the child's safety. This involves following legal and organizational protocols for reporting the abuse to the appropriate authorities and taking any necessary steps to protect the child from further harm. Waiting, advising the child to avoid the abuser, or discussing the disclosure with the family could put the child at further risk.

278. A community social work program aimed at supporting children of incarcerated parents should primarily focus on:
a) Advocating for the reduction of prison sentences across the board.
b) Providing therapeutic services and support groups for children and caregivers.
c) Encouraging children to visit their parents in prison as frequently as possible.
d) Focusing on legal advocacy to challenge the parents' convictions.

Answer: b) Providing therapeutic services and support groups for children and caregivers.
Explanation: Children of incarcerated parents face unique emotional and social challenges. A community program designed to support these children should prioritize therapeutic services and support groups that address their specific needs, provide emotional support, and foster resilience. While advocacy and prison visits might be components of comprehensive support, the primary focus should be on directly supporting the children and their caregivers.

279. What principle underlies person-centered care in gerontology?
a) Treating older adults as passive recipients of care.
b) Standardizing care practices for efficiency across all older adults.
c) Tailoring care practices and interventions to each older adult's preferences, values, and needs.
d) Prioritizing medical interventions over all other forms of care for older adults.

Answer: c) Tailoring care practices and interventions to each older adult's preferences, values, and needs.
Explanation: Person-centered care in gerontology emphasizes the importance of seeing older adults as unique individuals with their own preferences, values, and needs. This approach involves tailoring care and interventions to fit the individual rather than applying a one-size-fits-all method. It respects the autonomy and dignity of older adults, ensuring that their care is aligned with their personal life history, preferences, and goals, thereby enhancing their quality of life.

280. Which factor is considered a protective factor against cognitive decline in older adults?
a) Social isolation
b) Sedentary lifestyle
c) Engaging in regular physical and mental activities
d) High levels of stress

Answer: c) Engaging in regular physical and mental activities.
Explanation: Engaging in regular physical and mental activities is considered a protective factor against cognitive decline in older adults. These activities stimulate the brain and can help maintain cognitive functions, potentially delaying the onset or progression of cognitive impairments such as dementia. In contrast, factors like social isolation, a sedentary lifestyle, and high levels of stress may contribute to or exacerbate cognitive decline.

281. What is the primary goal of using reminiscence therapy with older adults?
a) To correct false memories and teach accurate historical facts.
b) To facilitate communication and recall of past experiences, enhancing well-being and identity.
c) To prepare older adults for end-of-life by focusing on past regrets.
d) To solely entertain older adults without any therapeutic goals.

Answer: b) To facilitate communication and recall of past experiences, enhancing well-being and identity.
Explanation: Reminiscence therapy involves encouraging older adults to recall and share memories from their past, facilitating communication and offering them an opportunity to reflect on their life experiences. This therapy aims to enhance well-being, provide a sense of continuity and identity, and can also improve mood and cognitive function. It acknowledges the value of older adults' life experiences and leverages these as a resource for their current well-being, rather than focusing on regrets or solely providing entertainment.

282. In assessing the needs of older adults, why is it important to consider "instrumental activities of daily living" (IADLs)?
a) Because IADLs focus exclusively on the medical needs of older adults.
b) Because IADLs are unrelated to an older adult's ability to live independently.
c) Because managing IADLs requires more complex skills related to independent living than basic self-care tasks.
d) Because IADLs only include leisure activities that are optional for older adults.

Answer: c) Because managing IADLs requires more complex skills related to independent living than basic self-care tasks.
Explanation: Instrumental activities of daily living (IADLs) include tasks such as managing finances, handling transportation, shopping, preparing meals, and using communication devices—skills that are necessary for an individual to live independently in the community. Assessing an older adult's ability to manage IADLs is crucial because these tasks require more complex organizational, cognitive, and physical skills than basic activities of daily living (ADLs), such as eating, bathing, and dressing. Difficulty in managing IADLs can indicate a need for support services to maintain independence and quality of life.

283. What is the significance of the "socioemotional selectivity theory" in understanding the social relationships of older adults?
a) It suggests that older adults tend to accumulate as many social contacts as possible.
b) It posits that older adults prioritize emotionally meaningful relationships and experiences as they age.
c) It indicates that older adults predominantly focus on new relationships, disregarding long-standing ones.
d) It claims that older adults' social relationships are exclusively determined by their physical health status.

Answer: b) It posits that older adults prioritize emotionally meaningful relationships and experiences as they age.
Explanation: Socioemotional selectivity theory, developed by Laura L. Carstensen, suggests that as people age, they become more selective about their social relationships and activities, prioritizing those that are most emotionally meaningful and satisfying. This change in social priorities is thought to be a result of older adults' increased awareness of their limited time, leading them to focus on what brings them joy and fulfillment. This theory helps explain why older adults may have smaller social circles but higher quality relationships.

284. How does "polypharmacy" potentially impact the health of older adults?
a) By reducing the risk of chronic diseases through the use of multiple medications.
b) By enhancing cognitive functions due to the synergistic effects of various medications.
c) By increasing the risk of adverse drug reactions and interactions due to taking multiple medications.
d) By significantly improving physical mobility and stamina with the use of diverse pharmaceuticals.

Answer: c) By increasing the risk of adverse drug reactions and interactions due to taking multiple medications.
Explanation: Polypharmacy, defined as the use of multiple medications by a patient, is particularly common among older adults due to the prevalence of multiple chronic conditions. However, it can lead to an increased risk of adverse drug reactions, drug-drug interactions, and medication non-adherence, potentially resulting in negative health outcomes. Careful management and regular review of all medications by healthcare providers are essential to mitigate these risks.

285. What role does "advance care planning" play in geriatric social work?
a) It ensures that older adults receive aggressive medical treatment regardless of their wishes.
b) It involves making decisions about the care of older adults only after they become incapacitated.
c) It facilitates discussions and decisions about future healthcare preferences, including end-of-life care.
d) It is a process exclusively focused on financial planning for older adults.

Answer: c) It facilitates discussions and decisions about future healthcare preferences, including end-of-life care.
Explanation: Advance care planning is a process that supports individuals in understanding and sharing their personal values, life goals, and preferences regarding future medical care, including end-of-life care. It ensures that older adults' healthcare preferences are known and can be respected, particularly in situations where they might not be able to communicate their wishes. This process involves discussing and

possibly documenting these preferences in advance directives or living wills, thereby empowering older adults and their families to make informed healthcare decisions that align with their values and desires.

286. Which of the following best describes a barrier to health care access for underserved populations?
a) An increase in health care providers in urban areas.
b) Expanded health insurance coverage under national health care reform.
c) High out-of-pocket costs for services not covered by insurance.
d) The implementation of electronic health records.

Answer: c) High out-of-pocket costs for services not covered by insurance.
Explanation: High out-of-pocket costs for medical services can significantly limit access to necessary health care for underserved populations. These costs can deter individuals from seeking care, leading to worse health outcomes. While an increase in providers, expanded insurance coverage, and the use of electronic health records generally improve access and efficiency of care, the financial burden of uncovered services remains a critical barrier.

287. In comparing health care systems, which characteristic is most associated with a single-payer health care system?
a) Health care services are primarily funded through private insurance companies.
b) Citizens are required to have health insurance, with the government providing it for those who cannot afford it.
c) Health care funding comes from a single public source, and all residents receive coverage.
d) Health care providers operate as for-profit entities competing in an open market.

Answer: c) Health care funding comes from a single public source, and all residents receive coverage.
Explanation: A single-payer health care system is characterized by a single public source funding health care for all residents, typically through taxes. This system aims to ensure universal coverage and equal access to health services, contrasting with systems heavily reliant on private insurance, mandatory insurance policies, or for-profit health care providers.

288. A social worker in a hospital setting is most likely to perform which of the following roles in facilitating access to health care?
a) Diagnosing health conditions based on medical tests.
b) Conducting surgeries and prescribing medications.
c) Assisting patients in navigating health insurance and connecting with community resources.
d) Designing public health campaigns at the national level.

Answer: c) Assisting patients in navigating health insurance and connecting with community resources.
Explanation: Social workers in health care settings often play a crucial role in helping patients understand their health insurance options, access community resources, and navigate the complex health care system. This support is essential in ensuring patients receive the care they need, especially in contrast to clinical roles like diagnosis or surgery, or broader public health responsibilities.

289. The Affordable Care Act (ACA) aimed to improve health care access in the United States by:

a) Reducing the number of health care providers in rural areas.
b) Increasing the reliance on emergency rooms for primary care.
c) Expanding Medicaid eligibility and creating health insurance marketplaces.
d) Mandating all citizens to purchase private health insurance without subsidies.

Answer: c) Expanding Medicaid eligibility and creating health insurance marketplaces.
Explanation: The ACA, or Obamacare, sought to increase health care access by expanding Medicaid to more low-income individuals and establishing health insurance marketplaces with subsidies to make coverage more affordable. This approach contrasts with reducing providers, increasing emergency room reliance for primary care, or mandating insurance purchase without financial assistance.

290. In addressing health disparities, community health workers (CHWs) often serve as:
a) Primary care providers offering medical treatments.
b) Intermediaries bridging the gap between underserved communities and the health care system.
c) Insurance agents determining eligibility for health coverage.
d) Pharmacists dispensing medications without prescriptions.

Answer: b) Intermediaries bridging the gap between underserved communities and the health care system.
Explanation: CHWs play a vital role in addressing health disparities by acting as intermediaries who connect underserved populations with health care services. They provide education, support, and advocacy, facilitating better access to care and improving health outcomes. This role is distinct from clinical care provision, insurance eligibility determination, or medication dispensing.

291. Telehealth has been recognized for its ability to:
a) Replace all forms of in-person health care delivery.
b) Eliminate the need for health insurance coverage.
c) Increase access to care for individuals in remote or underserved areas.
d) Discourage the use of technology in health care.

Answer: c) Increase access to care for individuals in remote or underserved areas.
Explanation: Telehealth, the use of telecommunications technology to provide health care, has significantly increased access for individuals in remote, rural, or underserved areas by allowing them to consult with health care providers without the need for travel. It complements, rather than replaces, in-person care and does not eliminate the need for health insurance or discourage technology use in health care.

292. Which policy intervention is directly aimed at improving health care equity?
a) Policies that exclusively increase pay for health care providers.
b) Legislation that restricts the use of telehealth services to urban areas.
c) Initiatives that provide health care subsidies for low-income populations.
d) Regulations that limit the number of hospitals in economically disadvantaged areas.

Answer: c) Initiatives that provide health care subsidies for low-income populations.
Explanation: Providing health care subsidies for low-income populations is a policy intervention aimed at improving health care equity by making health care more affordable and accessible to those who might otherwise be unable to obtain coverage. This approach targets financial barriers to care, in contrast to policies that might increase provider pay without addressing access, restrict telehealth services, or limit hospital numbers in disadvantaged areas.

293. A significant challenge in implementing electronic health records (EHRs) across different health care settings is:
a) The universal preference for paper records among health care providers.
b) Ensuring interoperability and secure sharing of information between systems.
c) The complete absence of technology in rural health care settings.
d) Legislation that prohibits the use of EHRs.

Answer: b) Ensuring interoperability and secure sharing of information between systems.
Explanation: One of the major challenges with EHRs is ensuring interoperability, or the ability of different EHR systems to communicate and share information securely and effectively. This is crucial for comprehensive care coordination across various health care settings, contrasting with the incorrect suggestions of universal preference for paper, the absence of technology in rural areas, or prohibitive legislation.

294. In analyzing the effectiveness of a new public health campaign to increase vaccination rates, a social worker should prioritize which outcome measure?
a) The number of social media likes on campaign posts.
b) The increase in public knowledge about vaccinations.
c) The change in actual vaccination rates within the target population.
d) The cost of producing campaign materials.

Answer: c) The change in actual vaccination rates within the target population.
Explanation: The primary indicator of a public health campaign's success in increasing vaccination rates is the actual change in vaccination rates within the target population. While awareness and knowledge are important, the ultimate goal is to influence behavior (i.e., increasing vaccination uptake). The cost of materials and social media engagement are secondary considerations to the campaign's impact on public health outcomes.

295. When implementing a bullying prevention program in a school, what key factor should a school social worker consider to ensure its effectiveness?
a) Increasing surveillance and punishment for bullies.
b) Focusing exclusively on older students, as they are more likely to engage in bullying.
c) Involving students, staff, and parents in creating a positive school culture.
d) Limiting the program to classroom activities without broader community involvement.

Answer: c) Involving students, staff, and parents in creating a positive school culture.

Explanation: The effectiveness of a bullying prevention program is significantly enhanced when it involves the whole school community, including students, staff, and parents, in creating a positive and inclusive school culture. This collaborative approach not only addresses bullying behavior but also promotes understanding, empathy, and respect among all members of the school community. Unlike the other options, this strategy provides a comprehensive and proactive approach to prevent bullying.

296. A school social worker is assessing a student who shows signs of anxiety. What initial step should they take?
a) Immediately refer the student to a psychiatrist for medication.
b) Conduct a comprehensive assessment to understand the sources of the student's anxiety.
c) Advise the student to avoid situations that trigger anxiety.
d) Inform the parents and recommend changing schools as a solution.

Answer: b) Conduct a comprehensive assessment to understand the sources of the student's anxiety.
Explanation: The first step in helping a student showing signs of anxiety is to conduct a comprehensive assessment. This assessment should aim to understand the various factors contributing to the student's anxiety, including academic pressures, social relationships, and any potential issues at home. This approach allows for the development of a tailored support plan that addresses the specific needs of the student, unlike the other options, which are either too drastic or bypass the crucial step of understanding the student's situation.

297. In developing an Individualized Education Program (IEP) for a student with disabilities, what is a critical role of the school social worker?
a) Serving as the primary instructor for the student.
b) Deciding independently what accommodations the student needs without consulting others.
c) Advocating for the student's needs and ensuring collaboration among teachers, parents, and specialists.
d) Excluding the student from the decision-making process to simplify discussions.

Answer: c) Advocating for the student's needs and ensuring collaboration among teachers, parents, and specialists.
Explanation: The school social worker plays a crucial role in the development of an IEP by advocating for the student's needs and facilitating collaboration among teachers, parents, and relevant specialists. This ensures that the program is tailored to the student's specific educational needs, fostering an inclusive and supportive learning environment. Unlike the other options, this approach emphasizes the importance of collaboration and student-centered planning.

298. A student discloses to the school social worker that they are experiencing homelessness. What should be the social worker's IMMEDIATE priority?
a) Discussing the student's academic performance to ensure it doesn't decline.
b) Connecting the student and their family with resources for housing and financial assistance.
c) Advising the student to keep their situation a secret to avoid stigma.
d) Encouraging the student to find part-time work to contribute financially.

Answer: b) Connecting the student and their family with resources for housing and financial assistance.

Explanation: When a student discloses they are experiencing homelessness, the immediate priority for the school social worker should be to connect the student and their family with resources to address their housing and financial needs. Ensuring the student has a stable living situation is critical for their overall well-being and ability to succeed academically. This approach directly addresses the student's most urgent needs, unlike the other options.

299. For a student struggling with substance abuse, what intervention strategy should a school social worker consider implementing FIRST?
a) Enforcing strict disciplinary actions to deter substance use.
b) Starting a school-wide anti-drug campaign focusing solely on the student.
c) Providing a referral for a comprehensive assessment and appropriate treatment services.
d) Isolating the student from their peers to prevent influence.

Answer: c) Providing a referral for a comprehensive assessment and appropriate treatment services.
Explanation: The first intervention for a student struggling with substance abuse should be to provide a referral for a comprehensive assessment to understand the extent of the substance use and to connect the student with appropriate treatment services. This approach ensures the student receives the specific support they need, focusing on recovery and health, rather than punitive measures or isolation, which do not address the root cause of the substance use.

300. In addressing chronic absenteeism, a school social worker should FIRST:
a) Implement a policy of automatic failure for missed days.
b) Investigate underlying causes, such as health issues, family problems, or bullying.
c) Exclude the student from extracurricular activities to encourage attendance.
d) Send legal notices to the parents without prior investigation.

Answer: b) Investigate underlying causes, such as health issues, family problems, or bullying.
Explanation: Addressing chronic absenteeism effectively requires understanding its root causes. A school social worker should first investigate potential underlying issues that may be contributing to the student's frequent absences, such as physical or mental health concerns, family challenges, or experiences of bullying. This comprehensive approach allows for targeted interventions that address the specific reasons behind the absenteeism, unlike punitive or exclusionary measures.

301. When a school social worker is implementing a peer mentorship program, what outcome should they MOST anticipate?
a) A decrease in the need for adult supervision in the school.
b) An improvement in the academic and social development of participating students.
c) Immediate resolution of all school conflicts.
d) Complete reliance on peers for emotional support.

Answer: b) An improvement in the academic and social development of participating students.
Explanation: Peer mentorship programs are designed to foster academic and social growth by providing students with support from their peers. These programs can lead to improvements in confidence, academic performance, and interpersonal skills among mentees and mentors alike. While such programs

contribute positively to the school environment, they do not eliminate the need for adult supervision, resolve all conflicts, or lead to complete reliance on peers for emotional support.

302. A school social worker facilitating a support group for students dealing with grief should prioritize:
a) Encouraging students to move on quickly from their loss.
b) Creating a safe and confidential space for students to share their feelings.
c) Advising students to avoid discussing the loss to prevent sadness.
d) Focusing exclusively on academic impacts of the grief.

Answer: b) Creating a safe and confidential space for students to share their feelings.
Explanation: When facilitating a support group for grief, the priority is to create a safe, confidential environment where students feel comfortable expressing their feelings and sharing their experiences of loss. This approach acknowledges the importance of processing grief and provides peer support, contrasting with methods that rush the grieving process, discourage open discussion, or focus narrowly on academic concerns.

303. In promoting mental health awareness in schools, a key strategy for a school social worker is to:
a) Limit discussions of mental health to prevent causing distress among students.
b) Provide education on mental health issues and resources to students, staff, and parents.
c) Focus solely on high-risk students while excluding the broader school community.
d) Assume students will seek out information independently when needed.

Answer: b) Provide education on mental health issues and resources to students, staff, and parents.
Explanation: A fundamental strategy in promoting mental health awareness involves educating the entire school community—students, staff, and parents—about mental health issues, signs of distress, and available resources. This inclusive and proactive approach fosters a supportive environment that encourages seeking help and reduces stigma, unlike limiting discussions, focusing narrowly on at-risk groups, or assuming autonomous information-seeking.

304. What is the primary mechanism through which trauma affects the brain's functioning?
a) Enhancing cognitive abilities for better coping strategies.
b) Inducing permanent amnesia for traumatic events.
c) Altering the response of the brain's stress systems.
d) Increasing intellectual capacity and memory retention.

Answer: c) Altering the response of the brain's stress systems.
Explanation: Trauma affects the brain primarily by altering the response of the brain's stress systems, including the hypothalamic-pituitary-adrenal (HPA) axis and the autonomic nervous system. These changes can lead to heightened or prolonged stress responses, impacting emotional regulation, memory, and cognition. Trauma can sensitize these systems to stress, making individuals more reactive to future stressors and potentially contributing to various trauma-related disorders.

305. How does trauma-informed care differ from traditional care models in social work practice?
a) Trauma-informed care disregards an individual's past experiences to focus solely on present issues.

b) Trauma-informed care treats only the psychological aspects of trauma, ignoring social and physical dimensions.
c) Trauma-informed care operates under the assumption that every individual has experienced trauma.
d) Trauma-informed care focuses on creating a safe environment and emphasizes understanding the impact of trauma.

Answer: d) Trauma-informed care focuses on creating a safe environment and emphasizes understanding the impact of trauma.
Explanation: Trauma-informed care is an approach that recognizes the widespread impact of trauma and understands potential paths for recovery. It seeks to avoid re-traumatization by creating a safe environment for clients and by acknowledging the role that trauma may play in their lives. This approach integrates knowledge about trauma into all aspects of service delivery, emphasizing physical, psychological, and emotional safety for both clients and providers, and helps survivors rebuild a sense of control and empowerment.

306. Which of the following best describes the concept of "complex trauma"?
a) A single, isolated event that is easily resolved through traditional therapy.
b) Repeated, chronic exposure to traumatic events, often resulting in more pervasive and severe impact on an individual.
c) Trauma that is only recognized and treated in complex, specialized medical settings.
d) A theoretical concept that has little practical application in the field of social work.

Answer: b) Repeated, chronic exposure to traumatic events, often resulting in more pervasive and severe impact on an individual.
Explanation: Complex trauma refers to the experience of multiple, chronic, and prolonged, developmentally adverse traumatic events, often of an interpersonal nature and early in life. This type of trauma is more pervasive and can severely impact an individual's emotional, cognitive, and social development. It often requires specialized, multi-dimensional approaches to treatment due to its deep and enduring effects on an individual's functioning and well-being.

307. In assessing trauma, why is it important to consider cultural factors?
a) Cultural factors have little to no impact on how trauma is experienced and can be safely ignored.
b) Cultural factors dictate the only acceptable ways to express and cope with trauma, without any individual variation.
c) Cultural factors influence the perception, expression, and coping mechanisms related to trauma, impacting assessment and intervention.
d) Considering cultural factors complicates the assessment process and should be avoided to simplify treatment.

Answer: c) Cultural factors influence the perception, expression, and coping mechanisms related to trauma, impacting assessment and intervention.
Explanation: Cultural factors play a significant role in how trauma is perceived, experienced, expressed, and addressed. These factors can influence an individual's understanding of trauma, acceptable ways of expressing distress, and coping mechanisms, as well as societal responses to trauma. Understanding

cultural context is essential for accurately assessing trauma and providing effective, culturally sensitive interventions that respect and incorporate an individual's cultural background and beliefs.

308. What is secondary traumatic stress, and how can it impact social workers?
a) A condition experienced by clients that results in secondary gains from traumatic events.
b) Stress that occurs from working in high-risk, high-stress environments, unrelated to trauma.
c) The stress resulting from helping or wanting to help a traumatized or suffering person, which can lead to symptoms similar to PTSD.
d) A temporary stress response that has minimal impact on social workers and requires no intervention.

Answer: c) The stress resulting from helping or wanting to help a traumatized or suffering person, which can lead to symptoms similar to PTSD.
Explanation: Secondary traumatic stress (STS) is the emotional duress that results when an individual hears about the firsthand trauma experiences of another. It can affect social workers and other helping professionals due to their close work with individuals who have experienced trauma. Symptoms of STS can mirror those of post-traumatic stress disorder (PTSD), including heightened anxiety, nightmares, and intrusive thoughts, impacting the well-being and effectiveness of social workers in their roles.

309. How does "resilience" factor into the recovery process for individuals who have experienced trauma?
a) Resilience negates any effects of trauma, making recovery unnecessary.
b) Resilience is a fixed trait; individuals either have it or they don't, determining their ability to recover from trauma.
c) Resilience involves dynamic processes that individuals can develop, contributing to adaptation and recovery after trauma.
d) Focusing on resilience in recovery is seen as blaming the victim for not overcoming trauma quickly enough.

Answer: c) Resilience involves dynamic processes that individuals can develop, contributing to adaptation and recovery after trauma.
Explanation: Resilience in the context of trauma recovery refers to the process of positive adaptation despite significant adversity. It is not a fixed trait but rather involves dynamic processes that can be fostered and developed over time. Factors that contribute to resilience include social support, coping skills, and positive outlooks. Recognizing and building resilience can be a crucial part of the healing process, helping individuals recover from trauma by utilizing their strengths and resources.

310. What role do support systems play in the trauma recovery process?
a) They have minimal impact compared to medical interventions.
b) They potentially re-traumatize individuals by forcing them to relive their experiences.
c) They provide essential emotional, psychological, and sometimes physical support, facilitating healing and resilience.
d) Support systems are beneficial only in the initial stages of trauma recovery.

Answer: c) They provide essential emotional, psychological, and sometimes physical support, facilitating healing and resilience.

Explanation: Support systems, including family, friends, community groups, and professional networks, play a crucial role in the trauma recovery process. They provide essential emotional and psychological support, offer practical assistance, and contribute to a sense of belonging and connectedness. This support can significantly facilitate healing, promote resilience, and encourage positive coping strategies, making it a vital component of effective trauma recovery.

311. What is the significance of "trauma-informed care" in social service settings?
a) It implies that all clients in social service settings have identifiable trauma histories.
b) It requires that all social workers have a background in clinical psychology.
c) It is an approach that recognizes the widespread impact of trauma and integrates this understanding into all aspects of service delivery.
d) It focuses exclusively on providing care to clients with trauma-related disorders.

Answer: c) It is an approach that recognizes the widespread impact of trauma and integrates this understanding into all aspects of service delivery.
Explanation: Trauma-informed care is an organizational framework that recognizes the prevalence and widespread impact of trauma on individuals, families, and communities. It involves understanding, recognizing, and responding to the effects of all types of trauma. Trauma-informed care integrates this awareness into all aspects of service delivery, ensuring that services are delivered in a way that is respectful, informed by an understanding of trauma, and seeks to avoid re-traumatization. This approach enhances safety, trustworthiness, and empowerment among clients and staff.

312. In the context of trauma and its effects, what is the primary challenge in applying a "one-size-fits-all" intervention strategy?
a) It respects the individual differences and unique recovery paths of those affected by trauma.
b) It is the most cost-effective method of delivering interventions.
c) Trauma affects individuals differently, requiring tailored approaches that consider personal histories, coping mechanisms, and current needs.
d) Standardized interventions are universally effective, rendering individualized approaches unnecessary.

Answer: c) Trauma affects individuals differently, requiring tailored approaches that consider personal histories, coping mechanisms, and current needs.
Explanation: The primary challenge of a "one-size-fits-all" intervention strategy in trauma care is that trauma affects individuals differently due to factors such as the nature of the trauma, personal histories, resilience factors, and existing support systems. Tailored approaches are necessary to effectively address the specific needs, strengths, and circumstances of each person. Recognizing and accommodating these individual differences is essential for providing effective, compassionate, and appropriate care that facilitates healing and recovery.

313. According to Erik Erikson's stages of psychosocial development, what is the primary challenge faced by adolescents?
a) Integrity vs. Despair
b) Industry vs. Inferiority
c) Identity vs. Role Confusion
d) Intimacy vs. Isolation

Answer: c) Identity vs. Role Confusion
Explanation: Erik Erikson's stage of Identity vs. Role Confusion is primarily faced by adolescents. This stage focuses on the development of a personal identity and sense of self. Adolescents explore various roles, beliefs, and ideas to form a cohesive identity. Success in this stage leads to a strong sense of self and direction in life, while failure results in confusion about one's place in the world and role in society.

314. In Jean Piaget's theory of cognitive development, which stage is characterized by the emergence of symbolic thought and the ability to use words and images to represent objects?
a) Sensorimotor stage
b) Preoperational stage
c) Concrete operational stage
d) Formal operational stage

Answer: b) Preoperational stage
Explanation: The Preoperational stage, according to Jean Piaget's theory of cognitive development, occurs approximately between the ages of 2 and 7 years. This stage is characterized by the emergence of symbolic thought, allowing children to use words and images to represent objects and events that are not present. It marks a significant advance in cognitive development but is also characterized by egocentrism and difficulty understanding the viewpoints of others.

315. Lev Vygotsky's concept of the Zone of Proximal Development (ZPD) refers to:
a) The range of tasks that a child can perform with the help of a more knowledgeable other.
b) The period during which a child must master certain skills to ensure successful development.
c) The difference between what children can achieve independently and what they can achieve with competition.
d) The geographical area in which a child grows up and its impact on cognitive development.

Answer: a) The range of tasks that a child can perform with the help of a more knowledgeable other.
Explanation: Lev Vygotsky's Zone of Proximal Development (ZPD) is a concept that describes the range of tasks that are too difficult for a child to master alone but can be learned with guidance and assistance from a more knowledgeable other (MKO), such as a teacher, peer, or parent. The ZPD emphasizes the importance of social interaction in cognitive development and the role of educators in scaffolding learning to just beyond the learner's current ability.

316. Attachment theory, developed by John Bowlby, suggests that:
a) Children are naturally detached from their caregivers and seek independence from birth.
b) A strong emotional and physical attachment to at least one primary caregiver is critical to personal development.
c) Attachment between a child and caregiver is primarily formed during adolescence.
d) The quality of attachment has no significant impact on relationships in adulthood.

Answer: b) A strong emotional and physical attachment to at least one primary caregiver is critical to personal development.

Explanation: Attachment theory, developed by John Bowlby, posits that having a strong emotional and physical attachment to at least one primary caregiver is essential for a child's personal development. This attachment is crucial for providing a sense of security that is necessary for exploring the environment and learning. Secure attachment in childhood forms the basis for healthy emotional development and influences the quality of relationships in adulthood.

317. Urie Bronfenbrenner's Ecological Systems Theory highlights:
a) The importance of genetic inheritance over environmental factors.
b) The role of cognitive processes in understanding the environment.
c) The interconnectedness of the various environmental systems that influence individual development.
d) The significance of peer interactions in early childhood only.

Answer: c) The interconnectedness of the various environmental systems that influence individual development.
Explanation: Urie Bronfenbrenner's Ecological Systems Theory emphasizes the complex layering of environmental systems from the microsystem (immediate environments like family and school) to the macrosystem (broader cultural values and laws) and how these layers interact to influence individual development. It highlights the dynamic interactions between the individual and their various environmental contexts over time, demonstrating that development is influenced by a multitude of social, cultural, and political factors.

318. According to Carol Gilligan's critique of Kohlberg's theory of moral development, what aspect does Kohlberg's theory overlook?
a) The role of intelligence in moral reasoning
b) The influence of punishment and reward on moral decisions
c) The ethical principle of justice only, neglecting the ethic of care
d) The importance of biological factors in moral development

Answer: c) The ethical principle of justice only, neglecting the ethic of care
Explanation: Carol Gilligan critiqued Lawrence Kohlberg's theory of moral development for its emphasis on the ethical principle of justice to the exclusion of the ethic of care. Gilligan argued that Kohlberg's theory was based primarily on male perspectives and failed to account for the female moral experience, which incorporates an ethic of care and relationships. She proposed that understanding moral development requires considering both justice and care perspectives.

319. What is the primary focus of the Disengagement Theory of aging?
a) Encouraging seniors to remain active and engaged in society to promote health
b) The mutual withdrawal between older adults and society as a natural, inevitable process of aging
c) The idea that older adults are more prone to social isolation due to technological advancements
d) The benefits of relocating older adults to specialized retirement communities

Answer: b) The mutual withdrawal between older adults and society as a natural, inevitable process of aging

Explanation: The Disengagement Theory of aging, proposed by Elaine Cumming and William Henry, suggests that aging involves an inevitable process of mutual withdrawal in which older adults naturally disengage from social roles and relationships, while society also disengages from them. This theory posits that such disengagement is a natural part of aging that allows for reflection and peace in later life, though it has been criticized and countered by other theories advocating for continued engagement and activity.

320. Understanding the cultural background of a client is crucial for effective social work practice because it:
a) Allows the social worker to apply the same set of interventions universally.
b) Enables the social worker to tailor interventions to align with the client's cultural values and beliefs.
c) Is only necessary when the social worker and client come from different countries.
d) Makes the process of social work quicker by reducing the need for assessment.

Answer: b) Enables the social worker to tailor interventions to align with the client's cultural values and beliefs.
Explanation: Recognizing and understanding a client's cultural background is essential in social work practice as it ensures that interventions are culturally sensitive and tailored to the individual's values, beliefs, and experiences. This approach respects the client's identity and fosters more effective and meaningful support, unlike applying a universal approach or assuming cultural understanding is only necessary for clients from different countries.

321. In social work practice, addressing socioeconomic disparities is important because:
a) It ensures that all clients receive the same treatment, regardless of their background.
b) It helps to identify and mitigate barriers to access and outcomes caused by these disparities.
c) Socioeconomic status is unrelated to a person's health and social needs.
d) Focusing on socioeconomic disparities allows social workers to avoid dealing with more complex issues.

Answer: b) It helps to identify and mitigate barriers to access and outcomes caused by these disparities.
Explanation: Socioeconomic disparities can significantly impact an individual's access to resources, services, and opportunities, affecting their health and social well-being. Social workers strive to understand and address these disparities to promote equity and justice, ensuring interventions consider the broader context of a client's life and are aimed at reducing barriers and improving outcomes.

322. A social worker designing a community program must consider the diverse needs of the community. This approach is an example of:
a) Cultural imposition.
b) Cultural competence.
c) Ethnocentrism.
d) Cultural relativism.

Answer: b) Cultural competence.
Explanation: Cultural competence involves recognizing and respecting diversity within a community and ensuring that programs and interventions are inclusive and responsive to the varied cultural, ethnic, and

linguistic needs. This approach enables social workers to create services that are accessible and relevant to all community members, fostering equity and respect.

323. When working with an LGBTQ+ client, it is essential for social workers to:
a) Assume that all LGBTQ+ clients face the same issues.
b) Use the client's self-identified pronouns and understand the specific challenges they may face.
c) Avoid discussing sexual orientation or gender identity to prevent discomfort.
d) Focus solely on issues related to being LGBTQ+.

Answer: b) Use the client's self-identified pronouns and understand the specific challenges they may face.
Explanation: Respectful and affirming communication, including the use of self-identified pronouns, and understanding the unique challenges faced by LGBTQ+ clients, are critical for providing supportive and effective social work practice. This approach recognizes the individuality of each client's experience and avoids assumptions, ensuring that interventions are relevant and respectful.

324. In working with older adults, social workers must be aware of ageism because it:
a) Enhances the therapeutic relationship by establishing clear boundaries.
b) Can lead to assumptions that overlook the individual strengths and needs of older clients.
c) Is a beneficial approach to simplify complex care needs.
d) Only affects those in late-stage geriatric care.

Answer: b) Can lead to assumptions that overlook the individual strengths and needs of older clients.
Explanation: Ageism, or discrimination based on age, can negatively impact social work practice by leading to stereotypes and assumptions that do not accurately reflect the abilities, needs, and preferences of older adults. Being aware of and addressing ageism is crucial for ensuring that services and interventions are respectful, individualized, and effective.

325. A social worker utilizing an empowerment approach with clients from marginalized communities primarily aims to:
a) Encourage dependency on social services.
b) Foster clients' independence and control over their own lives.
c) Focus on the social worker as the expert who knows what is best for the client.
d) Implement solutions without input from the clients to expedite the process.

Answer: b) Foster clients' independence and control over their own lives.
Explanation: The empowerment approach in social work focuses on supporting clients from marginalized communities to gain power and control over their own lives. This involves collaborating with clients to identify strengths, resources, and strategies to meet their goals, promoting independence rather than dependency, and recognizing the clients' expertise in their own lives.

326. In addressing racial disparities in access to mental health services, a social worker should FIRST:
a) Assume that these disparities are due to individual client preferences.
b) Work to understand systemic barriers and advocate for policies that promote equity.
c) Focus exclusively on increasing the number of minority mental health professionals.

d) Advise clients to seek services only within their racial or ethnic communities.

Answer: b) Work to understand systemic barriers and advocate for policies that promote equity.
Explanation: Understanding and addressing systemic barriers that contribute to racial disparities in access to mental health services are crucial. Social workers play a key role in advocating for systemic changes and policies that promote equity and improve access for all individuals, regardless of race. This approach is proactive and acknowledges the broader social determinants affecting access to care.

327. Incorporating language interpretation services in a community health center demonstrates an understanding of:
a) The need to standardize all health services in English.
b) Cultural homogeneity within the community.
c) The importance of linguistic competence in health care access.
d) The preference of health care providers to communicate in one language.

Answer: c) The importance of linguistic competence in health care access.
Explanation: Providing language interpretation services in health care settings is a critical aspect of linguistic competence, ensuring that individuals who speak different languages have equal access to health services. This approach acknowledges and respects cultural and linguistic diversity, facilitating effective communication and improving health outcomes.

328. When planning a support group for refugees, a social worker should consider which of the following to ensure cultural sensitivity?
a) Conducting all sessions in English to promote assimilation.
b) Understanding and incorporating the cultural backgrounds and experiences of the participants.
c) Discouraging discussions about cultural differences to avoid conflict.
d) Assuming all refugees have the same resettlement experiences and needs.

Answer: b) Understanding and incorporating the cultural backgrounds and experiences of the participants.
Explanation: Creating a culturally sensitive support group for refugees involves understanding and valuing the diverse cultural backgrounds, experiences, and needs of the participants. This approach fosters an inclusive environment where individuals feel respected and understood, promoting meaningful engagement and support. Assuming homogeneity or discouraging discussions of cultural differences undermines the group's potential effectiveness and relevance to participants' lives.

329. The presence of a large industrial plant in a small community is most likely to have which of the following impacts?
a) Increase in local employment opportunities and potential for economic growth.
b) Immediate improvement in air and water quality due to strict environmental regulations.
c) Reduction in community social cohesion as people move away from the area.
d) Elimination of all other forms of local business due to the dominance of the plant.

Answer: a) Increase in local employment opportunities and potential for economic growth.

Explanation: The establishment of a large industrial plant in a small community typically leads to an increase in local employment opportunities and has the potential to spur economic growth within the community. This can result in various socio-economic benefits, including higher incomes and increased local commerce. While there may be concerns about environmental impacts or changes in the community fabric, the direct and immediate effects often include job creation and economic development.

330. In a community affected by natural disaster, what role can a social worker play in addressing the immediate needs of residents?
a) Coordinating disaster response efforts and connecting individuals with emergency services and resources.
b) Focusing solely on long-term redevelopment projects without addressing immediate survival needs.
c) Advising residents to relocate permanently to avoid future disasters.
d) Limiting their involvement to providing psychological support without assisting in practical needs.

Answer: a) Coordinating disaster response efforts and connecting individuals with emergency services and resources.
Explanation: In the aftermath of a natural disaster, social workers play a crucial role in coordinating disaster response efforts. They help connect affected individuals and families with emergency services and resources, such as food, shelter, and medical care, addressing both immediate survival needs and emotional support. This multifaceted approach ensures that residents receive comprehensive support during critical times.

331. How does urbanization primarily affect community social structures?
a) By promoting homogeneity and reducing cultural diversity within communities.
b) Leading to the development of more tight-knit community relationships in urban areas.
c) Causing potential shifts in social networks and increased anonymity among residents.
d) Ensuring equal access to resources and opportunities for all community members.

Answer: c) Causing potential shifts in social networks and increased anonymity among residents.
Explanation: Urbanization can significantly alter community social structures, often leading to shifts in social networks and an increase in anonymity among residents. The density and diversity of urban environments can weaken traditional social ties and may result in more superficial relationships, contrasting with the closer-knit communities often found in rural areas. While urbanization brings numerous opportunities, it also presents challenges in maintaining strong, supportive community connections.

332. What impact does socioeconomic status have on access to healthcare?
a) It has no significant impact as healthcare access is universally equitable.
b) Higher socioeconomic status often correlates with better access to healthcare services and resources.
c) Lower socioeconomic status is associated with greater access to preventive healthcare services.
d) Socioeconomic status only affects access to healthcare in developing countries, not in developed ones.

Answer: b) Higher socioeconomic status often correlates with better access to healthcare services and resources.

Explanation: Socioeconomic status significantly impacts access to healthcare, with individuals from higher socioeconomic backgrounds generally having better access to healthcare services and resources. This disparity can be attributed to factors such as the ability to afford private insurance, proximity to quality healthcare facilities, and knowledge about health-related issues. Contrary to providing equal access, socioeconomic factors create inequalities in health outcomes across different populations.

333. Environmental racism is best described as:
a) A theory that suggests a preference for natural environments over urban ones.
b) Discrimination in enforcing environmental laws and regulations.
c) The disproportionate impact of environmental hazards on marginalized communities due to systemic discrimination.
d) The belief that environmental conservation is unnecessary.

Answer: c) The disproportionate impact of environmental hazards on marginalized communities due to systemic discrimination.
Explanation: Environmental racism refers to the way in which minority group neighborhoods (populated primarily by people of color and low-income residents) are burdened with a disproportionate number of hazards, including toxic waste facilities, garbage dumps, and other sources of environmental pollution and foul odors. It arises from systemic discrimination in environmental policy-making, the enforcement of regulations and laws, and the deliberate targeting of these communities for waste disposal and the siting of polluting industries.

334. A social worker is developing a program to support families in a low-income urban neighborhood. Which of the following factors should be prioritized to ensure the program's effectiveness?
a) Designing the program based on assumptions about the needs of low-income populations.
b) Engaging community members in the planning process to address their specific needs and concerns.
c) Limiting services to traditional office hours to maintain professional boundaries.
d) Focusing exclusively on immediate needs without considering long-term sustainability.

Answer: b) Engaging community members in the planning process to address their specific needs and concerns.
Explanation: The most effective approach to developing a support program for families in a low-income urban neighborhood involves actively engaging community members in the planning process. This ensures that the program is tailored to meet the specific needs, preferences, and concerns of those it aims to serve, fostering greater relevance, acceptance, and impact. Unlike top-down approaches or limited service hours, community engagement emphasizes collaboration and empowerment, leading to more sustainable and meaningful outcomes.

335. How do environmental factors like poor housing conditions affect child development?
a) They have no impact on development as long as children attend school regularly.
b) Poor housing conditions can lead to health problems, stress, and hindered educational achievement.
c) Children adapt quickly to their environment, so poor housing conditions improve resilience.
d) The effect of housing conditions on child development has been widely debunked by recent research.

Answer: b) Poor housing conditions can lead to health problems, stress, and hindered educational achievement.
Explanation: Poor housing conditions, such as overcrowding, inadequate heating, and exposure to toxins, can significantly impact child development. These conditions are associated with a range of health problems, including respiratory issues and lead poisoning, as well as psychological stress. Additionally, such environments can create barriers to learning and academic achievement, underscoring the need for interventions that address housing quality as part of supporting child development.

336. In addressing the effects of climate change on communities, social workers should prioritize:
a) Ignoring climate change as it is outside the scope of social work practice.
b) Advocating for policies that reduce emissions and supporting communities to adapt to environmental changes.
c) Focusing solely on immediate disaster relief without considering long-term environmental sustainability.
d) Advising communities to relocate to areas not affected by climate change.

Answer: b) Advocating for policies that reduce emissions and supporting communities to adapt to environmental changes.
Explanation: Social workers play a crucial role in addressing the effects of climate change by advocating for environmental justice, supporting policies that aim to reduce carbon emissions, and helping communities adapt to the changing environment. This involves both responding to immediate disasters and working on long-term sustainability efforts to mitigate future risks, highlighting the profession's commitment to holistic and preventative approaches.

337. A community experiencing a significant increase in air pollution levels is likely to face:
a) Improved overall health due to increased immunity.
b) Decreased need for public health interventions.
c) Higher rates of respiratory problems and other health issues.
d) Enhanced community cohesion as people come together to enjoy the outdoors.

Answer: c) Higher rates of respiratory problems and other health issues.
Explanation: An increase in air pollution levels is directly linked to a rise in health problems, particularly respiratory issues such as asthma, bronchitis, and other lung diseases. Additionally, air pollution can contribute to cardiovascular diseases and exacerbate existing health conditions, underscoring the need for public health interventions to address air quality and protect community health.

338. Which behavioral theory focuses on the learning of behaviors through the observation of others and the outcomes of those behaviors?
a) Classical conditioning
b) Operant conditioning
c) Social learning theory
d) Cognitive-behavioral theory

Answer: c) Social learning theory.

Explanation: Social learning theory, proposed by Albert Bandura, posits that people can learn new behaviors by observing others and the consequences that follow those behaviors. This theory emphasizes the role of observational learning, imitation, and modeling, suggesting that learning can occur in a social context without direct reinforcement. Bandura's concept of vicarious reinforcement highlights how individuals can learn from the experiences of others, not just their own.

339. In the context of operant conditioning, what does reinforcement aim to achieve?
a) Decrease the likelihood of a behavior being repeated
b) Increase the likelihood of a behavior being repeated
c) Ensure a behavior is never attempted again
d) Make the behavior more spontaneous and unpredictable

Answer: b) Increase the likelihood of a behavior being repeated.
Explanation: In operant conditioning, a theory developed by B.F. Skinner, reinforcement refers to any stimulus that strengthens or increases the probability of a behavior being repeated. Positive reinforcement involves the addition of a rewarding stimulus after a desired behavior is exhibited, making the behavior more likely to happen in the future. Negative reinforcement involves the removal of an adverse stimulus when the desired behavior is exhibited, also increasing the likelihood of the behavior being repeated.

340. How does the ecological systems theory explain the interaction between individuals and their environments?
a) By focusing solely on the individual's biological predispositions
b) By examining how different environmental systems impact and shape individual behavior
c) By asserting that individual behavior is unaffected by environmental factors
d) By emphasizing the role of genetic factors over environmental influences

Answer: b) By examining how different environmental systems impact and shape individual behavior.
Explanation: The ecological systems theory, proposed by Urie Bronfenbrenner, explains the interaction between individuals and their environments through the concept of multiple layers of environmental systems. These range from immediate settings such as family and school (microsystem) to broader societal and cultural influences (macrosystem). This theory highlights how individual development is influenced by the interactions within and between these systems, acknowledging the complex interplay between environmental contexts and individual behavior.

341. What role does "positive reinforcement" play in operant conditioning?
a) It is used to punish undesirable behaviors to decrease their occurrence.
b) It introduces an aversive stimulus to reduce a behavior.
c) It involves removing an unpleasant stimulus to increase a behavior.
d) It includes providing a reward following a desired behavior to increase its occurrence.

Answer: d) It includes providing a reward following a desired behavior to increase its occurrence.
Explanation: Positive reinforcement in operant conditioning involves the addition of a rewarding stimulus after a particular behavior is exhibited, with the purpose of increasing the likelihood of that behavior being

repeated in the future. By introducing a positive consequence following the desired action, the individual is more likely to repeat the behavior to receive the reward again.

342. How does the concept of "self-efficacy" influence behavior according to social learning theory?
a) It determines the genetic predisposition for learning new behaviors.
b) It refers to the belief in one's ability to execute behaviors necessary to produce specific performance attainments.
c) It diminishes the importance of observational learning.
d) It exclusively relies on external reinforcement for behavioral change.

Answer: b) It refers to the belief in one's ability to execute behaviors necessary to produce specific performance attainments.
Explanation: Self-efficacy, a key component of Albert Bandura's social learning theory, refers to an individual's belief in their capacity to execute the behaviors required to produce specific outcomes. This concept plays a crucial role in determining how people think, motivate themselves, and behave. High self-efficacy can enhance motivation and persistence in tasks, as individuals believe they can overcome challenges and achieve their goals, thus influencing their actions and learning.

343. In behavioral theories, what does the term "extinction" refer to in the context of operant conditioning?
a) The introduction of a new behavior to replace an old one
b) The process by which a learned behavior diminishes and eventually disappears when not reinforced
c) The immediate and permanent cessation of a behavior following punishment
d) The genetic elimination of behaviors over generations

Answer: b) The process by which a learned behavior diminishes and eventually disappears when not reinforced.
Explanation: Extinction in the context of operant conditioning refers to the process by which a previously reinforced behavior is no longer reinforced, leading to a decrease and eventual cessation of that behavior. When the reinforcement that maintains a behavior is withdrawn, the frequency of the behavior gradually decreases until it stops occurring, demonstrating how behavior is influenced by its consequences.

344. What principle is illustrated by a child cleaning their room to avoid being scolded by a parent?
a) Positive reinforcement
b) Negative reinforcement
c) Punishment
d) Observational learning

Answer: b) Negative reinforcement.
Explanation: Negative reinforcement involves the removal of an unpleasant stimulus to increase the likelihood of a behavior being repeated. In this scenario, the child cleans their room to avoid the negative consequence of being scolded, which is an unpleasant stimulus. The removal of the threat of scolding serves as a negative reinforcer, making it more likely that the child will clean their room in the future to avoid this negative outcome.

345. How does Bandura's concept of "reciprocal determinism" explain human behavior?
a) It suggests that behavior is solely determined by internal drives and instincts.
b) It posits that behavior is a result of the interplay between personal factors, environmental influences, and behavior itself.
c) It asserts that behavior is predetermined at birth and unchangeable.
d) It focuses on the unilateral impact of environmental factors on behavior, excluding personal choices.

Answer: b) It posits that behavior is a result of the interplay between personal factors, environmental influences, and behavior itself.
Explanation: Reciprocal determinism, a core concept of Albert Bandura's social learning theory, explains human behavior as a result of the dynamic and reciprocal interaction between personal factors (such as cognitive, emotional, and biological components), environmental influences, and behavior itself. This concept underscores the complexity of human behavior, highlighting how individuals both influence and are influenced by their environment and personal factors, leading to a continuous interaction that shapes behavior.

346. What is the primary focus of the "transactional model" of stress and coping proposed by Lazarus and Folkman?
a) Identifying universal stressors that affect all individuals equally
b) Examining how stress is transmitted from parents to children genetically
c) Understanding stress as a result of the interaction between an individual and their environment, focusing on appraisal and coping mechanisms
d) Focusing exclusively on environmental modifications to reduce stress

Answer: c) Understanding stress as a result of the interaction between an individual and their environment, focusing on appraisal and coping mechanisms.
Explanation: The transactional model of stress and coping, proposed by Richard Lazarus and Susan Folkman, focuses on the dynamic and reciprocal interaction between an individual and their environment regarding stress. It emphasizes the importance of cognitive appraisal (how an individual evaluates the significance of what is happening for their well-being) and coping mechanisms (how they respond to and manage the stressor). This model suggests that the experience of stress and the effectiveness of coping strategies are highly individualized, depending on how one appraises the situation and their available resources for coping.

347. What is the primary purpose of collecting a comprehensive biopsychosocial history during a social work assessment?
a) To diagnose medical conditions that may be impacting the client's psychological health.
b) To gather detailed information on all past social interactions without focusing on current issues.
c) To understand the client's psychological disorders without considering their physical health or social environment.
d) To obtain a holistic view of the client's biological, psychological, and social functioning to guide effective intervention planning.

Answer: d) To obtain a holistic view of the client's biological, psychological, and social functioning to guide effective intervention planning.
Explanation: Collecting a comprehensive biopsychosocial history is a foundational component of the social work assessment process. This approach ensures that the social worker considers all relevant aspects of the client's life, including biological (genetic, medical conditions), psychological (emotional, mental health), and social (relationships, environmental) factors. Understanding these dimensions enables the social worker to develop a more effective, individualized intervention plan that addresses the client's unique needs and circumstances.

348. In evaluating collateral data, why is it important to consult with multiple sources?
a) To extend the length of the assessment process unnecessarily.
b) To confirm biases and preconceived notions about the client.
c) To obtain a well-rounded, multi-perspective understanding of the client's situation.
d) To focus solely on the negative aspects of the client's history.

Answer: c) To obtain a well-rounded, multi-perspective understanding of the client's situation.
Explanation: Consulting with multiple sources when evaluating collateral data is crucial for obtaining a comprehensive and accurate understanding of the client's situation. Different sources can provide various perspectives and pieces of information that may not be apparent from a single viewpoint. This approach helps to ensure that the assessment is balanced, reduces the risk of bias, and allows for a more thorough evaluation of the client's needs and strengths.

349. What role does understanding a client's family history play in the biopsychosocial assessment?
a) It is irrelevant to the client's current functioning and should be disregarded.
b) It helps identify potential genetic factors and familial patterns that may impact the client's health and behavior.
c) It solely focuses on identifying negative traits inherited from family members.
d) It is used to place blame on family members for the client's challenges.

Answer: b) It helps identify potential genetic factors and familial patterns that may impact the client's health and behavior.
Explanation: Understanding a client's family history is an integral part of the biopsychosocial assessment process. It can reveal genetic predispositions, mental health conditions, behavioral patterns, and social dynamics within the family that may influence the client's current functioning. This information can guide the development of tailored interventions and support strategies, taking into account the broader familial context.

350. When incorporating collateral data into a biopsychosocial assessment, what ethical consideration must be prioritized?
a) Ensuring that all information collected is used to satisfy the curiosity of the social worker.
b) Sharing all collected data with the client's family and friends to obtain their opinions.
c) Obtaining informed consent from the client before collecting and using collateral information.
d) Using collateral information to make assumptions about the client without verification.

Answer: c) Obtaining informed consent from the client before collecting and using collateral information.
Explanation: Prioritizing ethical considerations when incorporating collateral data into a biopsychosocial assessment is paramount, with informed consent being a key factor. It is essential to obtain the client's consent before collecting and using information from other sources. This respects the client's autonomy and privacy, ensuring that they are aware of what information will be gathered, how it will be used, and who will have access to it, thus maintaining ethical standards in social work practice.

351. How can social workers ensure the accuracy of the biopsychosocial information collected during the assessment process?
a) By relying solely on the client's self-report without seeking any collateral data.
b) By using leading questions that guide clients towards providing specific answers.
c) By cross-referencing information from various sources and through direct observation.
d) By assuming that first impressions of the client are always correct.

Answer: c) By cross-referencing information from various sources and through direct observation.
Explanation: Ensuring the accuracy of the biopsychosocial information collected during the assessment process is crucial for developing an effective intervention plan. Social workers can achieve this by cross-referencing information provided by the client with collateral data from other reliable sources and through direct observation of the client's behavior and interactions. This comprehensive approach helps validate the information, provides a fuller picture of the client's situation, and reduces the risk of basing decisions on incomplete or inaccurate data.

352. In conducting a biopsychosocial assessment of a client, what is the PRIMARY reason a social worker includes questions about family history?
a) To fulfill a mandatory requirement for all social work assessments.
b) To understand potential hereditary and environmental factors that might impact the client's well-being.
c) Because it's a standard procedure that has no real impact on the assessment's outcome.
d) To gather information that will likely be used in legal settings.

Answer: b) To understand potential hereditary and environmental factors that might impact the client's well-being.
Explanation: A biopsychosocial assessment includes questions about family history to identify any hereditary conditions or environmental factors within the family that might affect the client's physical, psychological, and social well-being. This comprehensive approach allows the social worker to understand the client in the context of their unique background and experiences, which is essential for developing an effective intervention plan.

353. Which assessment tool is most appropriate for a social worker to use when evaluating a child for possible Attention-Deficit/Hyperactivity Disorder (ADHD)?
a) Minnesota Multiphasic Personality Inventory (MMPI)
b) Conners' Parent and Teacher Rating Scales
c) Beck Depression Inventory (BDI)
d) Myers-Briggs Type Indicator (MBTI)

Answer: b) Conners' Parent and Teacher Rating Scales
Explanation: Conners' Parent and Teacher Rating Scales are specifically designed to assess the behavior of children and adolescents, making them an appropriate tool for evaluating potential ADHD. These scales provide valuable information from both parents and teachers about the child's behavior in different settings, which is crucial for an ADHD assessment. In contrast, the other options are not specifically designed for diagnosing ADHD in children.

354. When assessing a client for Major Depressive Disorder, which of the following symptoms is a social worker MOST likely to inquire about?
a) Excessive energy
b) Persistent feelings of sadness or emptiness
c) Increased need for sleep
d) Heightened sensory perceptions

Answer: b) Persistent feelings of sadness or emptiness
Explanation: Persistent feelings of sadness, emptiness, or hopelessness are hallmark symptoms of Major Depressive Disorder. An assessment for depression will typically include questions designed to evaluate the presence and severity of these emotional states, as they directly relate to the diagnostic criteria for depression. The other options do not accurately represent common symptoms of Major Depressive Disorder.

355. A social worker using the DSM-5 for diagnostic purposes should understand that this manual is primarily used to:
a) Prescribe medication for mental disorders.
b) Provide a comprehensive biopsychosocial assessment.
c) Classify and diagnose mental disorders based on symptomatology.
d) Offer psychotherapy techniques specific to each disorder.

Answer: c) Classify and diagnose mental disorders based on symptomatology.
Explanation: The Diagnostic and Statistical Manual of Mental Disorders, Fifth Edition (DSM-5), is primarily used by mental health professionals to classify and diagnose mental disorders based on specific criteria and symptomatology. It does not prescribe medication, provide biopsychosocial assessments, or offer psychotherapy techniques but rather serves as a standardized classification system for diagnosing mental health conditions.

356. In using a strengths-based assessment with a client, a social worker focuses on:
a) Identifying the client's weaknesses and areas for improvement.
b) The problems and challenges that brought the client into therapy.
c) The client's resources, capabilities, and resilience.
d) External factors that the client cannot change.

Answer: c) The client's resources, capabilities, and resilience.
Explanation: A strengths-based assessment emphasizes the client's resources, capabilities, resilience, and potential for growth. By focusing on strengths rather than deficits, this approach empowers the client and

supports a more collaborative and optimistic framework for addressing challenges. It contrasts with traditional problem-focused assessments.

357. When evaluating a client for anxiety disorders, it's important to differentiate between symptoms of anxiety and:
a) Normal stress responses to life events.
b) Physical illnesses that mimic anxiety symptoms.
c) Personality traits.
d) Both A and B.

Answer: d) Both A and B.
Explanation: In assessing anxiety disorders, it is crucial to distinguish between symptoms of anxiety and normal stress responses to life events, as well as physical illnesses that can mimic anxiety symptoms. This differentiation ensures accurate diagnosis and treatment planning, avoiding misinterpretation of symptoms that may be attributable to other causes.

358. A culturally competent assessment should include:
a) Assumptions based on the client's cultural background.
b) Standardized questions applicable to all cultural groups.
c) Adaptations to consider the client's cultural, ethnic, and linguistic background.
d) A focus solely on the client's problems, ignoring cultural factors.

Answer: c) Adaptations to consider the client's cultural, ethnic, and linguistic background.
Explanation: Culturally competent assessments are adapted to acknowledge and respect the client's cultural, ethnic, and linguistic background, ensuring that the assessment is relevant and respectful of the client's identity and experiences. This approach helps build trust and rapport, enhancing the accuracy and effectiveness of the assessment process.

359. In selecting an assessment tool for evaluating the mental health of elderly clients, it's important to choose an instrument that:
a) Is designed exclusively for use with younger adults.
b) Considers the specific challenges and issues that may affect older adults.
c) Ignores age-related factors such as cognitive decline or physical health issues.
d) Focuses on assessing the client's past rather than current functioning.

Answer: b) Considers the specific challenges and issues that may affect older adults.
Explanation: When selecting an assessment tool for evaluating the mental health of elderly clients, it is crucial to use an instrument that considers age-related factors, including potential cognitive decline, physical health issues, and other challenges specific to older adults. This ensures that the assessment accurately reflects the client's current functioning and needs.

360. A social worker preparing to conduct a risk assessment for suicidality would MOST likely:
a) Wait for the client to bring up the topic of suicide before asking any questions.
b) Use a structured tool or checklist to systematically evaluate risk factors and warning signs.

c) Focus only on the client's current mood without considering historical or situational factors.
d) Conduct the assessment in a group setting to reduce the client's sense of isolation.

Answer: b) Use a structured tool or checklist to systematically evaluate risk factors and warning signs.
Explanation: When conducting a risk assessment for suicidality, it is best practice to use a structured tool or checklist. This approach ensures a comprehensive evaluation of risk factors, warning signs, and protective factors related to suicide, allowing for an accurate assessment and appropriate intervention planning.

361. In a school setting, a social worker assessing a child for potential learning disabilities should ensure the assessment:
a) Is conducted in the child's second language to test their language proficiency.
b) Focuses exclusively on academic performance, ignoring behavioral and emotional factors.
c) Is comprehensive, considering academic, cognitive, behavioral, and emotional domains.
d) Relies solely on teacher observations without involving parents or guardians.

Answer: c) Is comprehensive, considering academic, cognitive, behavioral, and emotional domains.
Explanation: A comprehensive assessment for potential learning disabilities in a school setting should encompass academic performance, cognitive abilities, behavior, and emotional well-being. This holistic approach ensures that all factors affecting the child's learning and school experience are considered, facilitating accurate diagnosis and effective support planning.

362. What is the primary purpose of collecting a comprehensive biopsychosocial history from a client in social work practice?
a) To fulfill mandatory reporting requirements to governmental agencies.
b) To provide a holistic understanding of the client's life situation, including biological, psychological, and social factors.
c) To focus exclusively on diagnosing mental health disorders.
d) To determine the client's financial eligibility for social services.

Answer: b) To provide a holistic understanding of the client's life situation, including biological, psychological, and social factors.
Explanation: Collecting a comprehensive biopsychosocial history is crucial in social work practice for providing a holistic understanding of the client's situation. This approach integrates biological (genetic, medical conditions), psychological (mental health, emotional, and cognitive functioning), and social (socioeconomic, environmental, cultural, familial relationships) factors. Understanding these dimensions allows social workers to develop more effective, personalized intervention plans.

363. When gathering collateral data for a biopsychosocial assessment, why is it important to include information from multiple sources?
a) To create a more comprehensive and accurate representation of the client's situation.
b) Because it is a legal requirement for all social work assessments.
c) To increase the length and detail of the assessment report.
d) Solely to confirm the social worker's initial hypotheses about the client.

Answer: a) To create a more comprehensive and accurate representation of the client's situation.
Explanation: Gathering collateral data from multiple sources, such as family members, teachers, medical professionals, and other relevant individuals, is crucial for creating a more comprehensive and accurate representation of the client's situation. Multiple perspectives can provide additional insights, verify information, and highlight areas that might not be apparent through a single source, leading to a more thorough understanding and better-informed intervention strategies.

364. In the context of a biopsychosocial assessment, what does the term "collateral data" refer to?
a) Information obtained from the client's social media profiles.
b) Information that is irrelevant to the client's current situation.
c) Information gathered from sources other than the client to supplement or corroborate the client's history.
d) Secondary data that is used only when primary data from the client is unavailable.

Answer: c) Information gathered from sources other than the client to supplement or corroborate the client's history.
Explanation: Collateral data refers to information collected from sources other than the client, such as family members, friends, teachers, healthcare providers, and previous records, to supplement, corroborate, or clarify the client's provided history. This data is valuable in creating a comprehensive understanding of the client's biopsychosocial situation, ensuring that assessments and plans are based on a wide range of information.

365. What role does understanding a client's family history play in a biopsychosocial assessment?
a) It is used to assign blame to family members for the client's issues.
b) To determine genetic predispositions and familial patterns that may impact the client's well-being.
c) Solely to fill in required sections of assessment forms.
d) Family history is considered outdated and is no longer included in assessments.

Answer: b) To determine genetic predispositions and familial patterns that may impact the client's well-being.
Explanation: Understanding a client's family history is critical in a biopsychosocial assessment as it can reveal genetic predispositions and familial patterns that may significantly impact the client's physical health, mental health, and social interactions. This information can inform risk assessments, intervention planning, and provide a context for understanding the client's experiences and behaviors within the framework of their family dynamics.

366. How can social workers effectively use collateral data when working with clients who have substance use disorders?
a) To confirm biases and preconceived notions about substance use.
b) As the sole basis for developing treatment plans without client input.
c) To gain additional insights into the client's use patterns, supports, and the impact on relationships.
d) To share personal information about the client with a wider audience for educational purposes.

Answer: c) To gain additional insights into the client's use patterns, supports, and the impact on relationships.
Explanation: Collateral data can be particularly valuable when working with clients who have substance use disorders by providing additional insights into their use patterns, the availability and effectiveness of support systems, and the impact of substance use on interpersonal relationships. This information can complement the client's self-report, offer a broader view of the client's situation, and help tailor interventions to address specific needs and dynamics effectively.

367. What is a key consideration when interpreting biopsychosocial assessments in culturally diverse populations?
a) Assuming that assessments have the same validity across all cultural groups.
b) Ignoring cultural factors as they are deemed insignificant in the assessment process.
c) Understanding and respecting cultural differences that may influence behavior, health beliefs, and family dynamics.
d) Focusing solely on biological factors as they are seen as more objective and reliable across cultures.

Answer: c) Understanding and respecting cultural differences that may influence behavior, health beliefs, and family dynamics.
Explanation: A key consideration when conducting biopsychosocial assessments with culturally diverse populations is the need to understand and respect cultural differences that can significantly influence behavior, health beliefs, family dynamics, and the interpretation of psychological symptoms. Recognizing these cultural factors ensures that assessments are culturally sensitive and accurate, leading to more effective and appropriate interventions.

368. In gathering biopsychosocial histories, why is it crucial to assess an individual's social support system?
a) Social support systems are only relevant in cases of severe mental illness.
b) To determine the financial wealth of the client's network.
c) Social support systems play a significant role in coping, recovery, and overall well-being.
d) It is a procedural formality with no impact on the assessment outcome.

Answer: c) Social support systems play a significant role in coping, recovery, and overall well-being.
Explanation: Assessing an individual's social support system is crucial in gathering biopsychosocial histories because social supports play a fundamental role in coping mechanisms, recovery processes, and overall well-being. Understanding the quality, availability, and effectiveness of an individual's social supports can inform the development of more comprehensive, tailored intervention plans that leverage these supports for improved outcomes.

369. When considering the biopsychosocial model, how should social workers view the interaction between biological, psychological, and social factors?
a) As independent factors that do not influence each other.
b) As a complex interplay where each factor can influence and be influenced by the others.
c) Solely focusing on biological factors as they are the most significant.
d) Disregarding psychological and social factors as irrelevant to social work practice.

Answer: b) As a complex interplay where each factor can influence and be influenced by the others.
Explanation: The biopsychosocial model posits that biological, psychological, and social factors are intricately interconnected, with each factor capable of influencing and being influenced by the others. This perspective encourages social workers to view clients' issues through a holistic lens, recognizing that addressing challenges in one area may require understanding and intervening in the others. This integrated approach facilitates comprehensive assessments and more effective interventions.

370. What is the primary purpose of utilizing evidence-based practice (EBP) in social work?
a) To adhere strictly to traditional methods that have been used for decades without change.
b) To enhance the professional autonomy of social workers by allowing them to use any methods they prefer.
c) To improve client outcomes through the integration of the best available research evidence with clinical expertise and client values.
d) To simplify the decision-making process by eliminating the need for critical thinking and individual assessment.

Answer: c) To improve client outcomes through the integration of the best available research evidence with clinical expertise and client values.
Explanation: Evidence-based practice in social work aims to enhance client outcomes by systematically integrating the most current and robust research evidence with social work expertise and the preferences, needs, and values of clients. This approach ensures that interventions are not only grounded in scientific evidence but also tailored to the unique circumstances of each client, promoting effective and personalized care.

371. When evaluating the outcomes of a program designed to reduce adolescent substance abuse, which indicator would be most relevant?
a) The number of adolescents enrolled in the program.
b) The percentage reduction in substance abuse among participants after completing the program.
c) The total cost of implementing the program.
d) The number of staff members involved in the program.

Answer: b) The percentage reduction in substance abuse among participants after completing the program.
Explanation: The most relevant indicator for evaluating the effectiveness of a substance abuse reduction program is the percentage reduction in substance abuse among participants. This outcome directly reflects the program's impact on changing the behavior it targets, providing a clear measure of its success. While other factors, like enrollment numbers, cost, and staffing, are important for program management and implementation, they do not directly measure program effectiveness in achieving its primary goal.

372. In the context of evidence-based practice, what is the significance of randomized controlled trials (RCTs)?
a) RCTs are considered the gold standard in research for determining the effectiveness of interventions due to their ability to minimize bias.
b) RCTs are discouraged in social work practice because they are too difficult to implement in real-world settings.

c) RCTs focus exclusively on the financial aspects of interventions, ignoring outcomes and client satisfaction.
d) RCTs are primarily used for assessing the aesthetic appeal of interventions rather than their effectiveness.

Answer: a) RCTs are considered the gold standard in research for determining the effectiveness of interventions due to their ability to minimize bias.
Explanation: Randomized controlled trials are highly valued in evidence-based practice because they randomly assign participants to either an intervention group or a control group, thereby minimizing selection bias and other confounding factors. This design allows for a more accurate assessment of whether observed outcomes are truly a result of the intervention, making RCTs a critical component of evidence-based evaluation.

373. What is a systematic review in the context of evidence-based practice?
a) A casual overview of available literature without any critical appraisal.
b) A detailed audit of an individual practitioner's case notes to ensure compliance with guidelines.
c) A comprehensive synthesis of research findings from multiple studies on a specific topic, using a standardized methodology.
d) An artistic critique of the presentation and readability of research publications.

Answer: c) A comprehensive synthesis of research findings from multiple studies on a specific topic, using a standardized methodology.
Explanation: A systematic review is a rigorous summary of existing research on a specific question or topic that uses standardized methods to identify, select, and critically appraise relevant research. By synthesizing findings from multiple studies, systematic reviews provide a high level of evidence about the effectiveness of interventions, informing evidence-based practice by identifying what works, for whom, and under what circumstances.

374. When implementing a new intervention based on evidence-based practice, what should a social worker do if the research evidence does not perfectly align with the client's values and circumstances?
a) Disregard the client's values and circumstances, strictly following the research evidence.
b) Modify the intervention, within ethical and professional guidelines, to better fit the client's unique values and circumstances.
c) Abandon evidence-based practice in favor of exclusively client-directed approaches.
d) Only use interventions that have been proven effective in randomized controlled trials, regardless of fit.

Answer: b) Modify the intervention, within ethical and professional guidelines, to better fit the client's unique values and circumstances.
Explanation: Evidence-based practice involves the integration of the best available research evidence with clinical expertise and client values. When there is a mismatch between research evidence and a client's values or circumstances, the social worker should adapt the intervention, as long as it is within ethical and professional boundaries, to ensure the intervention is both effective and respectful of the client's individuality. This approach maintains fidelity to the principles of evidence-based practice while honoring the client's autonomy and preferences.

375. What role does client feedback play in outcome evaluation of social work interventions?
a) It is considered irrelevant since the only valid outcomes are those measured by standardized tests.
b) It provides essential insights into the effectiveness and impact of interventions from the client's perspective.
c) Client feedback is only useful for marketing purposes and has no place in clinical evaluation.
d) It should be collected but ignored in favor of more objective measures of success.

Answer: b) It provides essential insights into the effectiveness and impact of interventions from the client's perspective.
Explanation: Client feedback is a crucial component of outcome evaluation in social work practice. It offers valuable perspectives on the effectiveness, relevance, and impact of interventions, reflecting the client's subjective experience and satisfaction. Collecting and incorporating client feedback into outcome evaluations ensures that services are responsive to client needs and perceptions of change, enhancing the overall quality and effectiveness of social work practice.

376. In assessing the effectiveness of a community mental health program, which type of data is MOST important?
a) The number of community members who are aware of the program.
b) Outcome data measuring changes in mental health status among participants.
c) The cost of the program per participant.
d) The qualifications of the staff running the program.

Answer: b) Outcome data measuring changes in mental health status among participants.
Explanation: Outcome data that measures changes in mental health status among participants is the most important when assessing the effectiveness of a community mental health program. This type of data provides direct evidence of whether the program is achieving its intended goals of improving mental health outcomes for participants. While awareness, cost, and staff qualifications are important aspects of program evaluation, the primary focus should be on the impact of the program on participants' mental health.

377. How does the concept of "practice-based evidence" complement evidence-based practice in social work?
a) By prioritizing traditional practices over current research findings.
b) Through generating evidence from the outcomes of everyday practice to inform and improve future practice.
c) By rejecting the findings of empirical research in favor of anecdotal evidence.
d) Practice-based evidence is seen as opposing evidence-based practice and is therefore not utilized.

Answer: b) Through generating evidence from the outcomes of everyday practice to inform and improve future practice.
Explanation: Practice-based evidence complements evidence-based practice by generating evidence from the outcomes and experiences of everyday clinical practice. This approach values the knowledge gained from direct practice, using it to inform and enhance evidence-based interventions. It recognizes that

valuable insights into effective practice can emerge from the systematic evaluation of real-world outcomes, thereby enriching the evidence base used to guide social work interventions.

378. When a social worker is evaluating the outcomes of a program aimed at reducing homelessness, what outcome measure is MOST directly relevant?
a) The number of media mentions the program receives.
b) The decrease in the number of individuals experiencing homelessness in the target area.
c) The total budget allocated to the program.
d) The number of staff employed by the program.

Answer: b) The decrease in the number of individuals experiencing homelessness in the target area.
Explanation: The most directly relevant outcome measure for a program aimed at reducing homelessness is the decrease in the number of individuals experiencing homelessness in the target area. This measure directly assesses the program's effectiveness in achieving its primary goal. While budget, staff numbers, and media mentions might indicate program scale or awareness, the ultimate indicator of success is the impact on homelessness itself.

379. What is the primary goal of Solution-Focused Brief Therapy (SFBT) when applied to individuals?
a) To uncover unconscious conflicts from the individual's past.
b) To identify and amplify existing strengths and resources to find solutions.
c) To change an individual's personality structure.
d) To provide long-term psychoanalysis and exploration of childhood experiences.

Answer: b) To identify and amplify existing strengths and resources to find solutions.
Explanation: Solution-Focused Brief Therapy (SFBT) centers on identifying the client's current resources and future hopes - helping them to build solutions rather than dwelling on problems. This approach aims to encourage individuals to develop a concrete vision of a preferred future and to identify and amplify their strengths and resources to achieve that vision. SFBT is action-oriented, future-focused, and goal-directed, making it distinct from therapies that focus on the past or on changing personality structures.

380. In working with families experiencing conflict, what is a key technique used in Structural Family Therapy?
a) Encouraging family members to change the subject when conflict arises.
b) Joining the family system to understand its dynamics and restructure relationships.
c) Focusing solely on individual therapy with the family member identified as the problem.
d) Avoiding discussions of family roles and boundaries to prevent further conflict.

Answer: b) Joining the family system to understand its dynamics and restructure relationships.
Explanation: Structural Family Therapy, developed by Salvador Minuchin, involves the therapist "joining" the family to observe and understand the structure, dynamics, and patterns of interaction that contribute to the family's issues. A key technique in this approach is restructuring, where the therapist actively works to alter the family's organization, including its hierarchies, roles, and boundaries, to reduce dysfunction and conflict. This may involve challenging unhelpful behaviors and encouraging healthier ways of relating to one another.

381. What intervention strategy is most associated with Cognitive Behavioral Therapy (CBT) when addressing maladaptive thought patterns?
a) Dream analysis and interpretation.
b) Cognitive restructuring to challenge and change negative thoughts.
c) Free association to uncover hidden meanings.
d) Prescribing medication to alter thought processes.

Answer: b) Cognitive restructuring to challenge and change negative thoughts.
Explanation: Cognitive Behavioral Therapy (CBT) employs cognitive restructuring as a core intervention strategy to address maladaptive thought patterns. This technique involves identifying negative or inaccurate thoughts and challenging them to consider more balanced and realistic perspectives. The goal is to change the way individuals perceive and interpret experiences, which can lead to more positive emotional states and behaviors. CBT focuses on the interconnection between thoughts, feelings, and behaviors, making cognitive restructuring pivotal in modifying dysfunctional thought patterns.

382. In group therapy, what is the purpose of establishing group norms?
a) To discourage any form of open communication and sharing.
b) To create a hierarchical structure within the group.
c) To set expectations for behavior and promote a safe environment.
d) To single out and identify the most problematic group member.

Answer: c) To set expectations for behavior and promote a safe environment.
Explanation: Establishing group norms in therapy is crucial for setting clear expectations for behavior and interaction among group members. Norms help create a therapeutic and safe environment where members feel comfortable sharing personal experiences and feelings. They contribute to building trust, respect, and cohesion within the group, facilitating effective therapy. Norms may include confidentiality, respect for each other's perspectives, and commitment to the group process.

383. When implementing a community-based intervention, what factor is crucial for ensuring its success?
a) Excluding community members from the planning process to maintain control.
b) Identifying and leveraging the community's strengths and resources.
c) Implementing the intervention without assessing community needs.
d) Assuming that all communities will benefit from the same type of intervention.

Answer: b) Identifying and leveraging the community's strengths and resources.
Explanation: For a community-based intervention to be successful, it is crucial to identify and leverage the community's strengths and resources. This strengths-based approach involves collaborating with community members to understand their needs, values, and goals, and to mobilize existing assets to address issues. Engaging community members in the planning and implementation process ensures that the intervention is relevant, culturally sensitive, and sustainable, increasing the likelihood of positive outcomes.

384. What approach would a social worker take in applying the ecological systems theory to client intervention?

a) Focusing solely on modifying the individual's behavior without considering environmental factors.
b) Analyzing the client's interactions across various environmental systems and addressing the influence of these systems on the client's situation.
c) Ignoring the broader social and cultural context that impacts the client.
d) Concentrating exclusively on changing the client's immediate family dynamics.

Answer: b) Analyzing the client's interactions across various environmental systems and addressing the influence of these systems on the client's situation.
Explanation: The ecological systems theory, proposed by Urie Bronfenbrenner, emphasizes the importance of understanding individuals within the context of various interacting environmental systems, from immediate settings like family and school to broader societal and cultural influences. Applying this theory, a social worker would analyze how these systems impact the client's situation and well-being. Interventions may target multiple levels of the client's environment to facilitate change, recognizing the complex interplay between individual and environmental factors.

385. In Narrative Therapy, what is the significance of "re-authoring" conversations?
a) To rewrite the client's past experiences so they are completely forgotten.
b) To identify and amplify problems within the client's narrative.
c) To help clients separate their identity from their problems and create new, empowering life narratives.
d) To convince clients to adopt the therapist's interpretation of their life story.

Answer: c) To help clients separate their identity from their problems and create new, empowering life narratives.
Explanation: Narrative Therapy focuses on the stories people construct and live by and how these narratives shape their identities and experiences. "Re-authoring" conversations are a technique wherein the therapist helps clients to identify and explore their problem-saturated stories, separate their sense of self from these problems, and construct new, empowering narratives. This process allows clients to view their problems from different perspectives, recognize their agency, and reimagine their life stories in ways that align with their values and goals.

386. What role does active listening play in motivational interviewing?
a) It is used to persuade clients to adopt the therapist's goals and objectives.
b) It demonstrates empathy and understanding, helping to build rapport and facilitate change.
c) It is a passive technique that has little impact on the therapeutic process.
d) Active listening is discouraged in motivational interviewing as it can reinforce resistance.

Answer: b) It demonstrates empathy and understanding, helping to build rapport and facilitate change.
Explanation: Active listening is a core component of motivational interviewing, a client-centered counseling style aimed at eliciting behavior change by helping clients explore and resolve ambivalence. Through active listening, the therapist demonstrates empathy, validates the client's feelings and perspectives, and fosters a supportive therapeutic relationship. This empathetic approach encourages clients to open up about their experiences and motivations, creating a collaborative atmosphere conducive to exploring change.

387. In the context of systems theory, how might a social worker address organizational dysfunction within a community agency?
a) By focusing solely on changing the behavior of individual employees.
b) By analyzing and intervening in the agency's structure, processes, and communication patterns.
c) By recommending the immediate dissolution of the agency.
d) By isolating the agency from the community to minimize external influences.

Answer: b) By analyzing and intervening in the agency's structure, processes, and communication patterns.
Explanation: Systems theory views organizations as complex systems composed of interrelated parts, including structure, processes, and communication patterns. When addressing organizational dysfunction, a social worker would analyze these components to understand how they contribute to the issue at hand. Interventions might include restructuring teams, improving communication channels, and modifying processes to enhance efficiency and effectiveness. This approach recognizes that changes in one part of the system can influence the functioning of the whole, aiming to promote systemic health and functionality.

389. When a social worker first responds to a crisis situation involving a client threatening self-harm, the INITIAL step should be to:
a) Immediately solve the underlying issues causing the client's distress.
b) Ensure the client's immediate safety and assess the risk of self-harm.
c) Advise the client to calm down and consider the consequences of their actions.
d) Encourage the client to apologize to affected family members and friends.

Answer: b) Ensure the client's immediate safety and assess the risk of self-harm.
Explanation: In a crisis situation, especially when there's a threat of self-harm, the initial step for a social worker is to ensure the client's immediate safety. This involves assessing the risk of self-harm and taking necessary actions to protect the client, which may include involving emergency services or crisis intervention resources. Addressing the underlying issues and involving family or friends come after ensuring the client's safety.

390. In a situation where a client has just experienced a traumatic event, which approach is MOST effective for immediate crisis intervention?
a) Encouraging the client to avoid discussing the event to prevent re-traumatization.
b) Providing psychoeducation about typical trauma responses and coping strategies.
c) Recommending the client take time off work or school to recover in isolation.
d) Focusing solely on long-term therapeutic goals and ignoring immediate emotional needs.

Answer: b) Providing psychoeducation about typical trauma responses and coping strategies.
Explanation: Providing psychoeducation about trauma responses and coping strategies is an effective immediate intervention following a traumatic event. This approach helps normalize the client's experiences, offers immediate coping strategies, and sets the groundwork for further therapeutic intervention. Avoiding discussion of the event, recommending isolation, or focusing only on long-term

goals without addressing immediate needs may not be helpful or could potentially exacerbate the client's distress.

391. In the aftermath of a community disaster, a social worker's priority should be to:
a) Offer detailed explanations about the causes of the disaster to all affected individuals.
b) Immediately begin long-term psychotherapy with survivors to address potential PTSD.
c) Assess the immediate needs of affected individuals and connect them with essential resources.
d) Encourage survivors to quickly rebuild physical structures without assessing mental health needs.

Answer: c) Assess the immediate needs of affected individuals and connect them with essential resources.
Explanation: Following a community disaster, a social worker's priority is to assess the immediate physical, emotional, and logistical needs of those affected and to connect them with essential resources such as food, shelter, medical care, and crisis counseling. This response addresses both the urgent survival needs and lays the foundation for longer-term recovery, including addressing mental health concerns like PTSD.

392. Which technique is most appropriate for a social worker to use when de-escalating a situation where a client is experiencing intense anger?
a) Challenging the client's reasons for being angry to demonstrate the irrationality of their feelings.
b) Maintaining a calm demeanor, using active listening, and acknowledging the client's feelings.
c) Ignoring the client's anger and redirecting the conversation to unrelated topics.
d) Telling the client that they will be refused service if they cannot control their anger.

Answer: b) Maintaining a calm demeanor, using active listening, and acknowledging the client's feelings.
Explanation: When de-escalating a situation where a client is experiencing intense anger, maintaining a calm demeanor, using active listening, and acknowledging the client's feelings are key techniques. These approaches help validate the client's emotions, promote a sense of being heard and understood, and can reduce the intensity of the anger, facilitating a more productive dialogue.

393. For a social worker providing support in an emergency shelter following a natural disaster, which action is MOST critical?
a) Ensuring that everyone in the shelter is aware of the social worker's credentials and expertise.
b) Organizing daily group therapy sessions for all shelter residents.
c) Identifying individuals with immediate health or safety needs and facilitating appropriate interventions.
d) Focusing exclusively on logistical support without addressing emotional or psychological needs.

Answer: c) Identifying individuals with immediate health or safety needs and facilitating appropriate interventions.
Explanation: In an emergency shelter setting following a natural disaster, the most critical action for a social worker is to identify individuals with immediate health or safety needs and to facilitate appropriate interventions. This may include connecting individuals with medical care, crisis counseling, or other necessary services. While providing emotional support and organizing therapeutic activities are important, addressing urgent health and safety needs is paramount to ensure the well-being of shelter residents.

394. When conducting a risk assessment for potential violence in a client, it is important for the social worker to:
a) Focus solely on the client's self-report without considering other sources of information.
b) Ignore any past incidents of violence as irrelevant to the current assessment.
c) Evaluate the presence of risk factors, warning signs, and protective factors.
d) Assure the client that all discussions about violence will remain confidential, regardless of the risk to others.

Answer: c) Evaluate the presence of risk factors, warning signs, and protective factors.
Explanation: Conducting a risk assessment for potential violence involves a comprehensive evaluation of risk factors (such as history of violence, substance use, access to weapons), warning signs (such as threats, escalation of risk behaviors), and protective factors (such as support systems, engagement in treatment). This balanced assessment helps in determining the level of risk and in planning appropriate interventions. Relying solely on self-report, disregarding past behavior, or promising unconditional confidentiality could overlook critical risks and hinder effective prevention and intervention strategies.

395. In responding to a call on a crisis hotline from someone expressing suicidal thoughts, the social worker's FIRST response should be to:
a) Immediately trace the call to send emergency services to the caller's location.
b) Assess the immediacy of the risk by asking about the caller's plan, means, and timeline.
c) Suggest the caller try to get some sleep and call back if they still feel suicidal later.
d) Offer reassurance that everyone feels suicidal at times and it will pass.

Answer: b) Assess the immediacy of the risk by asking about the caller's plan, means, and timeline.
Explanation: When responding to a crisis call from someone expressing suicidal thoughts, the first step is to assess the immediacy and severity of the suicide risk. This involves asking specific questions about the caller's plan for suicide, the means available to carry out the plan, and the timeline they are considering. This information is crucial for determining the level of intervention required, including whether there is a need to involve emergency services immediately.

396. A social worker designing a crisis intervention program for a high school should prioritize:
a) Mandatory psychological testing for all students to identify those at risk.
b) Training school staff in identifying and responding to signs of crisis in students.
c) Instituting punitive measures for students who express thoughts of self-harm or suicide.
d) Focusing exclusively on academic pressures, ignoring other potential stressors like bullying or family issues.

Answer: b) Training school staff in identifying and responding to signs of crisis in students.
Explanation: Designing a crisis intervention program for a high school should prioritize training school staff in identifying and appropriately responding to signs of crisis, including potential self-harm or suicidal thoughts. This approach builds a supportive environment where students at risk can be quickly identified and provided with the help they need. Mandatory testing and punitive measures can stigmatize students and may not effectively address the root causes of crises, while focusing solely on academic pressures overlooks other significant stressors.

397. In situations of domestic violence, the social worker's primary responsibility is to:
a) Convince the victim to leave the abuser immediately without assessing safety or readiness.
b) Ensure the safety of the victim and any children involved, developing a safety plan that considers their specific situation.
c) Focus on couples counseling to resolve the conflict between the victim and the abuser.
d) Advise the victim to ignore the abuse and focus on the positive aspects of the relationship.

Answer: b) Ensure the safety of the victim and any children involved, developing a safety plan that considers their specific situation.
Explanation: In cases of domestic violence, the social worker's primary responsibility is to ensure the safety of the victim (and any children involved). This involves developing a personalized safety plan that accounts for the victim's current situation, readiness to leave, and specific safety concerns. Immediate separation from the abuser may not always be safe or feasible, making it essential to assess and plan carefully. Couples counseling is not recommended in situations of abuse due to the power imbalances and risks to the victim.

398. What is the primary goal of case management in social work?
a) To ensure that clients adhere to prescribed medication schedules without fail.
b) To provide legal representation for clients in court proceedings.
c) To facilitate access to services and resources that meet clients' holistic needs.
d) To focus solely on immediate crisis intervention without planning for future needs.

Answer: c) To facilitate access to services and resources that meet clients' holistic needs.
Explanation: The primary goal of case management in social work is to assist clients in navigating and accessing a range of services and resources that address their holistic needs, including health, social, emotional, and economic needs. Case management involves assessing the client's needs, planning services, linking the client to services and resources, monitoring service delivery, and evaluating outcomes to ensure that the client's comprehensive needs are met effectively.

399. Which strategy is essential for effective coordination of services in case management?
a) Limiting communication with other service providers to protect client confidentiality.
b) Establishing and maintaining collaborative relationships with other service providers.
c) Recommending the same standardized services for all clients.
d) Avoiding the use of technology in managing and tracking client information.

Answer: b) Establishing and maintaining collaborative relationships with other service providers.
Explanation: Effective coordination of services requires case managers to establish and maintain collaborative relationships with a wide range of service providers. This collaborative approach ensures that all aspects of the client's needs are addressed through a coordinated effort, prevents service duplication, and facilitates a comprehensive support system for the client. Strong professional relationships among service providers enhance communication and teamwork, leading to better outcomes for clients.

400. In case management, what is the significance of conducting an initial assessment?
a) To determine the client's eligibility for case management services only.

b) To identify the client's strengths, needs, and goals to inform service planning.
c) To finalize the case management plan in the first meeting.
d) To persuade the client to accept the case manager's recommendations.

Answer: b) To identify the client's strengths, needs, and goals to inform service planning.
Explanation: Conducting an initial assessment is crucial in case management as it helps to identify the client's strengths, needs, and goals. This comprehensive understanding of the client's situation informs the development of a personalized case management plan that outlines the services and interventions required to meet the client's needs. The assessment process involves gathering information on various aspects of the client's life, including health, social, financial, and emotional domains, ensuring a holistic approach to service planning and delivery.

401. How does cultural competence impact the case management process?
a) It is irrelevant as case management does not involve understanding cultural differences.
b) It enhances the case manager's ability to provide services that respect the client's cultural background and preferences.
c) It limits the case manager to working only with clients from their own cultural background.
d) It encourages the use of a one-size-fits-all approach regardless of the client's cultural identity.

Answer: b) It enhances the case manager's ability to provide services that respect the client's cultural background and preferences.
Explanation: Cultural competence is a critical aspect of case management, as it enhances the case manager's ability to understand, respect, and effectively respond to the cultural background and preferences of their clients. Being culturally competent means recognizing and honoring cultural differences, including beliefs, values, practices, and customs, and incorporating this understanding into all stages of the case management process. This approach ensures that services are tailored to meet the unique needs of each client, leading to more effective and respectful service delivery.

402. What role does advocacy play in case management?
a) Advocacy is considered unethical in case management practices.
b) Case managers serve as advocates to challenge policies that negatively affect their clients and to empower clients to access necessary services.
c) Advocacy involves case managers making decisions on behalf of clients without their input.
d) Case managers only advocate for clients when it is convenient for the service providers.

Answer: b) Case managers serve as advocates to challenge policies that negatively affect their clients and to empower clients to access necessary services.
Explanation: Advocacy is a fundamental role of case managers, involving speaking up on behalf of clients to ensure they have access to needed services and resources. This can include challenging policies and practices that negatively impact clients, navigating bureaucratic obstacles, and empowering clients by supporting them to make informed decisions and understand their rights. Advocacy ensures that clients' voices are heard and their needs are adequately addressed within the service delivery system.

403. How do case managers use the "strengths-based approach" in their work with clients?

a) By focusing solely on the client's weaknesses and areas of need.
b) By identifying and leveraging the client's strengths and resources to achieve their goals.
c) By disregarding the client's input on their strengths and capabilities.
d) By using strengths as a way to ignore the challenges faced by clients.

Answer: b) By identifying and leveraging the client's strengths and resources to achieve their goals.
Explanation: The strengths-based approach in case management focuses on identifying and leveraging the inherent strengths, capabilities, and resources of clients to achieve their goals and address their needs. This approach is rooted in the belief that all clients have valuable skills and resources that can be mobilized to improve their situation. It involves working collaboratively with clients to recognize their strengths, build on them, and use them as a foundation for growth and problem-solving, leading to more empowering and effective outcomes.

404. When case managers monitor and evaluate the services provided to a client, what is their primary focus?
a) Ensuring that services meet the provider's needs.
b) Confirming that services are delivered according to the contract with minimal regard for outcomes.
c) Assessing whether the services are effectively meeting the client's needs and goals.
d) Reducing the frequency of services to minimize costs.

Answer: c) Assessing whether the services are effectively meeting the client's needs and goals.
Explanation: The primary focus of monitoring and evaluating the services provided to a client in case management is to assess whether these services are effectively meeting the client's articulated needs and goals. This ongoing process involves reviewing the appropriateness, quality, and outcomes of services and interventions. It ensures that the case management plan remains relevant and responsive to the client's evolving needs, leading to adjustments as necessary to achieve the best possible outcomes for the client.

405. What is the importance of "discharge planning" in case management?
a) It is a procedural step with little impact on the client's well-being.
b) To ensure a smooth transition and continued support for clients as they move from one level of care to another or return to their community.
c) To immediately terminate services once the client shows any improvement.
d) Discharge planning is only relevant in medical settings, not in case management.

Answer: b) To ensure a smooth transition and continued support for clients as they move from one level of care to another or return to their community.
Explanation: Discharge planning is a critical component of case management, focusing on ensuring a smooth and supported transition for clients either moving between levels of care (e.g., from hospital to home care) or returning to their community after receiving services. Effective discharge planning involves coordinating with service providers, arranging for necessary follow-up services, and ensuring that clients and their families are prepared for and supported during the transition. This process helps to prevent gaps in care, reduce the risk of relapse or rehospitalization, and support clients' ongoing recovery and well-being.

406. In the context of case management, how is "client self-determination" respected and promoted?
a) By making all decisions for the client to ensure their safety.
b) By informing clients about their options and supporting them in making their own informed choices.
c) By disregarding clients' preferences in favor of expert opinions.
d) By limiting information provided to clients to prevent overwhelm.

Answer: b) By informing clients about their options and supporting them in making their own informed choices.
Explanation: Respecting and promoting client self-determination is a fundamental principle in case management and involves recognizing clients as autonomous individuals with the right to make their own choices about their lives. Case managers respect this principle by providing clients with comprehensive information about their options, potential consequences, and resources available, and then supporting clients in making informed decisions based on their values, preferences, and goals. This empowers clients, promotes their independence, and ensures that interventions are aligned with their desires and needs.

407. Which of the following is a key principle of Cognitive Behavioral Therapy (CBT)?
a) Exploring unresolved issues from childhood to understand present behaviors.
b) Understanding that thoughts, feelings, and behaviors are interconnected and that changing negative thought patterns can lead to changes in feelings and behaviors.
c) Using dream analysis to uncover repressed thoughts and feelings.
d) Focusing on the client's past experiences as the root of current psychological problems.

Answer: b) Understanding that thoughts, feelings, and behaviors are interconnected and that changing negative thought patterns can lead to changes in feelings and behaviors.
Explanation: Cognitive Behavioral Therapy (CBT) is based on the premise that thoughts, feelings, and behaviors are interconnected, and that identifying and changing maladaptive thought patterns can alter behaviors and emotions. This approach is practical, problem-focused, and action-oriented, differing from methods that prioritize past experiences, such as psychoanalysis or that use techniques like dream analysis.

408. In the context of Person-Centered Therapy, the therapist's role is primarily to:
a) Provide direct advice and solutions to the client’s problems.
b) Interpret the client's unconscious conflicts that lead to psychological distress.
c) Create a supportive environment that promotes self-discovery and personal growth.
d) Challenge the client’s irrational beliefs through confrontation.

Answer: c) Create a supportive environment that promotes self-discovery and personal growth.
Explanation: Person-Centered Therapy, developed by Carl Rogers, emphasizes the therapist's role in providing a supportive, nonjudgmental environment that facilitates self-discovery and personal growth. The therapist offers empathy, unconditional positive regard, and congruence, allowing clients to explore their feelings and thoughts freely. This contrasts with approaches that focus on direct advice, interpretation of unconscious conflicts, or challenging irrational beliefs.

409. Which technique is commonly used in Dialectical Behavior Therapy (DBT) to help clients manage acute stress and emotional distress?
a) Free association
b) Dream analysis
c) Mindfulness exercises
d) Transference analysis

Answer: c) Mindfulness exercises
Explanation: Dialectical Behavior Therapy (DBT), developed by Marsha Linehan, incorporates mindfulness exercises as a core component to help clients become more aware of and present in the current moment. Mindfulness helps individuals observe their thoughts and feelings without judgment, aiding in emotion regulation and stress management. This contrasts with psychoanalytic techniques like free association, dream analysis, or transference analysis, which are not components of DBT.

410. In Narrative Therapy, the process of "externalization" refers to:
a) The therapist sharing personal stories to build rapport with the client.
b) Clients expressing their innermost thoughts and feelings through creative writing.
c) Viewing problems as separate from the individual, allowing them to rewrite their story.
d) Encouraging clients to adopt the therapist's interpretation of their life story.

Answer: c) Viewing problems as separate from the individual, allowing them to rewrite their story.
Explanation: Externalization is a technique in Narrative Therapy where problems are viewed as separate from the person. This approach allows individuals to distance themselves from issues, reducing personal blame and increasing their ability to address challenges. It encourages clients to rewrite their narrative in a more empowering way, contrasting with methods that involve the therapist's stories, creative writing without the purpose of distancing from problems, or adopting the therapist's interpretation of their story.

411. In Emotionally Focused Therapy (EFT) for couples, the therapist aims to:
a) Focus solely on improving communication skills without addressing underlying emotional issues.
b) Encourage partners to attribute their conflicts to external factors.
c) Facilitate the expression and understanding of underlying emotional needs to enhance emotional connection.
d) Advise couples to maintain emotional distance to avoid future conflicts.

Answer: c) Facilitate the expression and understanding of underlying emotional needs to enhance emotional connection.
Explanation: Emotionally Focused Therapy (EFT) for couples is centered on exploring and understanding the deeper emotional needs underlying partners' interactions and conflicts. By facilitating the expression of these needs and helping partners respond to each other more empathetically, EFT aims to strengthen the emotional bond and improve relationship dynamics. This approach contrasts with focusing solely on communication skills, attributing conflicts to external factors, or advising emotional distance.

412. Which of the following best represents the therapeutic goal of Existential Therapy?
a) To modify the client's behavior through reinforcement techniques.

b) To help the client achieve self-actualization and find meaning in life.
c) To uncover the client's unconscious motivations that influence current behavior.
d) To correct cognitive distortions and irrational thoughts.

Answer: b) To help the client achieve self-actualization and find meaning in life.
Explanation: Existential Therapy focuses on helping individuals confront the inherent challenges of human existence, such as freedom, isolation, meaninglessness, and mortality. The goal is to assist clients in finding meaning and purpose in life, encouraging them to live authentically and achieve self-actualization. This contrasts with behavior modification, uncovering unconscious motivations, or correcting cognitive distortions, which are goals of other therapeutic approaches.

413. Solution-Focused Brief Therapy (SFBT) emphasizes:
a) Delving into the client's past to identify the origins of current problems.
b) The development of coping strategies to deal with future problems.
c) Identifying and building upon the client's existing strengths and resources to solve problems.
d) The therapist identifying solutions for the client's problems.

Answer: c) Identifying and building upon the client's existing strengths and resources to solve problems.
Explanation: Solution-Focused Brief Therapy is centered on identifying the client's existing strengths, resources, and previous successes to develop solutions to current problems. This future-oriented, goal-directed approach focuses on what is working well for the client and how those successes can inform solutions, rather than delving into the past or the therapist prescribing solutions.

414. How does Gestalt Therapy view the importance of the here and now?
a) As irrelevant, with a focus instead on childhood experiences.
b) As central, emphasizing awareness and experience in the present moment to enhance self-awareness and resolve unfinished business.
c) Only important in terms of how it affects one's future goals.
d) Less important than understanding the client's dreams and subconscious messages.

Answer: b) As central, emphasizing awareness and experience in the present moment to enhance self-awareness and resolve unfinished business.
Explanation: Gestalt Therapy places a strong emphasis on the here and now, encouraging clients to focus on their current thoughts, feelings, and actions within the therapy session. This approach helps clients gain greater awareness of their present experiences and the ways they may be avoiding or interrupting contact with the present. It facilitates working through unresolved issues or "unfinished business" to achieve greater self-awareness and wholeness.

415. When utilizing Motivational Interviewing with a client resistant to change, the therapist is likely to:
a) Directly confront the client's denial and resistance.
b) Employ a directive, advice-giving approach to persuade the client to change.
c) Elicit the client's own motivations for change through open-ended questions and reflective listening.
d) Use a prescriptive approach, outlining the steps the client must take to change.

Answer: c) Elicit the client's own motivations for change through open-ended questions and reflective listening.
Explanation: Motivational Interviewing is a client-centered, guiding method of communication designed to enhance motivation for change by exploring and resolving ambivalence. It involves the use of open-ended questions, affirmations, reflective listening, and summarizing to elicit and strengthen the client's own motivation and commitment to change. This contrasts with confrontational, advice-giving, or prescriptive approaches, which may increase resistance.

416. In Psychodynamic Therapy, the concept of transference is used to:
a) Encourage clients to transfer their problems to the therapist to alleviate symptoms quickly.
b) Ignore the client-therapist relationship as it is considered irrelevant to therapy outcomes.
c) Analyze how clients project feelings about important figures from their past onto the therapist, revealing unresolved issues.
d) Focus exclusively on the client's future goals and aspirations, avoiding discussion of past relationships.

Answer: c) Analyze how clients project feelings about important figures from their past onto the therapist, revealing unresolved issues.
Explanation: Transference in Psychodynamic Therapy refers to the phenomenon where clients project onto their therapist feelings and attitudes they have toward significant figures from their past. This process is considered a valuable therapeutic tool, as it reveals unresolved issues and patterns in relationships that can then be addressed within the safety of the therapeutic relationship. This approach differs markedly from ignoring the client-therapist relationship, encouraging symptom transfer, or focusing solely on future goals.

417. What is the primary goal of advocacy in social work?
a) To ensure that social workers adhere to their professional code of ethics.
b) To empower clients and communities to gain access to resources and services.
c) To increase the social worker's visibility and professional reputation.
d) To standardize social services across different communities.

Answer: b) To empower clients and communities to gain access to resources and services.
Explanation: The primary goal of advocacy in social work is to empower and support clients and communities in gaining access to necessary resources and services. Advocacy involves representing, defending, or supporting clients' and communities' rights and needs, often by navigating complex social systems, challenging policies or practices that contribute to inequality, and working towards social justice and systemic change.

418. In the context of social justice interventions, what does "empowerment" typically involve?
a) Taking complete control over decisions to expedite service delivery.
b) Providing resources and support to enable individuals and communities to advocate for their own needs and rights.
c) Limiting client participation in planning to reduce complexity.
d) Encouraging dependency on social services for long-term support.

Answer: b) Providing resources and support to enable individuals and communities to advocate for their own needs and rights.
Explanation: Empowerment in the context of social justice interventions involves providing the resources, skills, knowledge, and support necessary for individuals and communities to effectively advocate for their own needs, rights, and interests. This approach fosters independence, self-determination, and strength-based collaboration, ensuring that those affected by issues have an active role in creating solutions and advocating for systemic change.

419. How do social workers utilize "policy advocacy" to promote social justice?
a) By avoiding involvement in political processes to remain neutral.
b) By engaging in direct service provision exclusively, without addressing policy issues.
c) By influencing and enacting changes in policies that negatively impact clients and communities.
d) By supporting policies that benefit social workers personally, rather than their clients.

Answer: c) By influencing and enacting changes in policies that negatively impact clients and communities.
Explanation: Policy advocacy involves social workers actively participating in the political and policy-making processes to influence and enact changes in policies and legislation that negatively affect clients and communities. This form of advocacy seeks to address and rectify systemic issues and inequalities at the policy level, promoting social justice by ensuring that laws and policies are fair, equitable, and supportive of all individuals' rights and well-being.

420. What role does "community organizing" play in social work advocacy?
a) To disengage clients from their communities and focus on individual issues.
b) To mobilize community members around shared concerns for collective action and systemic change.
c) To discourage community involvement in policy-making processes.
d) To centralize power among a small group of social workers and community leaders.

Answer: b) To mobilize community members around shared concerns for collective action and systemic change.
Explanation: Community organizing in social work advocacy involves mobilizing individuals and groups within a community around common issues, concerns, or goals to facilitate collective action and systemic change. This process empowers community members to identify their needs, develop strategies, and work together to advocate for changes that improve their collective well-being and address social injustices.

421. Why is cultural competence important in social justice advocacy?
a) It ensures that all advocacy efforts focus solely on the majority culture.
b) It diminishes the relevance of understanding diverse cultural perspectives.
c) It enhances the effectiveness of advocacy efforts by acknowledging and respecting diverse cultural identities and experiences.
d) It encourages the imposition of the advocate's cultural values on clients and communities.

Answer: c) It enhances the effectiveness of advocacy efforts by acknowledging and respecting diverse cultural identities and experiences.

Explanation: Cultural competence is crucial in social justice advocacy as it involves understanding, respecting, and valuing diverse cultural identities, perspectives, and experiences. This awareness and sensitivity enable social workers to tailor their advocacy efforts to be more inclusive, relevant, and effective, ensuring that the needs and rights of all individuals and communities, particularly those from marginalized or minority groups, are addressed and respected.

422. What is a key consideration when implementing social justice interventions at the organizational level?
a) Prioritizing organizational needs over the needs of clients and communities.
b) Encouraging organizations to adopt policies and practices that promote equity and inclusivity.
c) Maintaining the status quo to avoid disrupting existing power dynamics.
d) Isolating organizations from broader community issues and needs.

Answer: b) Encouraging organizations to adopt policies and practices that promote equity and inclusivity.
Explanation: A key consideration when implementing social justice interventions at the organizational level is to encourage and support organizations in adopting policies and practices that promote equity, inclusivity, and social justice. This involves examining and addressing systemic biases, barriers, and inequalities within the organization and its services to ensure that all individuals, particularly those from marginalized groups, have equitable access to resources, opportunities, and support.

423. How do social workers assess the impact of their advocacy and social justice interventions?
a) By assuming that any action taken is inherently successful without the need for evaluation.
b) By collecting and analyzing data on outcomes to determine the effectiveness of interventions.
c) By focusing exclusively on short-term outcomes without considering long-term effects.
d) By relying on anecdotal evidence alone without quantitative or qualitative analysis.

Answer: b) By collecting and analyzing data on outcomes to determine the effectiveness of interventions.
Explanation: Social workers assess the impact of their advocacy and social justice interventions by systematically collecting and analyzing data on the outcomes of these efforts. This involves using both quantitative and qualitative methods to evaluate whether the interventions have met their objectives, the extent to which they have addressed the targeted issues, and their effects on clients and communities. This evidence-based approach allows for continuous improvement and accountability in social work practice.

424. In social justice advocacy, why is it important to collaborate with other professionals and organizations?
a) To delegate all responsibilities and reduce the workload of social workers.
b) To create a unified front that strengthens efforts and resources for systemic change.
c) To avoid taking direct action and responsibility for challenging injustices.
d) To limit the perspectives and strategies considered in advocacy efforts.

Answer: b) To create a unified front that strengthens efforts and resources for systemic change.
Explanation: Collaborating with other professionals and organizations is important in social justice advocacy because it creates a unified front that amplifies the impact of advocacy efforts. By pooling

resources, expertise, and influence, collaborative efforts can more effectively address complex social injustices and systemic issues, leading to more substantial and sustainable changes.

425. What is an example of an "empowerment-based" intervention in social work practice?
a) Discouraging clients from participating in decision-making processes.
b) Providing clients with the resources, skills, and support needed to advocate for themselves and effect change in their lives.
c) Focusing solely on providing solutions rather than building clients' capacities.
d) Implementing top-down approaches that prioritize the social worker's expertise over the client's knowledge and experience.

Answer: b) Providing clients with the resources, skills, and support needed to advocate for themselves and effect change in their lives.
Explanation: Empowerment-based interventions in social work practice focus on providing clients with the resources, skills, and support necessary to advocate for themselves and effect positive change in their lives and communities. This approach recognizes the inherent strengths and capacities of clients, aiming to build their confidence and ability to navigate challenges, make informed decisions, and actively participate in shaping their own futures and the world around them.

426. The Charity Organization Society (COS), established in the late 19th century, was known for its approach to social work that emphasized:
a) Individual casework and investigation to determine the causes of poverty and distress.
b) Providing immediate financial assistance to all individuals in need without assessment.
c) Focusing solely on medical assistance to the poor and sick.
d) Advocating for the abolition of all forms of social welfare programs.

Answer: a) Individual casework and investigation to determine the causes of poverty and distress.
Explanation: The Charity Organization Society, established in the late 19th century, introduced a systematic approach to assisting the poor, which emphasized individual casework and the investigation of personal and environmental conditions causing poverty and distress. This method was aimed at offering more personalized and effective aid, distinguishing it from indiscriminate charity by seeking to address root causes and promoting self-sufficiency.

427. Jane Addams and Ellen Gates Starr founded Hull House in Chicago in 1889, marking a significant development in social work history. Their work is best described as:
a) Establishing a legal framework for child labor laws.
b) Creating a settlement house that offered various social services and educational opportunities to immigrants and the poor.
c) Developing psychoanalytic theory as a tool for social work practice.
d) Introducing the medical model into social work practice.

Answer: b) Creating a settlement house that offered various social services and educational opportunities to immigrants and the poor.

Explanation: Jane Addams and Ellen Gates Starr founded Hull House as a settlement house, which became a model for social reform in the United States and abroad. Hull House provided a wide range of services including education, art classes, child care, and legal aid, aiming to improve the lives of the immigrant and poor populations of Chicago. This approach to social work emphasized community-based assistance and empowerment, rather than the application of medical or psychoanalytic models.

428. The Social Security Act of 1935 is a landmark in the history of social work in the United States. Its significance lies in:
a) Introducing professional licensing requirements for all social workers.
b) Establishing a national system of unemployment insurance, old-age assistance, and aid to dependent children.
c) Outlawing child labor in manufacturing industries.
d) Creating the first code of ethics for social workers.

Answer: b) Establishing a national system of unemployment insurance, old-age assistance, and aid to dependent children.
Explanation: The Social Security Act of 1935 represented a significant advance in social welfare policy in the United States. It established a national system of unemployment insurance, old-age assistance, and aid to dependent children, laying the foundation for the modern welfare state. This act marked a shift towards federal responsibility for the social welfare of citizens, rather than relying solely on state, local, or private efforts.

429. The concept of "person-in-environment" (PIE) that is central to social work practice emphasizes:
a) The biological determinants of behavior.
b) The individual's financial status as the sole factor in assessing their needs.
c) The dynamic interaction between individuals and their physical, social, and cultural environments.
d) The use of psychotropic medication in managing social problems.

Answer: c) The dynamic interaction between individuals and their physical, social, and cultural environments.
Explanation: The "person-in-environment" (PIE) concept is a foundational principle in social work that recognizes the importance of understanding the dynamic interactions between individuals and their various environments, including physical, social, and cultural contexts. This perspective highlights the complexity of human behavior and the multifaceted nature of social problems, guiding social workers to consider a broad range of factors in assessment and intervention.

430. The settlement movement, initiated in the late 19th and early 20th centuries, contributed to social work by:
a) Emphasizing the importance of legal representation in court for the impoverished.
b) Advocating for community-based services and social reform through direct involvement in poor neighborhoods.
c) Focusing exclusively on providing vocational training to unemployed adults.
d) Introducing the use of technology in social work practice.

Answer: b) Advocating for community-based services and social reform through direct involvement in poor neighborhoods.
Explanation: The settlement movement was instrumental in shaping social work by advocating for community-based services and social reform. Settlement houses, like Hull House, were established in poor neighborhoods to offer a variety of services such as education, healthcare, and legal aid, and to work towards social reform by directly engaging with the community. This movement underscored the importance of addressing the social determinants of health and well-being through direct involvement and advocacy.

431. The National Association of Social Workers (NASW) was established primarily to:
a) Serve as a union for social workers.
b) Provide a platform for social workers to publish their research findings.
c) Set ethical standards for the profession and advocate for the interests of social workers and their clients.
d) Focus on the development of social work programs in universities.

Answer: c) Set ethical standards for the profession and advocate for the interests of social workers and their clients.
Explanation: The National Association of Social Workers (NASW) was established to set ethical standards for the profession and to advocate for the rights and interests of social workers and their clients. The NASW plays a critical role in promoting professional development, establishing professional practice standards, and advocating for social policies that uphold social justice and provide services to meet the needs of individuals and communities.

432. The ecological systems theory, often applied in social work, helps professionals understand:
a) Only the immediate family environment's impact on an individual.
b) The influence of genetic factors on personality development.
c) How different environmental systems interact and affect an individual's life.
d) The role of political systems in individual psychological disorders.

Answer: c) How different environmental systems interact and affect an individual's life.
Explanation: The ecological systems theory, introduced by Urie Bronfenbrenner, is a framework that helps social workers (and other professionals) understand how various environmental systems (microsystem, mesosystem, exosystem, macrosystem, and chronosystem) interact and influence an individual's development and behavior. This theory highlights the complexity of the interactions between individuals and their diverse environments, including family, school, community, and broader societal influences.

433. The strength-based approach in social work practice focuses on:
a) Identifying and diagnosing the individual's weaknesses and problems.
b) Utilizing the individual's strengths and resources to achieve goals and overcome challenges.
c) Relying on expert opinions rather than the client's perspective.
d) Standardized intervention strategies without customization.

Answer: b) Utilizing the individual's strengths and resources to achieve goals and overcome challenges.

Explanation: The strength-based approach in social work emphasizes identifying and leveraging the strengths, resources, and capabilities of individuals or communities to help them overcome challenges and achieve their goals. This approach is client-centered, focusing on empowerment and resilience rather than deficits and problems, encouraging clients to actively participate in the change process.

434. The development of the Code of Ethics by the National Association of Social Workers (NASW) serves to:
a) Provide legal protection for social workers in court cases.
b) Outline the professional values, principles, and standards to guide social workers' conduct.
c) Standardize social work education across all universities.
d) Regulate the financial management of social work agencies.

Answer: b) Outline the professional values, principles, and standards to guide social workers' conduct.
Explanation: The NASW Code of Ethics outlines the core values, principles, and standards that guide the conduct of social workers. It serves as a framework for ethical decision-making and professional behavior, ensuring that social workers act in the best interests of their clients and uphold the integrity of the profession. The Code of Ethics emphasizes principles such as service, social justice, dignity and worth of the person, the importance of human relationships, integrity, and competence.

435. What principle underlies the ethical standard of confidentiality in social work?
a) The necessity to inform the public about clients' personal issues.
b) The obligation to share all information obtained from clients with other professionals.
c) The duty to protect and keep private the information shared by clients.
d) The requirement to disclose client information in all group settings.

Answer: c) The duty to protect and keep private the information shared by clients.
Explanation: The ethical standard of confidentiality in social work is based on the principle that social workers have a duty to protect and keep private the information shared by clients, except in specific circumstances where mandated by law or where the client has given consent for the sharing of information. This principle is crucial in building trust between the social worker and the client, ensuring that clients feel safe to share personal and often sensitive information without fear of unauthorized disclosure.

436. In social work practice, the principle of self-determination primarily emphasizes:
a) The social worker’s authority to make decisions on behalf of the client.
b) The client's right to make their own choices and decisions.
c) The family's role in making decisions for the client.
d) The government's influence over personal decisions.

Answer: b) The client's right to make their own choices and decisions.
Explanation: The principle of self-determination emphasizes the client's right to make their own choices and decisions regarding their life. It is a fundamental ethical principle in social work that recognizes the autonomy and dignity of every individual. Social workers are expected to respect and support clients'

rights to self-determination, while also considering the client's capacity to make informed decisions and the potential consequences of those decisions.

437. Which ethical principle in social work aims at treating all people with fairness and equity, particularly those who are vulnerable or marginalized?
a) Social Justice
b) Integrity
c) Competence
d) Professionalism

Answer: a) Social Justice
Explanation: The ethical principle of social justice in social work is focused on treating all people with fairness and equity, striving to address and challenge social inequalities and injustices. This principle particularly emphasizes the importance of advocating for the rights and needs of vulnerable and marginalized populations. Social workers are encouraged to engage in practices that promote social change and development, as well as the empowerment and liberation of people to enhance social justice.

438. When a social worker encounters a situation where personal beliefs conflict with professional responsibilities, what ethical principle should guide their actions?
a) The social worker should always act according to personal beliefs.
b) The social worker should prioritize professional responsibilities over personal beliefs.
c) The social worker should terminate services with clients who do not share their beliefs.
d) The social worker should ignore ethical guidelines in favor of personal beliefs.

Answer: b) The social worker should prioritize professional responsibilities over personal beliefs.
Explanation: When personal beliefs conflict with professional responsibilities, the ethical principle of professional responsibility and integrity should guide the social worker's actions. Social workers are expected to put aside personal beliefs to uphold professional obligations, ethical standards, and the clients' best interests. If a social worker feels unable to do so effectively, they should seek supervision, consultation, or, if necessary, refer the client to another professional.

439. What ethical guideline should social workers follow when using social media and technology in practice?
a) Use social media to discuss clients with colleagues for advice.
b) Maintain the same ethical standards of confidentiality and professional boundaries as in offline interactions.
c) Share client stories on social media as educational examples without consent.
d) Use personal social media accounts to contact clients for convenience.

Answer: b) Maintain the same ethical standards of confidentiality and professional boundaries as in offline interactions.
Explanation: When using social media and technology in practice, social workers should maintain the same ethical standards of confidentiality and professional boundaries as they do in face-to-face interactions. This includes safeguarding clients' privacy, obtaining consent for electronic communications when

appropriate, and ensuring that their use of technology does not compromise their professional responsibilities or the client-worker relationship.

440. In what situation is it ethically permissible for a social worker to breach confidentiality?
a) When a client shares information that is not relevant to their treatment.
b) When the social worker believes that breaking confidentiality could benefit the client socially.
c) When required by law, such as in cases of suspected abuse or threats of harm to self or others.
d) Whenever the social worker deems it necessary for the client's well-being.

Answer: c) When required by law, such as in cases of suspected abuse or threats of harm to self or others.
Explanation: Confidentiality is a cornerstone of social work practice, but there are specific circumstances under which a social worker may ethically breach confidentiality, primarily when required by law. This includes situations where there is suspected abuse or neglect of children, elders, or dependent adults, or when a client poses a threat of harm to themselves or others. In these cases, social workers have a legal and ethical obligation to report the information to the appropriate authorities to protect the individuals involved.

441.How should a social worker handle a conflict of interest in professional practice?
a) Ignore the conflict and continue providing services to ensure continuity of care.
b) Seek to benefit personally from the conflict of interest.
c) Disclose the conflict of interest to relevant parties and take steps to resolve it, prioritizing the client's best interests.
d) Transfer the client to a colleague without explanation.

Answer: c) Disclose the conflict of interest to relevant parties and take steps to resolve it, prioritizing the client's best interests.
Explanation: When a conflict of interest arises in professional practice, the ethical response is for the social worker to disclose the conflict to all relevant parties, such as the client, the social worker's employer, or professional body. After disclosure, the social worker should take appropriate steps to address and resolve the conflict, ensuring that the client's best interests are prioritized. This might involve adjusting the service plan, seeking supervision, or, if necessary, arranging for the client to be transferred to another professional.

442. What is the ethical obligation of social workers regarding continuing education and competence?
a) Social workers are not required to update their skills once they have obtained their degree.
b) Social workers should only seek additional training if mandated by their employer.
c) Social workers have an ethical obligation to engage in continuing education to maintain and enhance professional competence.
d) Social workers should focus solely on their area of expertise and avoid expanding their knowledge base.

Answer: c) Social workers have an ethical obligation to engage in continuing education to maintain and enhance professional competence.
Explanation: Social workers are ethically obligated to engage in continuing education and professional development throughout their careers to maintain and enhance their professional competence. This

commitment ensures that social workers are up-to-date with the latest research, interventions, and best practices, enabling them to provide the highest quality of service to clients and communities. Continuing education also supports social workers in adapting to changes in the field and meeting the evolving needs of those they serve.

443. In advocating for clients' rights and access to services, social workers must navigate systems that may not always align with the clients' best interests. How should social workers approach this challenge?
a) By accepting the limitations of the system and adjusting clients' expectations accordingly.
b) By working within the system to identify, challenge, and change policies and practices that are unjust or inequitable.
c) By encouraging clients to navigate the system independently.
d) By using any means necessary, including unethical practices, to secure services for clients.

Answer: b) By working within the system to identify, challenge, and change policies and practices that are unjust or inequitable.
Explanation: Social workers have a responsibility to advocate for clients' rights and access to services, which includes working within systems to address and challenge policies and practices that may be unjust, oppressive, or inequitable. Ethical social work practice involves identifying these systemic barriers, advocating for change, and working collaboratively with clients, communities, and other stakeholders to promote social justice and ensure equitable access to services. This approach emphasizes the social worker's role as an agent of change within systems, always adhering to ethical principles and standards.

444. When a social worker receives a friend request on a social media platform from a current client, the MOST appropriate action would be to:
a) Accept the friend request to explore more about the client's social environment.
b) Politely decline the request and discuss the situation with the client, emphasizing the importance of professional boundaries.
c) Ignore the request without addressing it, to avoid any confrontation.
d) Accept the request but limit the client's access to personal information.

Answer: b) Politely decline the request and discuss the situation with the client, emphasizing the importance of professional boundaries.
Explanation: Maintaining professional boundaries is crucial in social work practice. Accepting a friend request from a current client on social media blurs these boundaries and can compromise the professional relationship. The most appropriate action is to politely decline the request and use the situation as an opportunity to discuss the importance of professional boundaries with the client, reinforcing the distinction between professional and personal relationships.

445. A social worker at a high school is asked by a teacher to share confidential information about a student's counseling sessions. The social worker should:
a) Share all requested information since both professionals are involved in the student's welfare.
b) Refuse to share any information and advise the teacher to ask the student directly.
c) Provide the information only if the student agrees to share it with the teacher.
d) Share only information that is directly relevant to the student's educational needs and with the student's consent, ensuring to respect confidentiality laws and ethical guidelines.

Answer: d) Share only information that is directly relevant to the student's educational needs and with the student's consent, ensuring to respect confidentiality laws and ethical guidelines.
Explanation: Confidentiality is a cornerstone of social work ethics, particularly when working with minors in educational settings. The social worker should balance the need to protect the student's confidentiality with the potential benefits of sharing information for the student's educational welfare. Information should only be shared with the student's informed consent and when it is directly relevant to their educational needs, in accordance with confidentiality laws and ethical guidelines.

446. In a therapeutic relationship, self-disclosure by the social worker:
a) Should be avoided under all circumstances to maintain strict professional boundaries.
b) Can be used judiciously if it is intended to benefit the therapeutic process and the client's well-being.
c) Is encouraged regularly to make the social worker appear more relatable and human.
d) Should focus on the social worker's personal problems to create empathy.

Answer: b) Can be used judiciously if it is intended to benefit the therapeutic process and the client's well-being.
Explanation: Self-disclosure by a social worker in a therapeutic context should be used sparingly and only when it serves the client's best interests or therapeutic goals. Any self-disclosure should be carefully considered for its potential impact on the client and the therapeutic relationship, ensuring it is intended to enhance understanding, empathy, or facilitate the client's progress, rather than to meet the social worker's needs.

447. When a client offers a social worker a gift of significant monetary value as a token of appreciation, the social worker should:
a) Accept the gift to avoid offending the client.
b) Politely decline the gift, explaining the policy and ethical considerations regarding gifts.
c) Accept the gift and donate it to charity.
d) Only accept the gift if it can be shared with the entire office or team.

Answer: b) Politely decline the gift, explaining the policy and ethical considerations regarding gifts.
Explanation: Social workers should be cautious about accepting gifts from clients, especially those of significant monetary value, as this could potentially influence the professional relationship and create a conflict of interest. The best course of action is to politely decline the gift, providing an explanation based on ethical standards and any applicable agency policies regarding the acceptance of gifts, thereby maintaining professional integrity and boundaries.

448. A social worker receives a subpoena to provide records for a client involved in a legal case. The FIRST step the social worker should take is to:
a) Immediately comply and send all requested documents to the court.
b) Contact the client to inform them about the subpoena and discuss the implications.
c) Consult with a legal advisor or the agency's legal department to understand the obligations and rights concerning client confidentiality and legal compliance.
d) Destroy any potentially incriminating records before they can be submitted.

Answer: c) Consult with a legal advisor or the agency's legal department to understand the obligations and rights concerning client confidentiality and legal compliance.
Explanation: Upon receiving a subpoena for client records, the social worker's first step should be to consult with a legal advisor or the agency's legal department. This consultation is crucial to understand the specific legal obligations and rights related to client confidentiality, legal compliance, and the appropriate course of action. This ensures that the social worker responds appropriately, balancing legal requirements with ethical obligations to protect client confidentiality.

449. During a group therapy session, one participant consistently dominates the conversation, limiting others' opportunities to speak. The social worker should:
a) Allow the participant to continue dominating to avoid confrontation.
b) Gently intervene, setting clear guidelines for participation and encouraging equitable sharing of time among all participants.
c) Ask the dominating participant to leave the group permanently.
d) Ignore the situation and hope it resolves on its own.

Answer: b) Gently intervene, setting clear guidelines for participation and encouraging equitable sharing of time among all participants.
Explanation: In group therapy, it's important for the facilitator to manage dynamics to ensure that all participants have the opportunity to contribute. When one participant dominates the conversation, the social worker should gently intervene to set clear guidelines for participation. This includes encouraging equitable sharing of time and ensuring that the group remains a supportive environment for all members. This approach fosters a more balanced and effective group dynamic.

450. A social worker practicing in a substance abuse treatment center is approached by a former client at a social event. The client begins discussing their ongoing recovery challenges. The social worker should:
a) Engage in the discussion, offering advice and support as if in a therapy session.
b) Politely redirect the conversation away from therapeutic topics and remind the client of the importance of maintaining professional boundaries outside of treatment settings.
c) Ignore the client and walk away to avoid any interaction.
d) Use the opportunity to informally assess the client's recovery progress.

Answer: b) Politely redirect the conversation away from therapeutic topics and remind the client of the importance of maintaining professional boundaries outside of treatment settings.
Explanation: When encountered by a former client in a social setting, it's important for social workers to maintain professional boundaries. This means politely redirecting the conversation away from therapeutic topics and reminding the client of the context and setting, thereby reinforcing the separation between professional therapeutic relationships and social interactions.

451. In a clinical supervisory relationship, the primary focus of supervision should be on:
a) The personal life and issues of the supervisee.
b) Enhancing the professional development and competency of the supervisee.
c) The supervisor's experiences and approaches to social work practice.
d) Administrative tasks and adherence to agency policies.

Answer: b) Enhancing the professional development and competency of the supervisee.
Explanation: The primary focus of clinical supervision in social work is to enhance the supervisee's professional development and competency. This includes reviewing cases, discussing interventions, addressing ethical dilemmas, and fostering reflective practice. While administrative issues and agency policies are relevant, the core of supervision is centered on the supervisee's growth as a professional and ensuring the delivery of effective, ethical services to clients.

452. When documenting client sessions, a social worker must ensure that records:
a) Are written in technical jargon to protect client confidentiality from unauthorized readers.
b) Include detailed personal opinions about the client's character and lifestyle choices.
c) Are accurate, objective, and protect the privacy and confidentiality of the client.
d) Focus exclusively on negative behaviors and outcomes to justify the need for continued services.

Answer: c) Are accurate, objective, and protect the privacy and confidentiality of the client.
Explanation: Documentation of client sessions must be accurate, objective, and written in a manner that protects the client's privacy and confidentiality. Records should accurately reflect the services provided, client progress, and any relevant clinical observations without including unnecessary personal information, subjective opinions, or technical jargon that obfuscates the content. The focus should be on providing a clear, professional account that supports the continuity and quality of care.

453. If a social worker is offered a significant promotion within their agency that would require supervising a close friend who is also a colleague, the MOST appropriate action would be to:
a) Decline the promotion to avoid any potential conflict of interest.
b) Accept the promotion and immediately terminate the friendship to maintain professional boundaries.
c) Discuss the situation with agency leadership to explore potential solutions that respect professional boundaries and address any conflicts of interest.
d) Accept the promotion and implement strict rules to govern the professional relationship with the friend.

Answer: c) Discuss the situation with agency leadership to explore potential solutions that respect professional boundaries and address any conflicts of interest.
Explanation: In situations where a promotion could lead to supervising a close friend, the best course of action is to openly discuss the potential conflict of interest with agency leadership. This approach allows for the exploration of solutions that maintain professional boundaries, ensure fair supervision, and address any ethical concerns. This may include adjustments in the supervisory arrangement or other measures to prevent conflicts of interest while allowing the social worker to accept the promotion if deemed appropriate.

454. What is the primary purpose of engaging in continuing education and professional development for social workers?
a) To meet the minimum legal requirements for licensure renewal.
b) To enhance their skills, knowledge, and competencies to provide high-quality services to clients.
c) Solely for the purpose of achieving higher salaries.
d) To specialize in a single area of practice, ignoring all other areas.

Answer: b) To enhance their skills, knowledge, and competencies to provide high-quality services to clients.
Explanation: The primary purpose of continuing education and professional development for social workers is to enhance their skills, knowledge, and competencies. This ongoing process ensures that social workers are up-to-date with the latest research, theories, techniques, and ethical standards, enabling them to provide the highest quality of service to clients and communities. While meeting legal requirements for licensure renewal is a necessary component of continuing education, the overarching goal is to improve practice and client outcomes.

455. Which method of professional development can provide social workers with the opportunity to reflect on their practice and gain insights from peers?
a) Independent reading of textbooks.
b) Attending large international conferences only.
c) Participating in case consultation groups or peer supervision.
d) Limiting professional interactions to within one's own workplace.

Answer: c) Participating in case consultation groups or peer supervision.
Explanation: Participating in case consultation groups or peer supervision offers social workers the opportunity to reflect on their practice and gain insights from peers. This method of professional development allows for the exchange of ideas, feedback, and support in a collaborative environment, fostering learning and growth. It helps social workers to explore different perspectives, enhance their problem-solving skills, and apply new knowledge to their practice.

456. How does attending interdisciplinary conferences benefit social workers?
a) It limits their exposure to ideas and practices within the field of social work.
b) It provides an opportunity to learn about developments and perspectives from related fields, enriching their practice.
c) It is discouraged as it may lead to confusion about social work's core identity.
d) It fulfills all continuing education requirements regardless of the conference content.

Answer: b) It provides an opportunity to learn about developments and perspectives from related fields, enriching their practice.
Explanation: Attending interdisciplinary conferences benefits social workers by providing them with the opportunity to learn about developments, theories, and practices from related fields. This exposure can enrich their practice by introducing new perspectives, enhancing understanding of complex issues, and fostering collaborative approaches to client care. Interdisciplinary knowledge encourages holistic and integrated service delivery, which is vital in addressing the multifaceted needs of clients.

457. What is the role of professional social work organizations in the continuing education of their members?
a) They discourage participation in educational activities outside the organization.
b) They serve as gatekeepers, limiting access to certain types of education.
c) They provide resources, accreditation for programs, and opportunities for professional development.
d) They only focus on providing theoretical knowledge without practical applications.

Answer: c) They provide resources, accreditation for programs, and opportunities for professional development.
Explanation: Professional social work organizations play a critical role in the continuing education of their members by providing resources, accrediting educational programs, and offering various opportunities for professional development. These organizations facilitate access to workshops, seminars, conferences, and online courses that cover a wide range of topics relevant to social work practice. They also often set standards for continuing education to ensure quality and relevance, supporting social workers in their commitment to lifelong learning and excellence in practice.

458. In what way does reflective practice contribute to professional development in social work?
a) By adhering strictly to established protocols without questioning them.
b) Through the uncritical acceptance of traditional practices.
c) By critically analyzing one's own practice to identify areas for improvement and learning.
d) Reflective practice is considered outdated and of no value in modern social work.

Answer: c) By critically analyzing one's own practice to identify areas for improvement and learning.
Explanation: Reflective practice is a valuable method for professional development in social work, involving the critical analysis of one's own practice to identify areas for improvement, learning, and growth. It encourages social workers to think deeply about their experiences, decisions, and actions, to understand their impact on clients, and to integrate theoretical knowledge with practical experience. Reflective practice fosters self-awareness, adaptability, and a commitment to ethical and effective practice.

459. What advantage does earning additional certifications or specializations offer social workers?
a) It automatically guarantees promotion and leadership positions.
b) It narrows their practice to a point where they only work with a specific type of client.
c) It enhances their expertise in specific areas of practice, meeting the diverse needs of clients more effectively.
d) Additional certifications are purely for personal satisfaction and have no professional value.

Answer: c) It enhances their expertise in specific areas of practice, meeting the diverse needs of clients more effectively.
Explanation: Earning additional certifications or specializations allows social workers to enhance their expertise in specific areas of practice, such as mental health, substance abuse, child welfare, or gerontology. This focused knowledge and skill set enable social workers to meet the diverse and complex needs of their clients more effectively, contribute to the field's body of knowledge, and often open up new career opportunities and pathways for professional growth.

460. What impact does lifelong learning have on social work practice?
a) It overwhelms social workers with too much information, leading to burnout.
b) It ensures that social workers remain informed, adaptable, and effective in their practice.
c) Lifelong learning is a concept that has been rejected by the social work profession.
d) It encourages social workers to rely solely on outdated knowledge and techniques.

Answer: b) It ensures that social workers remain informed, adaptable, and effective in their practice.

Explanation: Lifelong learning is crucial in social work practice as it ensures that social workers remain informed about the latest research, theories, techniques, and ethical standards. This commitment to ongoing education helps social workers to be adaptable in the face of changing societal needs, legislation, and professional guidelines, thereby enhancing their effectiveness in practice. Lifelong learning supports social workers in providing the highest quality of care and service to clients and communities.

461. In the context of clinical social work, supervision is primarily aimed at ensuring:
a) The supervisee's compliance with administrative tasks.
b) The professional development and ethical practice of the supervisee.
c) The supervisee achieves a minimum number of work hours.
d) The supervisor's methodologies are adopted by the supervisee.

Answer: b) The professional development and ethical practice of the supervisee.
Explanation: Supervision in clinical social work focuses on enhancing the professional development and ensuring the ethical practice of the supervisee. Through reflective discussion, case review, and guidance, supervision helps social workers to grow in their clinical skills, adhere to ethical standards, and provide effective services to clients. This process is critical for both novice and experienced practitioners to continually improve their practice and maintain professional standards.

462. A social worker feels overwhelmed by the complexities of a case involving multiple systems of care. The MOST appropriate use of supervision would be to:
a) Request reassignment to a less complex case.
b) Seek guidance on navigating the systems of care and integrating services for the client.
c) Discuss strategies for reducing workload and administrative duties.
d) Learn about the supervisor's personal experiences and coping mechanisms.

Answer: b) Seek guidance on navigating the systems of care and integrating services for the client.
Explanation: In situations where a social worker feels overwhelmed by the complexities of a case, especially one involving multiple systems of care, the most appropriate use of supervision is to seek guidance and support on effectively navigating these systems. Supervision provides an opportunity to explore strategies for integrating services, addressing the client's needs holistically, and managing the case's complexities. This approach helps in enhancing the social worker's competency and confidence in handling similar cases in the future.

463. A new social worker expresses anxiety about making decisions in client cases during supervision. The supervisor should:
a) Immediately take over the cases to ensure client safety.
b) Encourage the social worker to rely on intuition rather than formal training.
c) Facilitate the development of decision-making skills through case discussion and role-playing.
d) Suggest the social worker consider a different profession.

Answer: c) Facilitate the development of decision-making skills through case discussion and role-playing.
Explanation: When a new social worker expresses anxiety about decision-making, the supervisor should use the supervision process to build the supervisee's decision-making skills. This can be achieved through

case discussions that explore different scenarios and potential interventions, as well as role-playing exercises to practice decision-making in a supportive environment. This approach enhances the social worker's confidence and competence in making informed decisions in client cases.

464. During supervision, a social worker discusses feeling frustrated with a client's lack of progress. The supervisor's BEST response would be to:
a) Confirm that some clients are simply resistant to help and suggest focusing on more cooperative clients.
b) Explore the social worker's feelings and perceptions to identify potential countertransference issues.
c) Advise the social worker to confront the client about their lack of effort in sessions.
d) Recommend changing the therapeutic approach without further discussion.

Answer: b) Explore the social worker's feelings and perceptions to identify potential countertransference issues.
Explanation: When a social worker expresses frustration with a client's lack of progress, a supervisor should explore the social worker's feelings and perceptions to identify any potential countertransference issues that may be affecting the therapeutic relationship. This reflective process can uncover underlying biases or emotional reactions that might be influencing the social worker's approach to the case, thereby facilitating more effective and empathetic interventions.

465. If a social worker is unsure about the ethical implications of a proposed intervention in a complex case, supervision should focus on:
a) Reviewing the relevant ethical principles and codes of conduct to guide decision-making.
b) Encouraging the social worker to proceed with the intervention and learn from the outcome.
c) Suggesting that ethical considerations are secondary to clinical outcomes.
d) Recommending that the social worker avoid any intervention that poses ethical dilemmas.

Answer: a) Reviewing the relevant ethical principles and codes of conduct to guide decision-making.
Explanation: When faced with uncertainty about the ethical implications of a proposed intervention, supervision should involve a careful review of the relevant ethical principles and professional codes of conduct that govern social work practice. This process helps the social worker to critically evaluate the intervention, consider the ethical dimensions of the case, and make informed decisions that uphold the profession's ethical standards.

466. A supervisee is consistently late in submitting documentation. During supervision, addressing this issue should involve:
a) Ignoring the behavior as long as the supervisee's clinical work remains unaffected.
b) Discussing the importance of timely documentation, its impact on client care, and strategies for improvement.
c) Assigning additional paperwork as a form of punishment.
d) Threatening termination if the behavior does not change immediately.

Answer: b) Discussing the importance of timely documentation, its impact on client care, and strategies for improvement.

Explanation: When a supervisee is consistently late in submitting documentation, it is important to address the issue directly in supervision. The supervisor should discuss the importance of timely and accurate documentation, how it impacts client care and legal compliance, and collaboratively explore strategies for managing time more effectively. This approach is constructive and aims to improve professional practices while maintaining a supportive supervisory relationship.

467. In providing supervision to a group of social workers, the primary goal should be to:
a) Encourage competition among supervisees to motivate performance.
b) Focus solely on administrative compliance and case management efficiency.
c) Facilitate peer support, shared learning, and collective problem-solving.
d) Limit discussion to positive case outcomes to boost morale.

Answer: c) Facilitate peer support, shared learning, and collective problem-solving.
Explanation: The primary goal of group supervision in social work is to facilitate an environment of peer support, shared learning, and collective problem-solving. This approach allows supervisees to benefit from each other's experiences, perspectives, and feedback, enhancing their professional development and ability to address complex client needs collaboratively. It contrasts with focusing solely on competition, administrative tasks, or exclusively positive outcomes, which may not support comprehensive learning and growth.

468. When a supervisor observes a supervisee using techniques from a therapy modality in which they are not formally trained, the supervisor should:
a) Encourage the supervisee to continue experimenting with different modalities to discover what works best.
b) Address the issue by discussing the importance of competency in practice and the risks of practicing beyond one's scope.
c) Ignore the issue, assuming that the supervisee has good intentions.
d) Immediately report the supervisee to the licensing board for unethical practice.

Answer: b) Address the issue by discussing the importance of competency in practice and the risks of practicing beyond one's scope.
Explanation: When a supervisee uses techniques from a therapy modality in which they are not formally trained, it is crucial for the supervisor to address this issue by emphasizing the importance of practicing within one's areas of competency. This discussion should highlight the ethical and professional responsibilities to ensure safe and effective client care and the potential risks of practicing beyond one's scope of expertise. Encouraging ongoing professional development and training in desired modalities is also key.

469. In supervision, a social worker expresses interest in integrating a new evidence-based intervention into practice. The supervisor should FIRST:
a) Discourage the use of new interventions until they become more widely accepted.
b) Support the social worker in obtaining the necessary training and resources to implement the intervention competently.
c) Suggest focusing on traditional methods that the supervisor is more familiar with.
d) Recommend using the intervention with all clients to test its effectiveness.

Answer: b) Support the social worker in obtaining the necessary training and resources to implement the intervention competently.
Explanation: When a social worker expresses interest in integrating a new evidence-based intervention, the supervisor should first support the social worker in obtaining the necessary training, resources, and supervision to implement the intervention competently and ethically. This approach ensures that the social worker is prepared to apply the intervention effectively, maintaining a commitment to providing high-quality, evidence-based care to clients.

470. What principle underlies the social welfare policy of providing unemployment benefits?
a) Encouraging long-term dependence on government support.
b) Punishing individuals for job loss.
c) Supporting individuals during periods of involuntary unemployment to stabilize the economy and prevent poverty.
d) Discouraging job-seeking behavior.

Answer: c) Supporting individuals during periods of involuntary unemployment to stabilize the economy and prevent poverty.
Explanation: The principle behind providing unemployment benefits is to support individuals who are involuntarily unemployed, helping them to meet their basic needs during periods without work. This policy aims to stabilize the economy by maintaining consumer spending and preventing the spread of poverty, which can have broader societal impacts. It reflects a commitment to social protection and solidarity in facing economic challenges.

471. How do child welfare policies aim to protect children?
a) By ensuring children remain with their biological families, regardless of the circumstances.
b) Through prevention, intervention, and support services designed to ensure children's safety, well-being, and development.
c) By exclusively focusing on punitive measures against parents.
d) Child welfare policies do not involve the state in family matters.

Answer: b) Through prevention, intervention, and support services designed to ensure children's safety, well-being, and development.
Explanation: Child welfare policies are designed to protect children from harm and ensure their well-being and development through a range of prevention, intervention, and support services. These policies may involve working with families to address issues, providing services to support child development, and, when necessary, intervening to protect children from abuse or neglect. The aim is to promote safe, stable, and nurturing environments for children, whether with their biological families or in alternative care settings if required for their safety.

472. What is the purpose of the Social Security program in the United States?
a) To provide a universal income to all citizens, regardless of age or employment status.
b) To serve as the primary income source for working-age adults.
c) To provide financial assistance to retirees, disabled individuals, and survivors of deceased workers, contributing to economic stability.
d) To finance healthcare services exclusively.

Answer: c) To provide financial assistance to retirees, disabled individuals, and survivors of deceased workers, contributing to economic stability.
Explanation: The Social Security program in the United States is designed to provide financial assistance to retirees, disabled individuals, and survivors of deceased workers. It acts as a form of social insurance, funded through payroll taxes, aiming to ensure that these populations have a source of income when they are unable to work due to age, disability, or the loss of a breadwinner, thereby contributing to individual and economic stability.

473. Which policy is primarily associated with providing healthcare to low-income individuals and families in the United States?
a) Social Security
b) Medicare
c) Affordable Care Act (ACA)
d) Medicaid

Answer: d) Medicaid
Explanation: Medicaid is the policy primarily associated with providing healthcare services to low-income individuals and families in the United States. It is a joint federal and state program that helps with medical costs for some people with limited income and resources. Medicaid also offers benefits not typically covered by Medicare, including nursing home care and personal care services, making it a critical component of the social safety net.

474. How do housing policies contribute to social welfare?
a) By limiting access to affordable housing to increase market competition.
b) Through programs and initiatives that ensure individuals and families have access to affordable and safe housing.
c) Housing policies focus exclusively on high-income households.
d) By discouraging the construction of new housing developments.

Answer: b) Through programs and initiatives that ensure individuals and families have access to affordable and safe housing.
Explanation: Housing policies play a crucial role in social welfare by implementing programs and initiatives designed to ensure that individuals and families, especially those with low and moderate incomes, have access to affordable, safe, and stable housing. These policies can include public housing programs, housing vouchers, tax credits for low-income housing development, and support for homelessness prevention, addressing the fundamental need for shelter and its impact on overall well-being.

475. In the context of social welfare, what is the primary goal of education policies?
a) To restrict access to education for underserved populations.
b) To ensure equitable access to quality education for all individuals, promoting social mobility and reducing inequalities.
c) To focus educational resources on higher education exclusively.
d) Education policies do not address social welfare concerns.

Answer: b) To ensure equitable access to quality education for all individuals, promoting social mobility and reducing inequalities.
Explanation: Education policies in the context of social welfare aim to ensure that all individuals have equitable access to quality education, from early childhood through higher education. These policies are designed to promote social mobility, reduce inequalities, and equip individuals with the knowledge and skills necessary for personal development and economic participation. Efforts can include funding for public education, programs to support underserved populations, and measures to improve educational outcomes for all students.

476. What is the significance of the Americans with Disabilities Act (ADA) in the context of social welfare policies?
a) It limits the rights of individuals with disabilities in the workplace and public spaces.
b) The ADA is focused solely on providing financial assistance to individuals with disabilities.
c) It prohibits discrimination against individuals with disabilities in all areas of public life, including jobs, schools, transportation, and all public and private places open to the general public.
d) The ADA applies exclusively to the healthcare sector.

Answer: c) It prohibits discrimination against individuals with disabilities in all areas of public life, including jobs, schools, transportation, and all public and private places open to the general public.
Explanation: The Americans with Disabilities Act (ADA) is a landmark civil rights law that prohibits discrimination against individuals with disabilities in all areas of public life. Its significance in social welfare policies lies in its comprehensive approach to ensuring individuals with disabilities have the same rights and opportunities as everyone else. This includes equal access to employment, education, transportation, and other services and facilities, contributing to a more inclusive and equitable society.

477. When evaluating a new community mental health program, which indicator would be MOST crucial to assess its effectiveness?
a) The number of participants attending the program.
b) Participant satisfaction with the program services.
c) Changes in mental health status of participants before and after program participation.
d) The qualifications of the staff delivering the program.

Answer: c) Changes in mental health status of participants before and after program participation.
Explanation: Evaluating the effectiveness of a community mental health program requires direct measures of its impact on participants' mental health. Changes in the mental health status of participants before and after program participation provide concrete evidence of the program's effectiveness in achieving its intended outcomes. While participant satisfaction, program attendance, and staff qualifications are important aspects of program evaluation, the most critical indicator of a mental health program's success is its measurable impact on participants' mental health.

478. In the context of program development for a new youth mentoring program, the inclusion of stakeholder feedback is essential primarily to:
a) Satisfy grant requirements for community engagement.
b) Ensure the program aligns with the needs and preferences of the youth and community it serves.
c) Limit the need for future program revisions and updates.

d) Guarantee the program's eligibility for public funding.

Answer: b) Ensure the program aligns with the needs and preferences of the youth and community it serves.
Explanation: The inclusion of stakeholder feedback in the development of a youth mentoring program ensures that the program is designed to meet the actual needs, preferences, and circumstances of the target population and the broader community. This collaborative approach enhances the program's relevance and effectiveness, fostering greater community support and engagement. While meeting grant requirements and securing funding are important considerations, the primary reason for involving stakeholders is to ensure the program's alignment with community needs.

479. A social worker is tasked with developing an evaluation plan for a domestic violence support group. The MOST appropriate method to measure the program's impact on participants' sense of safety and well-being would be to:
a) Count the number of participants who complete the program.
b) Use a pre-and-post program survey measuring participants' feelings of safety and well-being.
c) Assess the qualifications of the group facilitators.
d) Calculate the cost-per-participant of running the program.

Answer: b) Use a pre-and-post program survey measuring participants' feelings of safety and well-being.
Explanation: Utilizing pre-and-post program surveys designed to measure changes in participants' feelings of safety and well-being provides direct, relevant data on the program's impact. This method allows for the assessment of subjective experiences of safety and well-being among participants, which are key outcomes for a domestic violence support group. It offers insight into the program's effectiveness in addressing the specific needs of participants beyond quantitative measures like completion rates or cost efficiency.

480. When developing a new program aimed at reducing homelessness in a community, a needs assessment is critical. The purpose of this needs assessment is to:
a) Identify the existing resources and gaps in services for the homeless population.
b) Allocate budget resources among the community social work staff.
c) Determine the geographical areas to exclude from the program.
d) Select which staff members will be promoted.

Answer: a) Identify the existing resources and gaps in services for the homeless population.
Explanation: Conducting a needs assessment at the beginning of program development for reducing homelessness is crucial for identifying the current landscape of resources, services available, and where there are gaps or unmet needs within the community. This information guides the program's design to effectively address specific needs, enhance existing services, and fill service gaps, ensuring that the program's efforts are targeted and efficient.

481. In the process of evaluating a school-based bullying prevention program, which of the following data sources would provide the MOST comprehensive understanding of the program's outcomes?
a) The program budget and expenses.

b) Testimonials from selected participants.
c) A combination of student surveys, teacher interviews, and incident reports.
d) The number of workshops held each year.

Answer: c) A combination of student surveys, teacher interviews, and incident reports.
Explanation: A comprehensive evaluation of a school-based bullying prevention program requires diverse data sources that capture various perspectives and indicators of change. Combining quantitative data from student surveys with qualitative data from teacher interviews, along with objective data from incident reports, offers a multifaceted view of the program's effectiveness. This approach allows evaluators to assess changes in bullying behavior, attitudes towards bullying, and the school environment's overall safety.

482. Incorporating logic models in program development helps to clarify:
a) The hierarchical structure of the organization running the program.
b) The program's theoretical framework without considering its practical application.
c) The sequence from program inputs and activities to desired outcomes and impacts.
d) Only the financial aspects involved in the program.

Answer: c) The sequence from program inputs and activities to desired outcomes and impacts.
Explanation: Logic models are valuable tools in program development and evaluation for mapping out the logical sequence from inputs (resources) and activities (what the program does) to outputs (direct products of program activities), outcomes (short and medium-term changes resulting from the program), and impacts (long-term changes). They help clarify how a program is intended to work and its theory of change, facilitating both planning and assessment by making explicit the connections between program elements and desired changes.

483. A critical component of evaluating the effectiveness of a substance abuse recovery program is to:
a) Focus exclusively on the number of participants who remain abstinent post-program.
b) Consider a range of outcomes, including reduction in use, improvements in mental health, and increased social support.
c) Evaluate the program based solely on the cost-effectiveness ratio.
d) Assess the program's effectiveness based on the personal opinions of the staff.

Answer: b) Consider a range of outcomes, including reduction in use, improvements in mental health, and increased social support.
Explanation: While abstinence can be an important outcome for substance abuse recovery programs, a comprehensive evaluation should consider a range of indicators of success. These might include reduction in substance use (not just complete abstinence), improvements in participants' mental health, enhancements in quality of life, and increases in social support and functioning. Such a holistic approach recognizes the complexity of recovery and the multifaceted nature of effective treatment outcomes.

484. When analyzing the sustainability of a community health initiative, it is important to examine:
a) The program's reliance on a single source of funding.
b) Only the initial outcomes achieved in the first year of operation.

c) The diversity of activities offered, regardless of their impact.
d) Long-term funding sources, partnerships, and community support mechanisms.

Answer: d) Long-term funding sources, partnerships, and community support mechanisms.
Explanation: Sustainability of a community health initiative is critical for its continued success and impact. Analyzing sustainability involves assessing long-term funding sources to ensure financial viability, the strength and diversity of partnerships that can provide support and resources, and community engagement and support mechanisms that contribute to the program's ongoing relevance and effectiveness. A focus on diverse, stable funding sources and strong community ties is essential for ensuring that a program can continue to operate and adapt over time.

485. To assess the fidelity of a program's implementation, an evaluator would MOST likely:
a) Compare the actual program delivery to the original program design and protocol.
b) Focus on the number of participants attending the program.
c) Evaluate the program based on its popularity in the community.
d) Consider only the feedback from the program staff.

Answer: a) Compare the actual program delivery to the original program design and protocol.
Explanation: Program fidelity assessment involves comparing how a program is being implemented in practice against the original program design and protocol. This evaluation ensures that the program is delivered as intended, which is crucial for attributing outcomes directly to the program. Assessing fidelity helps identify deviations from the planned implementation, allowing for adjustments to enhance effectiveness and ensure that the program's impacts are due to its core components and not to variations in delivery.

486. How does the implementation of the Affordable Care Act (ACA) influence social work practice in community health settings?
a) It limits the scope of practice to only those with private insurance.
b) It expands access to mental health and substance use disorder services for individuals, affecting case management and referral processes.
c) It mandates social workers to prioritize physical health issues over mental health concerns.
d) It discourages social workers from engaging in advocacy and policy change efforts.

Answer: b) It expands access to mental health and substance use disorder services for individuals, affecting case management and referral processes.
Explanation: The Affordable Care Act (ACA) significantly impacts social work practice in community health settings by expanding access to healthcare services, including mental health and substance use disorder treatments. This expansion affects social workers by broadening the scope of clients they can serve and enhancing the availability of services for referral and case management. It underscores the importance of integrated care models and increases the role of social workers in navigating healthcare systems for their clients, promoting holistic well-being.

487. In the context of child welfare, how have policies advocating for family preservation impacted social work interventions?

a) They have decreased the emphasis on child safety in favor of maintaining family unity at all costs.
b) They have led to a reduced role for social workers in child welfare cases.
c) They have emphasized interventions that support families staying together, when safe and possible, through services like in-home counseling and support.
d) They have mandated that all children be removed from their homes at the first sign of trouble as a precautionary measure.

Answer: c) They have emphasized interventions that support families staying together, when safe and possible, through services like in-home counseling and support.
Explanation: Family preservation policies in child welfare have shifted the focus towards supporting interventions that allow families to stay together safely. These policies advocate for providing families with services such as in-home counseling, substance abuse treatment, and parenting education to address issues within the family context. This approach recognizes the importance of the family unit while ensuring child safety, significantly impacting social work practice by promoting more holistic, family-centered interventions.

488. How do housing first policies affect social work practice with homeless populations?
a) They prioritize long-term employment as a precondition for housing assistance.
b) They shift the focus towards providing permanent housing solutions without preconditions, impacting case management strategies.
c) They discourage the use of social services until individuals are housed.
d) They mandate that all homeless individuals pass a drug test before receiving housing.

Answer: b) They shift the focus towards providing permanent housing solutions without preconditions, impacting case management strategies.
Explanation: Housing first policies represent a paradigm shift in addressing homelessness, focusing on providing individuals with permanent housing solutions without preconditions such as sobriety or employment. This approach impacts social work practice by changing case management strategies to prioritize securing stable housing as a foundation for addressing other needs. Social workers in this context work to integrate housing solutions with other support services, recognizing stable housing as critical to the well-being and recovery of homeless populations.

489. The introduction of mandatory reporting laws for suspected child abuse and neglect primarily requires social workers to:
a) Obtain parental consent before making a report.
b) Use their discretion on whether to report, based on their relationship with the client.
c) Report suspected cases of child abuse and neglect to appropriate authorities, as part of legal and ethical responsibilities.
d) Focus solely on providing therapy to the child, ignoring legal reporting requirements.

Answer: c) Report suspected cases of child abuse and neglect to appropriate authorities, as part of legal and ethical responsibilities.
Explanation: Mandatory reporting laws for suspected child abuse and neglect obligate social workers and other professionals to report any suspected cases to appropriate authorities. This legal requirement

underscores the ethical responsibility to protect vulnerable children from harm. Social workers must adhere to these laws, prioritizing the safety and welfare of the child, which often involves making difficult decisions that impact their practice and client relationships.

490. What impact do social security policies have on elderly clients from a social work perspective?
a) They decrease the need for social work services as financial needs are fully met by social security benefits.
b) They increase dependency on government assistance, discouraging personal responsibility.
c) They provide a foundation of financial support, affecting social work interventions related to aging, poverty, and healthcare.
d) They are irrelevant to social work practice as they do not address health or emotional well-being.

Answer: c) They provide a foundation of financial support, affecting social work interventions related to aging, poverty, and healthcare.
Explanation: Social security policies play a critical role in providing elderly clients with a foundational level of financial support, significantly influencing social work practice. These policies impact interventions related to aging, poverty, healthcare access, and quality of life. Social workers utilize this knowledge to advocate for their clients, navigate benefits systems, and integrate financial planning into broader care plans, addressing the holistic needs of the elderly population.

491. In analyzing the impact of the Americans with Disabilities Act (ADA) on client systems, social workers recognize that this policy:
a) Has limited applicability in social work practice, focusing only on employment rights.
b) Primarily increases the administrative burden on social service agencies.
c) Enhances access to public services and accommodations, promoting client advocacy and accessibility in social work interventions.
d) Reduces the need for social work advocacy by completely solving issues of accessibility and discrimination.

Answer: c) Enhances access to public services and accommodations, promoting client advocacy and accessibility in social work interventions.
Explanation: The Americans with Disabilities Act (ADA) significantly impacts social work practice by enhancing access to public services, accommodations, and employment for individuals with disabilities. This policy promotes greater inclusion and equity, guiding social workers in advocating for clients' rights, ensuring accessibility in community programs and services, and addressing barriers faced by individuals with disabilities. Social workers integrate the principles of the ADA into their practice, emphasizing the importance of accessible and inclusive environments for all clients.

492. The implementation of welfare reform policies, such as the Personal Responsibility and Work Opportunity Reconciliation Act, has influenced social work practice by:
a) Eliminating the need for social services by providing ample employment opportunities.
b) Requiring social workers to focus exclusively on job placement services.
c) Shifting the focus towards supporting clients in meeting work requirements and accessing education and training programs.
d) Discouraging social workers from engaging in policy advocacy and systemic change efforts.

Answer: c) Shifting the focus towards supporting clients in meeting work requirements and accessing education and training programs.
Explanation: Welfare reform policies, including the Personal Responsibility and Work Opportunity Reconciliation Act, have reshaped social work practice by emphasizing work requirements for receiving benefits. This shift necessitates that social workers assist clients in meeting these requirements, which often involves supporting access to education, training programs, and employment services. Social workers adapt their practice to help clients navigate these policies, balancing the need to comply with requirements while advocating for clients' broader needs and systemic changes.

493. When a social worker aims to influence policy change at the state level, their FIRST step should typically be to:
a) Organize a protest to garner media attention for the issue.
b) Draft a bill and present it directly to the governor for endorsement.
c) Identify and collaborate with legislators who have shown interest in their cause.
d) Immediately implement a social media campaign to raise public awareness.

Answer: c) Identify and collaborate with legislators who have shown interest in their cause.
Explanation: The most strategic first step for a social worker aiming to influence policy change is to identify and collaborate with legislators who have demonstrated interest in their cause. This collaboration can provide an informed pathway to introducing legislation, as these legislators can serve as champions for the cause within the legislative body. Building relationships with sympathetic legislators can also help in navigating the complexities of the legislative process more effectively than immediate public campaigns or protests.

494. In the legislative process, the purpose of a committee hearing is to:
a) Vote on whether to pass a bill to become law immediately.
b) Provide a platform for the public and interest groups to present their views on the bill.
c) Allow the governor or president to veto legislation in front of a committee.
d) Redraft legislation without any further input from other legislators or the public.

Answer: b) Provide a platform for the public and interest groups to present their views on the bill.
Explanation: Committee hearings are a critical stage in the legislative process, serving as a platform where public testimony, expert opinions, and interest group perspectives on a bill are presented. These hearings allow for detailed examination and discussion of the proposed legislation, offering insights that can influence committee members' decisions on whether to move the bill forward, amend it, or halt its progress.

495. A bill that has been passed by both houses of Congress is sent to the President. What action can the President take?
a) Sign the bill into law.
b) Do nothing, after which the bill automatically becomes law after 10 days (excluding Sundays) if Congress is in session.
c) Veto the bill.
d) All of the above.

Answer: d) All of the above.
Explanation: Once a bill has passed both houses of Congress, the President has several options: sign the bill into law, allow the bill to become law without a signature by not acting on it within 10 days (excluding Sundays) while Congress is in session, or veto the bill. Each of these actions represents a critical checkpoint in the legislative process, with the veto offering a powerful means for the President to express disapproval of legislation.

496. The role of a social worker in the legislative process could include:
a) Drafting legislation and voting on bills in Congress.
b) Lobbying, providing expert testimony, and educating policymakers about issues affecting their clients.
c) Directly amending the Constitution to reflect social work ethics.
d) Acting as a judge in legal disputes related to policy.

Answer: b) Lobbying, providing expert testimony, and educating policymakers about issues affecting their clients.
Explanation: Social workers can play a vital role in the legislative process through lobbying efforts, offering expert testimony during committee hearings, and educating policymakers about the implications of proposed legislation on vulnerable populations. While they do not draft legislation as members of Congress or directly amend the Constitution, their expertise and advocacy can significantly influence policy development and legislative outcomes.

497. A social worker advocating for policy change should understand the importance of "grassroots advocacy," which primarily involves:
a) Mobilizing community members to support or oppose legislation through public demonstrations.
b) Paying for advertisements in national media to influence public opinion.
c) Holding private meetings with high-ranking officials without public involvement.
d) Starting a petition that will automatically result in legislative change if it receives enough signatures.

Answer: a) Mobilizing community members to support or oppose legislation through public demonstrations.
Explanation: Grassroots advocacy refers to the process of mobilizing community members at the local level to support or oppose legislation, often through activities like public demonstrations, writing letters to representatives, and engaging in public forums. This type of advocacy relies on the power of collective action and public pressure to influence policy decisions, emphasizing the importance of broad-based community involvement and action.

498. When a social work organization is planning an advocacy campaign focused on a specific policy issue, a key strategic step would include:
a) Disregarding opposing viewpoints to maintain a strong stance.
b) Developing a clear message and call to action that resonates with a broad audience.
c) Limiting the campaign's reach to social work professionals only.
d) Avoiding the use of social media to prevent controversy.

Answer: b) Developing a clear message and call to action that resonates with a broad audience.

Explanation: For an advocacy campaign to be effective, especially when focused on a specific policy issue, it is critical to develop a clear, compelling message and call to action that can engage and resonate with a broad audience. This includes articulating the issue's importance, how it affects individuals and communities, and what actions supporters can take to help. A well-crafted message helps to unify supporters, mobilize action, and increase the campaign's impact.

499. In advocating for social justice, social workers must be aware of the significance of "policy analysis." This process involves:
a) Examining the potential impacts of proposed legislation or policies on individuals, families, and communities.
b) Creating policies without consulting affected populations.
c) Focusing solely on the financial aspects of policy implementation.
d) Promoting policies that benefit social workers over their clients.

Answer: a) Examining the potential impacts of proposed legislation or policies on individuals, families, and communities.
Explanation: Policy analysis is a critical tool in social work advocacy that involves a thorough examination of how proposed legislation or policies could affect various populations, particularly vulnerable groups. This process considers the potential benefits, drawbacks, and unintended consequences of policies, providing a foundation for informed advocacy efforts that seek to promote social justice and equitable outcomes.

500. Effective policy advocacy campaigns often require social workers to engage in "coalition building," which means:
a) Forming alliances solely with other social workers to strengthen the profession's voice.
b) Establishing partnerships with a diverse array of stakeholders, including other professionals, organizations, and community groups, to support a common cause.
c) Avoiding collaborations with organizations that have different viewpoints.
d) Focusing exclusively on building internal consensus within a single organization.

Answer: b) Establishing partnerships with a diverse array of stakeholders, including other professionals, organizations, and community groups, to support a common cause.
Explanation: Coalition building is a strategic approach in policy advocacy that involves forming partnerships with a wide range of stakeholders who share a common interest in a particular cause or policy issue. By bringing together diverse groups and individuals, coalitions can amplify their voice, resources, and influence, enhancing their ability to effect policy change. This collaborative effort is essential for tackling complex social issues that require collective action.

501. A social worker's use of evidence-based research in advocacy is important because it:
a) Provides a basis for making emotional appeals to policymakers.
b) Can help to substantiate claims and demonstrate the need for policy change based on empirical data.
c) Is only useful for academic purposes and has no place in the legislative process.
d) Complicates the advocacy process by introducing unnecessary information.

Answer: b) Can help to substantiate claims and demonstrate the need for policy change based on empirical data.
Explanation: Utilizing evidence-based research in advocacy efforts is crucial for substantiating claims and articulating the need for policy change. By presenting empirical data and research findings, social workers can provide policymakers with a solid foundation for understanding the issues at hand, the potential impacts of policy decisions, and the evidence supporting specific interventions or reforms. This approach enhances the credibility and persuasiveness of advocacy efforts, facilitating informed decision-making.

502. Transactional leadership is characterized by:
a) The use of charisma to inspire and motivate followers towards a vision.
b) A focus on the exchange process between leaders and followers, where compliance is rewarded.
c) An emphasis on the leader's role as a servant to meet the needs of followers.
d) The development of followers into leaders through mentoring and empowerment.

Answer: b) A focus on the exchange process between leaders and followers, where compliance is rewarded.
Explanation: Transactional leadership is centered around the exchange process between the leader and their followers. In this model, leaders provide clear instructions and expectations, and followers are rewarded for compliance and achieving set goals. This leadership style is often contrasted with transformational leadership, which focuses on inspiring followers towards a vision or change.

503. Transformational leadership is BEST described as:
a) Leadership that maintains the status quo and focuses on completing tasks efficiently.
b) Leadership that relies on disciplinary power and control to achieve organizational goals.
c) Leadership that inspires and motivates followers to exceed their own interests for the good of the group or organization.
d) Leadership that delegates all decision-making to followers to encourage independence.

Answer: c) Leadership that inspires and motivates followers to exceed their own interests for the good of the group or organization.
Explanation: Transformational leadership involves inspiring and motivating followers to achieve more than they originally intended and to exceed their own self-interests for the sake of the group or organization. Transformational leaders are characterized by their ability to bring about significant change by focusing on the organization's vision, encouraging innovation, and fostering a strong sense of commitment and loyalty among followers.

504. The Situational Leadership Model suggests that effective leadership depends on:
a) The leader's ability to maintain control over all situations.
b) The leader's personal charisma and intelligence.
c) The specific needs of the situation, including the maturity level of followers.
d) The leader’s adherence to traditional leadership practices without deviation.

Answer: c) The specific needs of the situation, including the maturity level of followers.

Explanation: The Situational Leadership Model posits that there is no single "best" style of leadership. Instead, effective leadership is contingent upon the situation, including factors like the task at hand and the maturity level (readiness and competence) of the followers. Leaders adjust their style—from directing to coaching, supporting, and finally delegating—based on what is most needed to achieve success in a particular context.

505. Which leadership theory emphasizes the leader's role in clarifying paths for followers to achieve their goals and the use of rewards and punishments?
a) Trait Theory
b) Path-Goal Theory
c) Authentic Leadership
d) Laissez-faire Leadership

Answer: b) Path-Goal Theory
Explanation: Path-Goal Theory focuses on how leaders motivate their followers to achieve designated goals. The leader's role is to clarify the path to these goals, remove any obstacles, and provide the necessary support. This theory also emphasizes the use of rewards for achieving goals and the application of corrective measures for failure to meet objectives, making leadership adaptable based on followers' needs and the task characteristics.

506. Authentic Leadership is BEST described as:
a) Leadership based on adherence to bureaucratic principles and procedures.
b) Leadership that derives authority solely from a formal position within the organization.
c) Leadership that is genuine and transparent, with a focus on ethical values and trust.
d) Leadership that avoids direct involvement in the work of followers.

Answer: c) Leadership that is genuine and transparent, with a focus on ethical values and trust.
Explanation: Authentic Leadership emphasizes the importance of leaders being genuine, transparent, and ethical. Authentic leaders are self-aware and maintain strong relationships with their followers based on trust. They are consistent in word and deed, base their actions on ethical values, and are driven by a commitment to lead with their true selves.

507. In Servant Leadership, the leader's primary focus is on:
a) Serving their own interests and ensuring personal power and influence.
b) The needs and growth of followers and the community before their own.
c) Establishing strict controls and monitoring follower performance closely.
d) Achieving high profits and shareholder value above all else.

Answer: b) The needs and growth of followers and the community before their own.
Explanation: Servant Leadership is a philosophy where the main goal of the leader is to serve others. This type of leader focuses on the needs, development, and wellbeing of their followers and the community before considering their own. Servant leaders prioritize empowering and uplifting others, which in turn fosters a strong sense of community and encourages high levels of engagement and performance.

508. Which organizational structure is characterized by a clear hierarchy, strict roles, and top-down communication?
a) Flat organization
b) Matrix structure
c) Bureaucratic organization
d) Network structure

Answer: c) Bureaucratic organization
Explanation: A bureaucratic organization is defined by its clear hierarchy, strict roles and responsibilities, and top-down communication flow. This type of structure is traditional and emphasizes order, standardization, and control, with decisions typically made at the top and communicated down through the ranks.

509. In terms of organizational culture, which component is critical for fostering a positive work environment that supports change?
a) Rigid adherence to policies
b) Strong hierarchical communication
c) Shared values and beliefs
d) Centralized decision-making

Answer: c) Shared values and beliefs
Explanation: Shared values and beliefs are crucial components of organizational culture that contribute to a positive work environment supportive of change. When an organization's members share common values, it facilitates unity, collaboration, and an openness to adapt and embrace new ideas, which are essential for navigating change effectively.

510. Which management theory emphasizes the importance of understanding human behaviors, needs, and attitudes within the workplace?
a) Scientific management
b) Classical management
c) Human relations theory
d) Systems theory

Answer: c) Human relations theory
Explanation: Human relations theory focuses on the importance of understanding workers' behaviors, needs, and attitudes in the workplace. It suggests that employees are motivated not just by money but also by social needs and job satisfaction, emphasizing the significance of creating a supportive work environment and considering employees' emotional welfare.

511. The concept of "transformational leadership" is best described as:
a) Leading by strictly enforcing rules and maintaining a distance from followers.
b) Leading by setting clear objectives and providing rewards or punishments based on performance.
c) Leading by inspiring and motivating followers to exceed their own interests for the good of the group or organization.
d) Leading by consensus, allowing followers to have equal say in decision-making processes.

Answer: c) Leading by inspiring and motivating followers to exceed their own interests for the good of the group or organization.
Explanation: Transformational leadership involves leaders who inspire and motivate their followers to achieve more than they originally intended and even more than they thought possible. They focus on transforming followers' beliefs, values, and capabilities, thereby promoting organizational change and innovation.

512. An organization implementing a "matrix structure" would most likely experience which of the following?
a) Clear lines of authority with decisions made at the top
b) Reduced need for communication among departments
c) Flexibility and increased collaboration across different functional areas
d) Simplification of tasks and reduction in employee autonomy

Answer: c) Flexibility and increased collaboration across different functional areas
Explanation: A matrix structure is characterized by its cross-functional teams and dual-reporting system, where employees report to both a functional manager and a project or product manager. This structure is designed to enhance flexibility and foster collaboration across different areas of expertise, breaking down traditional departmental barriers.

513. In organizational management, "SWOT analysis" is used to:
a) Determine the optimal pricing strategy for new products.
b) Assess an organization's strengths, weaknesses, opportunities, and threats.
c) Evaluate employee performance against predetermined benchmarks.
d) Calculate the financial health of an organization over a fiscal year.

Answer: b) Assess an organization's strengths, weaknesses, opportunities, and threats.
Explanation: SWOT analysis is a strategic planning tool used to identify and evaluate an organization's Strengths, Weaknesses, Opportunities, and Threats. This analysis helps organizations understand internal resources and capabilities (strengths and weaknesses) and external factors that could impact their success (opportunities and threats), facilitating informed decision-making and strategy development.

514. Which approach to conflict resolution focuses on finding a solution that is mutually satisfying to all parties involved?
a) Avoidance
b) Competition
c) Accommodation
d) Collaboration

Answer: d) Collaboration
Explanation: Collaboration is a conflict resolution approach that involves working together with all parties to find a solution that satisfies everyone's needs and concerns. It is considered a win-win approach, as it seeks to address the interests of all parties and often leads to innovative and lasting solutions.

515. The most effective approach for a social service program to identify areas for quality improvement is to:
a) Wait for client complaints to highlight what needs to be changed.
b) Conduct annual performance reviews of individual staff members.
c) Implement a continuous feedback loop that includes client satisfaction surveys, staff input, and program outcome data.
d) Focus exclusively on financial audits to determine where budget adjustments are needed.

Answer: c) Implement a continuous feedback loop that includes client satisfaction surveys, staff input, and program outcome data.
Explanation: A continuous feedback loop that incorporates client satisfaction surveys, staff input, and analysis of program outcome data offers a comprehensive approach to identifying areas for quality improvement. This method ensures that feedback is consistently gathered from all stakeholders, providing a well-rounded perspective on the program's performance and areas for enhancement. It allows for timely adjustments and improvements, rather than waiting for annual reviews or relying solely on financial audits, which may not capture the full scope of the program's effectiveness or areas needing improvement.

516. In evaluating the impact of a new intervention within a social service program, it is important to:
a) Compare the outcomes of clients who received the intervention with those who did not.
b) Solely rely on qualitative feedback from clients about their experience.
c) Disregard any changes in staff satisfaction or turnover rates.
d) Focus on the short-term outcomes, ignoring long-term effects.

Answer: a) Compare the outcomes of clients who received the intervention with those who did not.
Explanation: Comparing the outcomes of clients who received the new intervention with those who did not (a control or comparison group) allows for a clearer assessment of the intervention's effectiveness. This approach provides evidence on whether the intervention led to better outcomes, accounting for other variables that could influence results. While client feedback is valuable, combining qualitative and quantitative data, including long-term effects and staff experiences, offers a more comprehensive evaluation of the intervention's impact.

517. When planning a quality improvement initiative in a social service agency, it is crucial to:
a) Make decisions based solely on the highest-ranking officials' opinions within the agency.
b) Involve a cross-section of stakeholders, including clients, front-line staff, and management, in the planning process.
c) Limit feedback to quantitative data, as qualitative feedback is often too subjective.
d) Implement changes quickly, without pilot testing, to achieve immediate results.

Answer: b) Involve a cross-section of stakeholders, including clients, front-line staff, and management, in the planning process.
Explanation: Involving a diverse group of stakeholders in the planning process of a quality improvement initiative ensures that multiple perspectives are considered, leading to more effective and comprehensive solutions. Engaging clients, front-line staff, and management helps identify a wider range of issues and

opportunities for improvement, fostering buy-in and support across the organization. This collaborative approach is more likely to result in meaningful and sustainable changes than decisions made unilaterally by high-ranking officials or without adequate testing.

518. For a program aimed at reducing youth recidivism rates, the most indicative measure of success would be:
a) The number of participants who complete the program.
b) Feedback from community members about their perceptions of youth behavior.
c) A decrease in recidivism rates among participants compared to a control group.
d) The amount of media coverage the program receives.

Answer: c) A decrease in recidivism rates among participants compared to a control group.
Explanation: The most direct measure of success for a program aimed at reducing youth recidivism is a decrease in recidivism rates among program participants, especially when compared to a similar group that did not receive the intervention. This outcome-focused metric directly assesses the program's effectiveness in achieving its primary goal, whereas other measures such as program completion rates, community perceptions, or media coverage, while important, do not directly indicate whether the program successfully reduced recidivism.

519. In ensuring the sustainability of a social service program, it is vital to:
a) Focus solely on securing long-term funding, ignoring other aspects of program management.
b) Develop a comprehensive plan that includes funding strategies, staff training, program evaluation, and stakeholder engagement.
c) Assume that initial success guarantees future funding and support.
d) Rely on one-time grants and donations without exploring other revenue sources.

Answer: b) Develop a comprehensive plan that includes funding strategies, staff training, program evaluation, and stakeholder engagement.
Explanation: Sustainability of a social service program requires a multi-faceted approach that goes beyond securing funding. A comprehensive sustainability plan should include strategies for ongoing funding, staff development and training to maintain program quality, regular program evaluation to demonstrate effectiveness, and active engagement with stakeholders to ensure continued support and relevance. This holistic approach addresses the various dimensions that contribute to a program's long-term viability and impact.

520. In the process of budgeting for a non-profit organization, which of the following is the MOST critical factor to ensure financial stability and program sustainability?
a) Projected entertainment expenses for fundraising events.
b) Allocation of funds for unforeseen legal battles.
c) Accurate estimation of revenue from various sources including grants, donations, and service fees.
d) Investment in high-risk financial markets for quick returns.

Answer: c) Accurate estimation of revenue from various sources including grants, donations, and service fees.

Explanation: Accurate estimation of revenue from various sources such as grants, donations, service fees, and other funding streams is crucial for the financial management and budgeting process in non-profit organizations. This ensures that the organization can plan effectively, allocate resources to key programs and services, and maintain financial stability and sustainability. While managing expenses is also important, the ability to accurately forecast and track incoming revenue allows for more informed decision-making and strategic planning.

521. When evaluating a new program proposal, a social work manager should FIRST consider:
a) The popularity of the program with the organization's staff.
b) Potential media coverage the program might attract.
c) The alignment of the program with the organization's mission and strategic goals.
d) The program's potential to generate profit.

Answer: c) The alignment of the program with the organization's mission and strategic goals.
Explanation: For a social work manager, the first and foremost consideration when evaluating a new program proposal is how well it aligns with the organization's mission and strategic goals. This alignment ensures that the program contributes meaningfully to the organization's overall purpose and long-term objectives, rather than being driven by profitability, staff preferences, or potential media attention. Ensuring program alignment with the mission and goals is essential for maintaining the integrity and focus of the organization's efforts.

522. A critical component of financial management in social work organizations involves:
a) Prioritizing expenditures on new technologies regardless of their immediate applicability.
b) Regularly reviewing and adjusting the budget to reflect changes in funding levels and program needs.
c) Allocating a fixed percentage of the budget to every program annually without review.
d) Focusing exclusively on cutting costs to maintain a lean operation.

Answer: b) Regularly reviewing and adjusting the budget to reflect changes in funding levels and program needs.
Explanation: Effective financial management in social work organizations requires the regular review and adjustment of budgets to accurately reflect both the availability of funds and the evolving needs of programs. This adaptive approach ensures that resources are allocated efficiently, programs are adequately supported, and the organization can respond flexibly to changes in funding or operational priorities. Unlike rigid or cost-cutting-only strategies, this method supports sustainable program delivery and organizational health.

523. When a social work agency is planning its annual budget, incorporating a "contingency fund" is important for:
a) Covering the costs of annual staff retreats.
b) Ensuring there are resources available to address unexpected expenses or financial shortfalls.
c) Allocating additional funds to the highest-grossing programs.
d) Investing in stock options as a means of generating additional income.

Answer: b) Ensuring there are resources available to address unexpected expenses or financial shortfalls.

Explanation: Including a contingency fund in the annual budget is a prudent financial practice that allows an organization to have a reserve of funds specifically set aside to address unexpected expenses, emergencies, or financial shortfalls. This foresight ensures that the organization can maintain stability and continuity of operations even when faced with unforeseen financial challenges, without having to divert funds from essential programs or services suddenly.

524. In managing a grant-funded project, effective financial oversight includes:
a) Spending all allocated funds as quickly as possible to ensure full utilization.
b) Keeping detailed records of expenditures and matching them against the budget and grant requirements.
c) Ignoring grant restrictions to prioritize organizational needs.
d) Relying solely on verbal agreements with funders regarding budget changes.

Answer: b) Keeping detailed records of expenditures and matching them against the budget and grant requirements.
Explanation: Effective financial oversight of a grant-funded project requires meticulous record-keeping of all expenditures, ensuring they align with both the approved budget and the specific requirements or restrictions set forth by the grant. This level of financial management and accountability helps to maintain transparency, build trust with funders, and ensure that funds are being used appropriately and efficiently to achieve the intended project outcomes.

525. In a study examining the effects of a new therapeutic intervention for depression, which research method would best allow for the control of variables and determination of cause-and-effect relationships?
a) Case study
b) Ethnography
c) Experimental design
d) Narrative analysis

Answer: c) Experimental design
Explanation: An experimental design is the most appropriate method for examining cause-and-effect relationships between variables, such as the efficacy of a new therapeutic intervention for depression. By randomly assigning participants to either a treatment group or a control group and controlling for external variables, researchers can isolate the effects of the intervention on depression outcomes, thereby providing strong evidence for its effectiveness or lack thereof.

526. When assessing the cultural impact of social programs within a diverse community, which qualitative research method is MOST appropriate?
a) Surveys with closed-ended questions
b) Structured interviews
c) Participant observation
d) Randomized controlled trials

Answer: c) Participant observation

Explanation: Participant observation is a qualitative research method well-suited for deeply understanding the cultural impact of social programs within a diverse community. By immersing themselves in the community and observing interactions and behaviors directly, researchers can gain nuanced insights into how cultural factors influence the effectiveness and reception of social programs. This method allows for the capture of complex dynamics that might not be evident through more structured or quantitative approaches.

527. A researcher interested in exploring how individuals with chronic illness navigate daily challenges is likely to use which of the following research methods?
a) Meta-analysis
b) Phenomenology
c) Correlational study
d) Quasi-experimental design

Answer: b) Phenomenology
Explanation: Phenomenology is a qualitative research method focused on understanding individuals' lived experiences and perceptions. For a study aimed at exploring how individuals with chronic illness navigate daily challenges, phenomenology would enable the researcher to delve into the personal and subjective experiences of those living with chronic illness, capturing the depth and complexity of their daily realities in a way that quantitative methods may not.

528. To determine the relationship between social media use and loneliness among teenagers, a researcher is most likely to employ:
a) Content analysis
b) Ethnomethodology
c) A correlational study
d) Grounded theory

Answer: c) A correlational study
Explanation: A correlational study is designed to identify and analyze the relationships between variables without inferring causality. In this case, examining the relationship between social media use and loneliness among teenagers would involve collecting data on both variables and statistically analyzing them to see if there is a correlation, such as whether higher levels of social media use are associated with greater feelings of loneliness.

529. In qualitative research, the process of coding data involves:
a) Assigning numerical values to different responses for statistical analysis
b) Organizing data into categories and themes for in-depth analysis
c) Randomly selecting data points for inclusion in the study
d) Calculating the mean, median, and mode of responses

Answer: b) Organizing data into categories and themes for in-depth analysis
Explanation: Coding in qualitative research refers to the process of organizing data into categories and themes that emerge from the data itself. This allows researchers to systematically analyze the data for

patterns, meanings, and insights related to the research questions. Coding is a fundamental step in qualitative data analysis, facilitating a deep, nuanced understanding of complex human experiences.

530. To evaluate the long-term outcomes of a community intervention program, a researcher would most likely use a:
a) Cross-sectional study
b) Longitudinal study
c) Case-control study
d) Cross-sequential study

Answer: b) Longitudinal study
Explanation: A longitudinal study, which involves observing the same subjects over a period of time, is best suited for evaluating the long-term outcomes of a community intervention program. This research design allows the researcher to track changes and developments in the program's impact on the community, providing valuable insights into its effectiveness, sustainability, and any long-term benefits or consequences.

531. The use of focus groups in social work research is particularly effective for:
a) Determining the statistical significance of observed effects
b) Exploring participants' perceptions and experiences in depth
c) Establishing cause-and-effect relationships between variables
d) Generalizing findings to a larger population

Answer: b) Exploring participants' perceptions and experiences in depth
Explanation: Focus groups are a qualitative research method that brings together a small group of people to discuss specific topics of interest in a guided conversation. This method is particularly effective for exploring participants' perceptions, experiences, and attitudes in depth, as it allows for dynamic interaction, discussion, and reflection among group members, providing rich, detailed data that might not emerge from individual interviews or quantitative methods.

532. When comparing the effectiveness of two different social work interventions, the MOST suitable research design would be:
a) Ethnographic study
b) Experimental study with a control group
c) Narrative inquiry
d) Discourse analysis

Answer: b) Experimental study with a control group
Explanation: An experimental study with a control group is the most suitable research design for comparing the effectiveness of two different social work interventions. This design allows researchers to randomly assign participants to either intervention or a control group, thereby controlling for extraneous variables and making it possible to directly compare the outcomes of the interventions. This approach provides rigorous evidence on the relative effectiveness of each intervention.

533. When applying the findings of an evaluation research study to social work practice, it is MOST important to consider:
a) The popularity of the intervention among social work professionals.
b) The statistical significance of the results without regard to their practical importance.
c) Whether the findings are directly applicable to the client population and context of practice.
d) Only the most expensive and complex interventions, as they are presumed to be more effective.

Answer: c) Whether the findings are directly applicable to the client population and context of practice.
Explanation: The most crucial aspect of applying evaluation research findings to social work practice is the applicability of these findings to the specific client population and practice context. This ensures that interventions are not only evidence-based but also relevant and likely to be effective in the given circumstances. Consideration must be given to the characteristics of the client population, the social work setting, and the feasibility of implementing the intervention as studied.

534. In conducting evaluation research of a new therapeutic intervention for adolescents with anxiety, the MOST appropriate research design would be:
a) A cross-sectional survey of adolescents' self-reported anxiety levels.
b) A longitudinal study tracking changes in anxiety levels over time without any intervention.
c) A randomized controlled trial comparing the new intervention with a standard treatment or placebo.
d) An open-ended interview study with parents about their perceptions of adolescents' anxiety.

Answer: c) A randomized controlled trial comparing the new intervention with a standard treatment or placebo.
Explanation: A randomized controlled trial (RCT) is considered the gold standard for evaluating the effectiveness of therapeutic interventions. This design allows for the clear comparison of outcomes between participants receiving the new intervention and those receiving standard treatment or a placebo, controlling for other variables that might influence anxiety levels. RCTs provide rigorous evidence on the efficacy of interventions, making them highly appropriate for evaluating new therapeutic approaches for adolescents with anxiety.

535. When evaluating the outcomes of a community-based elder care program, it is crucial to use outcome measures that are:
a) Based solely on the cost-effectiveness of the program.
b) Focused on short-term outcomes, disregarding long-term effects.
c) Sensitive to the specific needs and life contexts of older adults.
d) Uniform for all age groups to simplify the analysis.

Answer: c) Sensitive to the specific needs and life contexts of older adults.
Explanation: In evaluating a community-based elder care program, outcome measures must be sensitive to the particular needs, challenges, and life contexts of older adults. This ensures that the evaluation accurately reflects the program's impact on this specific population's quality of life, health, and well-being. Using age-appropriate and relevant outcome measures is crucial for assessing the effectiveness and relevance of elder care programs.

536. A social worker involved in program evaluation must understand the difference between qualitative and quantitative research methods because:
a) Qualitative methods are always superior to quantitative methods.
b) Quantitative methods cannot provide insights into program participants' experiences.
c) Different research questions and objectives may require the use of one method over the other, or a combination of both, to gather comprehensive data.
d) Qualitative research is cheaper and easier to conduct than quantitative research.

Answer: c) Different research questions and objectives may require the use of one method over the other, or a combination of both, to gather comprehensive data.
Explanation: Understanding the distinction between qualitative and quantitative research methods is crucial for social workers conducting program evaluation. This knowledge allows them to choose the most appropriate method(s) based on the specific research questions and objectives of the evaluation. While quantitative methods can provide numerical data on outcomes and patterns, qualitative methods offer in-depth insights into participants' experiences and perceptions. Often, a mixed-methods approach combining both qualitative and quantitative data is most effective in capturing a comprehensive view of a program's impact.

537. In the dissemination phase of an evaluation study, the PRIMARY goal is to:
a) Ensure the study remains unpublished to maintain the program's proprietary methods.
b) Share the findings with a broad audience, including practitioners, policymakers, and the community, to inform practice and decision-making.
c) Limit the sharing of findings to academic circles to enhance the researchers' reputations.
d) Focus exclusively on the program's successes, omitting any negative outcomes.

Answer: b) Share the findings with a broad audience, including practitioners, policymakers, and the community, to inform practice and decision-making.
Explanation: The primary goal of disseminating the findings of an evaluation study is to share the results with a wide range of stakeholders, including social work practitioners, policymakers, program participants, and the broader community. This ensures that the evidence generated can inform practice, guide policy decisions, and potentially lead to the replication or adaptation of effective programs. Dissemination aims to enhance the utility and impact of the research by making its findings accessible and actionable for those who can benefit from them.

538. When analyzing data from a program aimed at reducing substance abuse, the use of inferential statistics would be MOST appropriate to:
a) Describe the characteristics of program participants at a single point in time.
b) Determine if observed changes in substance use among participants are statistically significant.
c) Summarize the program's budget and expenses in detail.
d) Collect detailed narratives about participants' experiences in the program.

Answer: b) Determine if observed changes in substance use among participants are statistically significant.
Explanation: Inferential statistics are used to analyze data in a way that allows researchers to make conclusions about the population based on a sample and to determine if the observed changes are

statistically significant and not due to chance. In the context of a program aimed at reducing substance abuse, inferential statistics would enable the evaluation of whether the intervention effectively led to significant changes in substance use among participants, thereby assessing the program's impact.

539. The choice of a control or comparison group in program evaluation research is essential because it:
a) Simplifies the research design by eliminating the need for pre-tests.
b) Allows for the assessment of program impact by comparing outcomes with those who did not receive the intervention.
c) Is required for all types of qualitative research.
d) Automatically guarantees the success of the program being evaluated.

Answer: b) Allows for the assessment of program impact by comparing outcomes with those who did not receive the intervention.
Explanation: Using a control or comparison group in program evaluation research is critical for assessing the program's impact effectively. This group, which does not receive the intervention, serves as a benchmark against which the outcomes of the program participants (treatment group) can be compared. This comparison helps to isolate the effects of the program from other factors that could influence the outcomes, providing stronger evidence of the program's effectiveness or lack thereof.

540. The process of logic modeling in program evaluation is MOST useful for:
a) Predicting the exact financial return on investment for program funders.
b) Providing a detailed job description for every staff member involved in the program.
c) Outlining the program's intended chain of outcomes from inputs through to impacts.
d) Ensuring that the program will never require adjustments or revisions.

Answer: c) Outlining the program's intended chain of outcomes from inputs through to impacts.
Explanation: Logic models are valuable tools in program evaluation for visually representing a program's logic or theory of change. They outline how program inputs (resources) lead to activities (what the program does), outputs (direct products of program activities), outcomes (short and medium-term changes resulting from the program), and impacts (long-term changes in the community or population). This helps stakeholders understand the expected process through which the program aims to achieve its goals and provides a framework for evaluating whether and how these goals are met.

541. In ensuring ethical considerations are met in evaluation research, obtaining informed consent from participants is crucial to:
a) Guarantee the program receives additional funding.
b) Ensure participants are fully aware of the research purposes, procedures, and their rights before agreeing to take part.
c) Make the data collection process faster and easier.
d) Avoid any need for data analysis.

Answer: b) Ensure participants are fully aware of the research purposes, procedures, and their rights before agreeing to take part.

Explanation: Obtaining informed consent is a fundamental ethical requirement in evaluation research. It involves ensuring that all participants are fully informed about the study's aims, what participation entails, any potential risks and benefits, and their rights (including the right to withdraw at any time). This process respects participants' autonomy and ensures they voluntarily agree to participate based on a clear understanding of the research.

542. Informed consent in social work research is critical because it ensures that:
a) Participants are randomly assigned to study groups without bias.
b) Participants are fully aware of the research purpose, procedures, risks, and benefits, and agree to participate voluntarily.
c) All participants receive financial compensation for their involvement.
d) The results will be statistically significant and generalizable.

Answer: b) Participants are fully aware of the research purpose, procedures, risks, and benefits, and agree to participate voluntarily.
Explanation: Informed consent is a foundational ethical principle in research, ensuring that participants understand the nature of the study, what it involves, any potential risks, and benefits, and agree to participate on a voluntary basis. This process respects participants' autonomy and right to make an informed decision about their involvement in research.

543. When conducting research with vulnerable populations, ethical considerations include:
a) Prioritizing the research outcomes over the well-being of the participants.
b) Ensuring that the benefits of the research justify any potential risks to participants.
c) Using deception as necessary to obtain unbiased data.
d) Withholding information about the purpose of the research to prevent data contamination.

Answer: b) Ensuring that the benefits of the research justify any potential risks to participants.
Explanation: Research with vulnerable populations requires a careful ethical balance to ensure that the benefits of the research outweigh any potential risks. Researchers must take extra precautions to protect these participants from harm, ensuring their well-being is the priority. This involves minimizing risks, obtaining informed consent, and ensuring that participants are treated with respect and dignity.

544. Anonymity and confidentiality in research are important to:
a) Guarantee that the research findings are valid and reliable.
b) Ensure that participants' identities are not disclosed without their consent, protecting their privacy.
c) Make sure that all research is published, regardless of the results.
d) Ensure that researchers gain recognition for their work.

Answer: b) Ensure that participants' identities are not disclosed without their consent, protecting their privacy.
Explanation: Anonymity and confidentiality are key ethical principles in research that protect participants' privacy. Anonymity means that participants' identities are unknown even to the researchers, while confidentiality means that information participants provide is not disclosed to others without their

consent. These principles help to ensure that participants feel safe to provide honest responses and participate in research without fear of harm or privacy invasion.

545. In the case of research involving minors, ethical research practice requires:
a) Only the minors' consent is necessary for participation.
b) Consent from a parent or guardian, in addition to assent from the minor, when appropriate.
c) Minors can be included in the research without consent if the study poses minimal risk.
d) Parental consent is not required if the research benefits the minor directly.

Answer: b) Consent from a parent or guardian, in addition to assent from the minor, when appropriate.
Explanation: When research involves minors, obtaining consent from a parent or guardian is generally required due to minors' legal inability to give informed consent themselves. Additionally, researchers should seek the assent of minors, which means agreeing to participate in an age-appropriate manner. This dual process respects the autonomy of the minor while ensuring their protection through parental or guardian oversight.

546. The principle of beneficence in research ethics primarily focuses on:
a) Ensuring the research contributes to the body of knowledge.
b) Maximizing benefits and minimizing harm to participants.
c) Guaranteeing that all participants receive the intervention being tested.
d) Ensuring that the research is financially beneficial to the sponsors.

Answer: b) Maximizing benefits and minimizing harm to participants.
Explanation: The principle of beneficence is a fundamental ethical guideline in research that focuses on maximizing potential benefits to participants while minimizing possible harm. This principle compels researchers to consider the welfare of participants as central to the research design and conduct, ensuring that any risks are justified by the potential benefits.

547. When a social work researcher discovers that their study unexpectedly poses greater risks to participants than initially thought, the ethically responsible action is to:
a) Continue the study as planned to maintain the integrity of the research design.
b) Immediately halt the study and review the ethical implications and safety protocols.
c) Only inform new participants about the increased risks.
d) Increase the financial compensation for participants.

Answer: b) Immediately halt the study and review the ethical implications and safety protocols.
Explanation: If a study poses greater risks than initially anticipated, the researcher has an ethical obligation to pause the research to reassess the risks, potential benefits, and ethical implications. This might involve modifying the study protocol, implementing additional safety measures, or, in some cases, terminating the study if the risks cannot be adequately mitigated.

548. Dual relationships in research, similar to practice, are ethically problematic because they can:
a) Enhance the trust between the researcher and the participant.
b) Lead to conflicts of interest and compromise the integrity of the research.

c) Increase the number of participants willing to join the study.
d) Make the research process more efficient and straightforward.

Answer: b) Lead to conflicts of interest and compromise the integrity of the research.
Explanation: Dual relationships, where the researcher has another significant relationship with a participant (e.g., clinician-client, teacher-student), can lead to conflicts of interest and potentially harm the participant or the research integrity. They can compromise objectivity, confidentiality, and participant welfare, thus are generally avoided in ethical research practices.

549. When evaluating the ethical considerations of a new research study, an Institutional Review Board (IRB) primarily assesses:
a) The statistical methods used for data analysis.
b) The potential for the research to lead to published papers in high-impact journals.
c) The balance of risks and benefits to participants and the protection of their rights and welfare.
d) The financial budget of the research project.

Answer: c) The balance of risks and benefits to participants and the protection of their rights and welfare.
Explanation: The primary role of an Institutional Review Board (IRB) is to ensure that research involving human participants is conducted ethically. This involves assessing the balance of risks and benefits to participants, ensuring that risks are minimized and benefits maximized, and that participants' rights and welfare are protected throughout the research process. The IRB review includes evaluating informed consent processes, privacy protections, and the overall ethical implications of the study design.

550. When interpreting the results of a regression analysis in a study on the factors affecting client satisfaction in social work practice, a significant positive coefficient for the variable "number of counseling sessions attended" would suggest:
a) Clients who attend more counseling sessions are less likely to be satisfied with social work services.
b) There is no relationship between the number of counseling sessions attended and client satisfaction.
c) Clients who attend more counseling sessions are more likely to be satisfied with social work services.
d) The number of counseling sessions attended is the only factor affecting client satisfaction.

Answer: c) Clients who attend more counseling sessions are more likely to be satisfied with social work services.
Explanation: In regression analysis, a positive coefficient for an independent variable (in this case, "number of counseling sessions attended") indicates a positive relationship with the dependent variable (client satisfaction). This means that as the number of counseling sessions increases, client satisfaction also tends to increase, suggesting that more frequent engagement in counseling is associated with higher levels of satisfaction among clients.

551. A social worker evaluating the effectiveness of a new group therapy program for teenagers with anxiety analyzes pre- and post-test scores using a paired t-test. This statistical test is chosen because it is designed to:
a) Compare the mean scores of two unrelated groups.
b) Determine the correlation between two variables.

c) Compare the mean scores of the same group of participants at two different times.
d) Identify the median score improvement in the group.

Answer: c) Compare the mean scores of the same group of participants at two different times.
Explanation: The paired t-test is utilized to compare the means of the same group at two different points in time (pre- and post-intervention) to assess whether there is a statistically significant difference in scores, such as a decrease in anxiety levels after participating in the group therapy program. This test is appropriate for evaluating changes within the same group, offering insights into the program's effectiveness.

552. In analyzing data from a survey on barriers to accessing mental health services, a social worker uses chi-square tests. The primary purpose of using this test is to:
a) Assess the average number of barriers reported by participants.
b) Determine if there are significant differences in the reported barriers among different demographic groups.
c) Calculate the strength of association between two continuous variables.
d) Predict the number of barriers an individual might face based on their demographic profile.

Answer: b) Determine if there are significant differences in the reported barriers among different demographic groups.
Explanation: The chi-square test is used to examine whether there are significant differences in categorical variables across different groups. In the context of a survey on barriers to accessing mental health services, this test can help determine if the distribution of reported barriers significantly varies among different demographic categories (e.g., age, gender, socioeconomic status), suggesting potential disparities in access to care.

553. A longitudinal study on the impact of a new social policy on child welfare outcomes collects data at multiple points over five years. The primary statistical approach to analyzing this data to understand trends over time would be:
a) Cross-sectional analysis.
b) Repeated measures ANOVA.
c) Simple linear regression.
d) Descriptive statistics only.

Answer: b) Repeated measures ANOVA.
Explanation: Repeated measures ANOVA is particularly suited for analyzing data from a longitudinal study where the same subjects are observed multiple times. This approach allows the researcher to assess changes in child welfare outcomes over the five years, accounting for the correlation between repeated observations of the same subjects and providing insights into the policy's long-term impact.

554. To understand the relationship between socioeconomic status (SES) and mental health outcomes in a community survey, the most appropriate statistical analysis would be:
a) A chi-square test.
b) An independent samples t-test.

c) Pearson's correlation coefficient.
d) A one-way ANOVA.

Answer: c) Pearson's correlation coefficient.
Explanation: Pearson's correlation coefficient is used to measure the strength and direction of the relationship between two continuous variables. In examining the relationship between socioeconomic status (SES), a continuous variable, and mental health outcomes (assuming they are quantitatively measured), this statistical tool can assess whether higher or lower SES is associated with better or worse mental health outcomes, providing a correlation coefficient that ranges from -1 to +1.

555. In preparing a report on the outcomes of a substance abuse treatment program, a social worker finds a standard deviation of 4.2 on the post-treatment addiction severity index. The standard deviation indicates:
a) The average severity of addiction post-treatment.
b) The range of addiction severity scores post-treatment.
c) The variance from the mean addiction severity score post-treatment.
d) The minimum effectiveness of the treatment program.

Answer: c) The variance from the mean addiction severity score post-treatment.
Explanation: The standard deviation is a measure of the amount of variation or dispersion from the average (mean) score. A standard deviation of 4.2 on the post-treatment addiction severity index indicates how much the individual scores vary from the mean score, providing insights into the spread of outcomes

556. When assessing a client for substance use disorders, it is important to consider:
a) Only the physical signs of substance use.
b) The frequency and amount of substance use alone.
c) Environmental, genetic, and behavioral factors in addition to substance use patterns.
d) The client's self-report as the sole indicator of substance use.

Answer: c) Environmental, genetic, and behavioral factors in addition to substance use patterns.
Explanation: A comprehensive assessment of a client for substance use disorders requires consideration of a broad range of factors beyond just the observable physical signs or the frequency and amount of substance use. Environmental factors (such as access to substances and peer influences), genetic predispositions, and behavioral indicators (including changes in behavior, mood, or social functioning) all play crucial roles in understanding the complexity of substance use disorders. This holistic approach ensures a more accurate diagnosis and informs the development of an effective treatment plan.

557. Motivational Interviewing (MI) is an effective approach for clients with substance use disorders because it:
a) Uses confrontation to force clients to recognize their substance use issues.
b) Focuses on directing the client towards admitting they have a problem.
c) Emphasizes collaboration, evoking clients' own motivations for change, and autonomy.
d) Relies on the therapist to set goals for the client's recovery.

Answer: c) Emphasizes collaboration, evoking clients' own motivations for change, and autonomy.
Explanation: Motivational Interviewing (MI) is particularly effective for treating substance use disorders as it is a client-centered, directive method for enhancing intrinsic motivation to change by exploring and resolving ambivalence. Unlike approaches that use confrontation or direct persuasion, MI emphasizes collaboration between the therapist and client, respects the client's autonomy, and focuses on eliciting the client's personal motivations for making changes. This approach facilitates a supportive and non-judgmental environment that encourages clients to openly discuss their feelings about substance use and change.

558. The stages of change model in treating addictive behaviors include all of the following EXCEPT:
a) Precontemplation
b) Action
c) Determination
d) Maintenance

Answer: c) Determination
Explanation: The stages of change model (also known as the Transtheoretical Model) describes the process by which individuals overcome addiction and includes the stages of Precontemplation, Contemplation, Preparation, Action, and Maintenance. "Determination" is not recognized as a stage within this model. The model helps professionals understand where a client is in their readiness to change and to apply appropriate interventions tailored to each stage.

559. In treating clients with substance use disorders, harm reduction strategies might include:
a) Insisting on abstinence as the only acceptable goal.
b) Providing clean syringes to reduce the risk of HIV transmission.
c) Punishing relapses to discourage future substance use.
d) Ignoring minor substance use to focus on more severe cases only.

Answer: b) Providing clean syringes to reduce the risk of HIV transmission.
Explanation: Harm reduction is a set of practical strategies aimed at reducing negative consequences associated with drug use. It acknowledges that while not all individuals are ready or able to stop substance use, steps can still be taken to minimize harm. Providing clean syringes to individuals who use injectable drugs is an example of a harm reduction strategy designed to reduce the spread of infectious diseases like HIV and hepatitis C, without necessarily requiring abstinence from substance use.

510. A client in the Maintenance stage of change for overcoming addiction is MOST likely to:
a) Deny the negative impact of their substance use.
b) Be actively engaging in treatment and recovery behaviors.
c) Be considering the possibility of making a change but not yet ready.
d) Have sustained change over time and be working to prevent relapse.

Answer: d) Have sustained change over time and be working to prevent relapse.
Explanation: The Maintenance stage of the stages of change model is characterized by individuals having made significant changes in their behavior regarding substance use and working to maintain these

changes and prevent relapse. This stage involves ongoing commitment to sustaining new behaviors and implementing strategies to avoid returning to substance use, reflecting a long-term approach to recovery.

511. When selecting a treatment approach for a client with a substance use disorder, it is ESSENTIAL to consider:
a) The most expensive option, as it is likely the most effective.
b) A one-size-fits-all method that has been generally effective in the past.
c) The client's specific needs, preferences, and situation.
d) The opinion of the client's family over the client's own wishes.

Answer: c) The client's specific needs, preferences, and situation.
Explanation: An effective treatment plan for a client with a substance use disorder must be individualized, taking into account the client's unique needs, preferences, situation, and readiness for change. Substance use disorder treatment is not one-size-fits-all; what works well for one individual may not be effective for another. Considering the client's specific circumstances allows for the development of a tailored treatment approach that is more likely to be successful and meaningful for the client.

512. The concept of "dual diagnosis" refers to individuals who:
a) Have been diagnosed with both substance use and eating disorders.
b) Present with two different substance use disorders simultaneously.
c) Experience both physical and psychological effects of substance use.
d) Have a co-occurring mental health disorder and substance use disorder.

Answer: d) Have a co-occurring mental health disorder and substance use disorder.
Explanation: Dual diagnosis refers to the co-occurrence of a mental health disorder and a substance use disorder within the same individual. This condition presents unique challenges for treatment, as both disorders may influence each other and require an integrated approach to address the complex needs of the client effectively. Recognizing and treating both disorders simultaneously is crucial for successful recovery outcomes.

513. Relapse prevention in substance use disorder treatment primarily focuses on:
a) Increasing the severity of consequences for relapse to deter future occurrences.
b) Identifying and managing high-risk situations and triggers that may lead to relapse.
c) Ensuring that clients remain in a controlled environment at all times.
d) Focusing solely on physical detoxification processes.

Answer: b) Identifying and managing high-risk situations and triggers that may lead to relapse.
Explanation: Relapse prevention is a critical component of treatment for substance use disorders, emphasizing the identification and management of situations, emotions, and triggers that could lead to a return to substance use. By developing strategies to cope with these high-risk scenarios, clients are better equipped to maintain their recovery and reduce the likelihood of relapse. This approach acknowledges relapse as a part of the recovery process and focuses on building resilience and coping mechanisms.

514. Screening for substance use disorders in a social work setting is important because:

a) It allows for the immediate imposition of legal penalties for drug use.
b) Substance use may be a contributing factor to other social and health issues clients are experiencing.
c) All clients in social work settings are likely to have substance use disorders.
d) It eliminates the need for further assessment or intervention.

Answer: b) Substance use may be a contributing factor to other social and health issues clients are experiencing.
Explanation: Screening for substance use disorders in social work settings is a critical first step in identifying clients who may need further assessment or intervention for substance use issues. Substance use can significantly impact various areas of an individual's life, including health, relationships, employment, and legal status. Early identification allows social workers to address these issues holitically, integrating substance use treatment with other forms of social and health support to improve overall outcomes for clients.

515. Understanding the psychosocial challenges faced by older adults, which theory best explains the process of maintaining or developing new friendships in later life to adapt to changes such as retirement or widowhood?
a) Disengagement Theory
b) Continuity Theory
c) Activity Theory
d) Socioemotional Selectivity Theory

Answer: d) Socioemotional Selectivity Theory.
Explanation: Socioemotional Selectivity Theory suggests that as people age, they become more selective in their social relationships, focusing on those that are most meaningful or bring emotional satisfaction. This selectivity helps older adults maintain or develop new friendships that are emotionally gratifying, serving as a coping mechanism for changes and losses such as retirement or the death of a spouse. This theory contrasts with Disengagement Theory, which posits that older adults naturally withdraw from social contacts as they age, and Activity Theory, which emphasizes staying active and engaged. Continuity Theory suggests that older adults try to maintain the same activities, behaviors, and relationships as they age, which doesn't directly address the development of new relationships in response to life changes.

516. In assessing the needs of older adults, why is it important to consider the concept of "functional age" rather than just chronological age?
a) Because functional age reflects the social roles and stereotypes associated with being elderly.
b) Because it is a more accurate measure of the biological effects of aging.
c) Because it assesses the individual's physical, emotional, and cognitive abilities, providing a more comprehensive view of their capacity and needs.
d) Because it determines the eligibility for age-related social services.

Answer: c) Because it assesses the individual's physical, emotional, and cognitive abilities, providing a more comprehensive view of their capacity and needs.
Explanation: Functional age provides a more nuanced understanding of an older adult's abilities and needs by considering their physical, emotional, and cognitive functions, rather than simply categorizing them by

chronological age. This approach recognizes the significant variability among individuals in aging processes and outcomes, allowing for tailored assessments and interventions that more accurately address the specific needs and capacities of each older adult.

517. Which intervention is MOST effective in addressing social isolation in the elderly?
a) Implementing strict daily routines to provide structure
b) Encouraging the use of technology for social networking and communication
c) Increasing surveillance and monitoring for safety
d) Limiting their participation in community activities to avoid overstimulation

Answer: b) Encouraging the use of technology for social networking and communication.
Explanation: Encouraging older adults to use technology for social networking and communication can significantly reduce social isolation by providing them with tools to connect with family, friends, and community services. This intervention promotes social engagement and participation, which is critical for mental and emotional well-being. Unlike increasing surveillance or limiting community activities, which can reinforce isolation, using technology empowers older adults to maintain and expand their social networks.

518. What is the primary goal of geriatric interdisciplinary teams in healthcare settings?
a) To reduce healthcare costs by limiting access to specialized services
b) To provide comprehensive care that addresses the complex needs of older adults through collaboration among healthcare professionals
c) To focus care exclusively on physical health, as it is the most significant concern in aging
d) To transition care responsibilities solely to family members

Answer: b) To provide comprehensive care that addresses the complex needs of older adults through collaboration among healthcare professionals.
Explanation: Geriatric interdisciplinary teams aim to provide comprehensive, integrated care for older adults by bringing together professionals from various healthcare disciplines. This collaborative approach ensures that the complex and multifaceted needs of older adults are fully addressed, including physical, emotional, cognitive, and social aspects of health, thereby enhancing the quality of care and improving outcomes.

519. In planning programs for older adults, why is it important to incorporate elements of life review or reminiscence therapy?
a) Because focusing on the past helps older adults disengage from current social relationships.
b) Because it satisfies older adults' preference for passive activities.
c) Because it can enhance psychological well-being by allowing older adults to reflect on and find meaning in their life experiences.
d) Because it primarily serves as a distraction from health issues.

Answer: c) Because it can enhance psychological well-being by allowing older adults to reflect on and find meaning in their life experiences.

Explanation: Life review and reminiscence therapy involve discussing past experiences and significant life events, which can help older adults process their experiences, resolve past conflicts, and find meaning and continuity in their lives. This can significantly enhance their psychological well-being and sense of identity, rather than serving merely as a distraction or promoting disengagement from social relationships.

520. When addressing elder abuse, what factor is MOST important for social workers to consider in their intervention plans?
a) The older adult's chronological age
b) The cultural and familial context of the older adult
c) The geographic location of the older adult
d) The older adult's educational background

Answer: b) The cultural and familial context of the older adult.
Explanation: Understanding the cultural and familial context of the older adult is crucial in addressing elder abuse. Cultural norms and family dynamics can significantly impact the perception, reporting, and resolution of abuse. Interventions must be culturally sensitive and considerate of family structures and values to be effective. This approach ensures respect for the older adult's background and promotes interventions that are both appropriate and sustainable within their specific context.

521. In the context of child welfare, a safety assessment primarily aims to:
a) Evaluate the educational achievements of the child.
b) Determine the financial stability of the family.
c) Identify immediate threats to a child's safety within their living environment.
d) Assess the psychological well-being of the parents or guardians.

Answer: c) Identify immediate threats to a child's safety within their living environment.
Explanation: A safety assessment in child welfare is a critical process used to identify any immediate threats to a child's safety within their current living environment. This assessment focuses on factors that may pose a risk to the child's physical well-being and security, allowing social workers and child protection agencies to take necessary actions to ensure the child's safety. This might include interventions to remove the child from harm's way or to implement safeguards within the home.

522. The primary goal of family preservation services in child welfare is to:
a) Prepare children for adoption.
b) Facilitate the long-term foster care placement of children.
c) Keep families together, whenever safely possible, through supportive services.
d) Ensure that children are removed from their homes.

Answer: c) Keep families together, whenever safely possible, through supportive services.
Explanation: Family preservation services are designed to support families facing challenges that might lead to child welfare intervention. The primary goal is to keep families together by providing the necessary supportive services that address the underlying issues, such as substance abuse, domestic violence, or mental health challenges, thereby preventing the need for removing children from their homes. These

services are provided with the belief that it is generally in the best interest of the child to remain with their family, provided their safety can be ensured.

523. When a child is identified as being at risk of harm, the immediate response by child welfare professionals should:
a) Wait for a formal complaint to be filed before taking any action.
b) Contact the child's family to warn them of potential legal consequences.
c) Ensure the child's safety through appropriate protective measures.
d) Immediately move the child into a long-term foster care placement.

Answer: c) Ensure the child's safety through appropriate protective measures.
Explanation: The paramount concern in child welfare is the safety and well-being of the child. When a child is identified as being at risk of harm, child welfare professionals are obligated to take immediate protective measures. These actions are based on an assessment of the situation and can range from developing a safety plan with the family to, if necessary, removing the child from the home to a safe environment. The initial response focuses on protection, with long-term solutions developed based on the child's needs and family circumstances.

524. A comprehensive assessment of a child in need involves evaluating:
a) Only the child's academic performance.
b) The child's physical, emotional, social, and educational needs.
c) The family's willingness to participate in community events.
d) The child's preference for living with relatives or in foster care.

Answer: b) The child's physical, emotional, social, and educational needs.
Explanation: A comprehensive assessment of a child in need extends beyond academic performance or living preferences. It encompasses a holistic evaluation of the child's physical health, emotional well-being, social interactions, and educational needs. This assessment helps in identifying all areas where the child may require support, intervention, or services, ensuring a tailored approach to their welfare and development.

525. Kinship care as a child welfare option is preferred because it:
a) Requires no background checks or home assessments.
b) Is less expensive than other forms of child welfare services.
c) Provides the child with the opportunity to maintain family connections and cultural identity.
d) Automatically grants legal guardianship to relatives.

Answer: c) Provides the child with the opportunity to maintain family connections and cultural identity.
Explanation: Kinship care, where children are placed with relatives or close family friends when they cannot remain with their parents, is preferred for several reasons, notably the opportunity it provides for children to maintain important family connections and cultural identity. This form of care supports the child's emotional and psychological well-being by preserving continuity in their relationships and environment. Kinship care does involve assessments and background checks to ensure the child's safety and well-being in the new living arrangement.

526. Child welfare interventions aimed at supporting at-risk families BEFORE a crisis occurs are known as:
a) Tertiary prevention.
b) Secondary prevention.
c) Primary prevention.
d) Crisis intervention.

Answer: c) Primary prevention.
Explanation: Primary prevention strategies in child welfare are proactive measures designed to support families and prevent issues from escalating to the point of crisis. These interventions may include community education programs, parental support groups, and access to resources such as childcare and healthcare, aimed at reducing the risk factors associated with child abuse and neglect. Unlike secondary prevention (which targets families already identified at risk) or tertiary prevention (which addresses families where harm has occurred), primary prevention seeks to avert the development of such situations altogether.

527. When considering the placement of a child in foster care, it is VITAL to:
a) Focus solely on the availability of foster care slots in the immediate area.
b) Ensure the placement is the least disruptive and most family-like setting that meets the child's needs.
c) Prioritize placements that are the most cost-effective for the child welfare system.
d) Place the child based on the convenience of the child welfare professionals involved.

Answer: b) Ensure the placement is the least disruptive and most family-like setting that meets the child's needs.
Explanation: The paramount consideration in the placement of a child in foster care is to ensure that the setting is as least disruptive as possible and closely resembles a family environment, addressing the child's specific needs. This approach promotes stability and continuity in the child's life, contributing to their emotional and psychological well-being. The focus is on the child's best interests, rather than cost, convenience, or availability factors.

528. In the case of suspected child abuse or neglect, mandatory reporting laws require that social workers:
a) Discuss their suspicions with the family before making a report.
b) Only report if they have direct evidence of abuse or neglect.
c) Report their suspicions to the appropriate authorities, regardless of evidence.
d) Wait for a colleague's opinion before making a report.

Answer: c) Report their suspicions to the appropriate authorities, regardless of evidence.
Explanation: Mandatory reporting laws compel social workers and other professionals to report any suspicions of child abuse or neglect to the appropriate authorities, such as child protection services. The obligation to report is based on suspicion or reasonable concern, not necessarily the presence of direct evidence. This legal requirement is designed to ensure that potential cases of abuse or neglect are investigated by professionals who can assess the risk and take necessary protective actions.

529. The concept of "best interest of the child" in child welfare decisions primarily emphasizes:
a) The preferences of the child welfare agency.

b) Adhering strictly to the most cost-effective solutions.
c) The child's well-being, safety, and stability above all other considerations.
d) The legal rights of the parents or guardians over the child's needs.

Answer: c) The child's well-being, safety, and stability above all other considerations.
Explanation: The "best interest of the child" standard is a guiding principle in child welfare that prioritizes the child's well-being, safety, and stability in all decisions affecting them. This includes considerations related to custody, placement, and interventions. The standard seeks to ensure that decisions are made based on what will most benefit the child, taking into account their physical, emotional, and educational needs, rather than the preferences or conveniences of adults or agencies involved.

530. The principle of Universal Health Coverage (UHC) aims to ensure:
a) Health care services are available only to employed individuals and their families.
b) Only emergency health services are provided free of charge to all citizens.
c) Every individual has access to quality health services without suffering financial hardship.
d) Health insurance is optional for those under a certain income level.

Answer: c) Every individual has access to quality health services without suffering financial hardship.
Explanation: Universal Health Coverage (UHC) is a health care system concept where every individual has access to the necessary health services, including prevention, treatment, rehabilitation, and palliative care, without experiencing financial hardship. It aims to ensure equitable access to health care services for all, regardless of their socio-economic status, thereby improving health outcomes and protecting citizens from the financial risks associated with health care costs.

531. In a health care system characterized by a single-payer model, the funding for health care services is:
a) Collected from multiple private insurance companies that compete in an open market.
b) Directly paid by patients out-of-pocket at the point of service.
c) Provided by a single public source, typically the government.
d) Generated through donations and charitable contributions.

Answer: c) Provided by a single public source, typically the government.
Explanation: In a single-payer health care system, funding for health care services comes from a single public source, often the government. This system simplifies health care financing by having the government collect taxes and use those funds to provide health care services to all citizens. It aims to ensure that access to health care does not depend on an individual's ability to pay, thereby promoting equity and efficiency in the delivery of health care services.

532. The Affordable Care Act (ACA) in the United States was designed to:
a) Reduce the role of private insurance companies in the health care system.
b) Expand access to health insurance, increase consumer protections, and emphasize preventive care.
c) Eliminate public health care programs such as Medicaid and Medicare.
d) Make health insurance mandatory only for those above the poverty line.

Answer: b) Expand access to health insurance, increase consumer protections, and emphasize preventive care.
Explanation: The Affordable Care Act (ACA), also known as Obamacare, was enacted with the primary goals of expanding access to health insurance, increasing consumer protections (such as preventing denial of coverage due to pre-existing conditions), and emphasizing preventive care to improve health outcomes. The ACA aimed to reduce the number of uninsured Americans through various mechanisms, including individual mandates, subsidies for private insurance, and the expansion of Medicaid.

533. A major barrier to accessing health care services in rural areas is:
a) The overabundance of health care facilities leading to competition.
b) The presence of too many insurance options confusing the residents.
c) A lack of health care providers and facilities.
d) Strict regulations preventing the construction of new hospitals.

Answer: c) A lack of health care providers and facilities.
Explanation: Rural areas often face significant barriers to accessing health care services, primarily due to a lack of health care providers and facilities. This shortage can lead to long travel distances for care, longer wait times for appointments, and a lack of specialized services, significantly impacting the health outcomes of rural populations. Efforts to address these disparities focus on incentives for health care providers to practice in rural areas, telehealth, and other strategies to improve access.

534. In discussing health care disparities, the term "social determinants of health" refers to:
a) The genetic factors that predispose individuals to certain health conditions.
b) The availability of health care services within a 5-mile radius of one's residence.
c) Conditions in the environments where people are born, live, learn, work, play, and age that affect health and quality of life.
d) The level of health care insurance coverage individuals can afford.

Answer: c) Conditions in the environments where people are born, live, learn, work, play, and age that affect health and quality of life.
Explanation: Social determinants of health encompass a wide range of factors that influence individuals' health and well-being. These include socioeconomic status, education, neighborhood and physical environment, employment, and social support networks, as well as access to health care. By addressing these social determinants, public health initiatives aim to reduce health disparities and promote equity within health care systems.

535. Understanding the concept of "trauma-informed care" is critical in social work practice because it emphasizes:
a) The use of psychiatric medications as the primary treatment for trauma symptoms.
b) A focus on the biological underpinnings of trauma without addressing social or environmental factors.
c) The necessity of re-traumatizing clients to help them process their trauma fully.
d) Recognizing the widespread impact of trauma and integrating knowledge about trauma into policies, procedures, and practices.

Answer: d) Recognizing the widespread impact of trauma and integrating knowledge about trauma into policies, procedures, and practices.
Explanation: Trauma-informed care is a framework that involves understanding, recognizing, and responding to the effects of all types of trauma. It emphasizes physical, psychological, and emotional safety for both providers and survivors and helps rebuild a sense of control and empowerment for the clients. This approach integrates awareness of the prevalence and impact of trauma in all aspects of service delivery and aims to avoid re-traumatization while promoting healing and resilience.

536. The concept of "secondary traumatic stress" (STS) is important for social workers because it highlights:
a) The increased risk of physical illnesses among individuals who have experienced direct trauma.
b) The stress experienced by service providers when they are exposed to the trauma stories of the people they help.
c) The importance of implementing punitive measures to manage clients who exhibit trauma-related behaviors.
d) The necessity for social workers to focus exclusively on the financial aspects of clients' lives.

Answer: b) The stress experienced by service providers when they are exposed to the trauma stories of the people they help.
Explanation: Secondary traumatic stress (STS) refers to the emotional duress that results when an individual hears about the firsthand trauma experiences of another. For social workers and other helping professionals, STS highlights the impact of empathetic engagement with clients who have experienced trauma. This stress can mimic symptoms of PTSD and underscores the need for self-care strategies, workplace support, and possibly professional help to manage the effects of vicarious trauma.

537. In assessing the impact of trauma on an individual, it's essential to consider:
a) Only the most recent traumatic event the individual has experienced.
b) Trauma as an isolated event that does not influence or interact with other life experiences.
c) Trauma impacts in a vacuum, disregarding the individual's support systems and coping mechanisms.
d) The cumulative nature of trauma, including historical, interpersonal, and recent events, and its interaction with the individual's environment, support systems, and coping mechanisms.

Answer: d) The cumulative nature of trauma, including historical, interpersonal, and recent events, and its interaction with the individual's environment, support systems, and coping mechanisms.
Explanation: The impact of trauma on an individual is complex and multifaceted, requiring an understanding of the cumulative nature of trauma. This includes recognizing how past and present traumas, including historical and interpersonal events, interact with each other and with the individual's current environment, support systems, and coping strategies. A comprehensive assessment of trauma impacts considers the broader context of the individual's life, acknowledging that trauma does not occur in isolation and its effects are influenced by various factors.

538. Which strategy is MOST effective in building resilience in individuals who have experienced trauma?
a) Encouraging avoidance of any reminders of the trauma.
b) Promoting connections with supportive and empathetic relationships.
c) Focusing exclusively on negative outcomes and challenges.

d) Isolating the individual from community and social support to strengthen independence.

Answer: b) Promoting connections with supportive and empathetic relationships.
Explanation: Building resilience in individuals who have experienced trauma involves fostering connections with supportive and empathetic relationships. These connections can provide emotional support, understanding, and a sense of belonging, which are crucial for healing and resilience. Encouraging positive relationships helps individuals feel less isolated, enhances their ability to cope with trauma, and promotes recovery by providing a supportive network.

539. Post-Traumatic Stress Disorder (PTSD) can manifest in various ways. Which of the following is NOT typically a symptom of PTSD?
a) Increased desire for socialization to distract from traumatic memories.
b) Re-experiencing the traumatic event through flashbacks or nightmares.
c) Avoidance of reminders of the trauma.
d) Hypervigilance and increased startle response.

Answer: a) Increased desire for socialization to distract from traumatic memories.
Explanation: Increased desire for socialization is not typically a symptom of PTSD. Common symptoms of PTSD include re-experiencing the traumatic event through flashbacks or nightmares, avoidance of reminders of the trauma, negative changes in thoughts and mood associated with the traumatic event, and heightened reactions such as hypervigilance or an increased startle response. Individuals with PTSD may actually avoid social situations and become more isolated as a way to cope with their trauma.

540. Which of the following best describes a Health Maintenance Organization (HMO)?
a) A healthcare system where patients pay directly for each service to increase transparency.
b) An insurance model that provides health services for a fixed annual fee with an emphasis on preventive care, requiring members to use a specific network of providers.
c) A type of health insurance plan that charges patients a fee for each service provided.
d) A government-operated system that provides healthcare to all citizens regardless of their ability to pay.

Answer: b) An insurance model that provides health services for a fixed annual fee with an emphasis on preventive care, requiring members to use a specific network of providers.
Explanation: Health Maintenance Organizations (HMOs) are a type of health insurance plan that offers health services for a fixed annual fee. They focus on preventive care and require members to use healthcare providers and facilities within the HMO's network. HMOs often require members to choose a primary care physician who coordinates their care and provides referrals to specialists within the network.

541. What is the primary goal of integrated healthcare delivery systems?
a) To separate mental health care from physical health care to specialize treatment options.
b) To maximize profits by increasing the efficiency of billing systems.
c) To provide comprehensive care by coordinating all aspects of a patient's health care needs.
d) To limit patient access to specialists to control healthcare costs.

Answer: c) To provide comprehensive care by coordinating all aspects of a patient's health care needs.

Explanation: Integrated healthcare delivery systems aim to provide comprehensive care by coordinating all aspects of a patient's health care needs. This approach seeks to improve patient outcomes and satisfaction by ensuring that care is seamless across different types of services, including primary care, specialty care, and mental health services. Integration emphasizes the whole person, rather than treating different health issues in isolation.

542. In the context of healthcare, what does the term "medical home" refer to?
a) A residential care facility for individuals with chronic medical conditions.
b) A healthcare setting that provides patients with access to acute, emergency, and surgical care.
c) A model of primary care that is patient-centered, comprehensive, team-based, coordinated, accessible, and focused on quality and safety.
d) A government program that offers free medical care at home for underprivileged populations.

Answer: c) A model of primary care that is patient-centered, comprehensive, team-based, coordinated, accessible, and focused on quality and safety.
Explanation: The term "medical home," also known as a patient-centered medical home (PCMH), refers to a model of primary care that is designed to be patient-centered, comprehensive, coordinated, and focused on quality and safety. It involves a team-based approach to healthcare, where the primary care provider leads a team of professionals that collectively take responsibility for the ongoing care of patients, ensuring that healthcare needs are met in a holistic and coordinated manner.

543. Which factor is a common barrier to accessing healthcare services?
a) Increased use of technology in healthcare settings.
b) Comprehensive insurance coverage for all citizens.
c) Geographic location and availability of healthcare providers.
d) Lower healthcare costs.

Answer: c) Geographic location and availability of healthcare providers.
Explanation: Geographic location and the availability of healthcare providers are common barriers to accessing healthcare services. Individuals living in rural or underserved areas may have difficulty accessing healthcare due to a lack of nearby facilities or specialists. This can lead to delays in receiving care, increased travel costs, and overall poorer health outcomes.

544. What role do social workers play in healthcare settings?
a) Only to administer medical treatments under the supervision of physicians.
b) To provide counseling services exclusively for patients with mental health issues.
c) To assist patients and their families in navigating the healthcare system, including accessing services and understanding treatment options.
d) To conduct medical research and develop new treatment protocols.

Answer: c) To assist patients and their families in navigating the healthcare system, including accessing services and understanding treatment options.
Explanation: Social workers in healthcare settings play a crucial role in assisting patients and their families with navigating the complexities of the healthcare system. They provide support in accessing services,

understanding treatment options, dealing with social and financial issues related to health conditions, and coordinating care among various healthcare providers. Social workers address the holistic needs of patients, including their psychological, social, and economic well-being.

545. How does telehealth impact access to healthcare services?
a) It decreases access by requiring patients to have advanced technical skills.
b) It has no significant impact on healthcare access.
c) It increases access by allowing patients to receive care remotely, especially in underserved areas.
d) It limits access to only the most technologically advanced healthcare facilities.

Answer: c) It increases access by allowing patients to receive care remotely, especially in underserved areas.
Explanation: Telehealth has significantly impacted access to healthcare services by enabling patients to receive care remotely through digital communication tools. This is particularly beneficial for individuals in rural or underserved areas, where access to healthcare providers may be limited. Telehealth can facilitate consultations, follow-up appointments, and even some types of therapy and monitoring without the need for patients to travel, thereby expanding access to necessary healthcare services.

546. Medicaid is a program that:
a) Offers health insurance to all citizens regardless of income.
b) Provides health coverage primarily to low-income individuals and families.
c) Is only available to employees of the federal government.
d) Covers the cost of private health insurance plans for middle-income families.

Answer: b) Provides health coverage primarily to low-income individuals and families.
Explanation: Medicaid is a public insurance program in the United States that provides health coverage to low-income individuals and families. It is jointly funded by the state and federal governments and administered by the states. Medicaid covers a wide range of health services, including hospital care, doctor visits, long-term care, and preventive care, for eligible participants, including children, pregnant women, elderly adults, and individuals with disabilities.

547. Patient advocacy in healthcare involves:
a) Encouraging patients to accept all medical advice without question.
b) Actively supporting and promoting the interests and rights of patients within the healthcare system.
c) Limiting patients' access to information about their conditions to reduce anxiety.
d) Representing the healthcare providers' interests to the patients.

Answer: b) Actively supporting and promoting the interests and rights of patients within the healthcare system.
Explanation: Patient advocacy refers to activities and efforts aimed at supporting and promoting the interests and rights of patients within the healthcare system. This can involve helping patients navigate the healthcare system, ensuring they have access to necessary services, assisting them in making informed decisions about their care, and protecting their rights to privacy and dignified treatment. Advocates work to ensure that the patient's voice is heard and considered in their care.

548. In the context of health care systems, the term "universal health coverage" is best defined as:
a) A system where health care services are provided exclusively by private sector entities.
b) A health care system that covers only the employed population and their dependents.
c) A system where only emergency health services are guaranteed for all citizens.
d) A system that ensures all individuals and communities have access to quality health services without suffering financial hardship.

Answer: d) A system that ensures all individuals and communities have access to quality health services without suffering financial hardship.
Explanation: Universal health coverage aims to provide all individuals and communities with access to the health services they need, including prevention, treatment, rehabilitation, and palliative care, without experiencing financial hardship. This encompasses a wide range of services and is not limited by the financial, geographical, or social status of individuals, ensuring equity in access to health care services.

549. The Affordable Care Act (ACA) was designed to increase health care access primarily through:
a) Introducing a single-payer health care system in the United States.
b) Expanding Medicaid eligibility and establishing health insurance marketplaces.
c) Requiring all citizens to seek health care only through private insurance companies.
d) Eliminating all forms of health insurance, relying on out-of-pocket payments.

Answer: b) Expanding Medicaid eligibility and establishing health insurance marketplaces.
Explanation: The Affordable Care Act (ACA), enacted in 2010, aimed to increase access to health care in the United States primarily by expanding Medicaid eligibility to more low-income individuals and families and creating health insurance marketplaces (exchanges) where individuals could purchase affordable and subsidized health insurance plans. These measures were designed to reduce the number of uninsured Americans and improve access to health care services.

550. A social worker is assisting a client who is unable to afford their medication. This scenario underscores the importance of:
a) Pharmaceutical companies' role in setting drug prices.
b) The need for medication adherence programs.
c) Addressing the social determinants of health that impact access to care.
d) Implementing stricter regulations on health care providers.

Answer: c) Addressing the social determinants of health that impact access to care.
Explanation: This scenario highlights the broader issue of the social determinants of health, which include factors like income, housing, education, and access to services that significantly impact an individual's ability to obtain necessary health care and medications. Addressing these determinants is crucial for ensuring equitable access to health care and improving health outcomes for all segments of the population.

551. In comparing health care systems, a single-payer system is characterized by:
a) Multiple insurance providers competing in an open marketplace.
b) Health care funding and administration by one entity, usually the government.

c) Private health care providers operating without governmental regulation.
d) Direct payment for services by patients without the involvement of insurance.

Answer: b) Health care funding and administration by one entity, usually the government.
Explanation: A single-payer system refers to a health care system in which a single public or quasi-public agency organizes health care financing, but the delivery of care remains largely in private hands. In such systems, the government typically collects taxes and uses those funds to provide health insurance for all citizens, ensuring universal coverage. This system contrasts with models where multiple insurance companies provide health coverage, and health care providers operate independently of government administration.

552. The concept of "health disparities" is best understood as:
a) The differences in health insurance premiums across different regions.
b) Variations in health services provided by urban versus rural hospitals.
c) Preventable differences in the burden of disease, injury, violence, or opportunities to achieve optimal health experienced by socially disadvantaged populations.
d) The distinction between primary care and specialty care services.

Answer: c) Preventable differences in the burden of disease, injury, violence, or opportunities to achieve optimal health experienced by socially disadvantaged populations.
Explanation: Health disparities refer to the preventable differences in health status that are seen among various population groups based on social, economic, and environmental disadvantages. These disparities are rooted in inequities in access to healthcare services, exposure to unhealthy environments, and other social determinants of health. Addressing health disparities involves targeted efforts to improve the conditions and access to care for underserved and marginalized populations.

553. When advocating for improved health care access, social workers may employ strategies such as:
a) Encouraging clients to avoid seeking medical care to reduce system burden.
b) Lobbying for policies that increase healthcare costs to improve quality.
c) Promoting legislation that expands insurance coverage and access to preventative services.
d) Supporting laws that restrict access to healthcare based on employment status.

Answer: c) Promoting legislation that expands insurance coverage and access to preventative services.
Explanation: Social workers advocate for policies and legislation that improve access to health care for all individuals, particularly the underserved and marginalized populations. This includes supporting measures that expand health insurance coverage, increase affordability and accessibility of care, and promote preventive health services. Through advocacy, social workers play a critical role in addressing barriers to health care access and improving public health outcomes.

554. An effective health care system is one that balances:
a) The interests of insurance companies over patient care needs.
b) Cost containment with the provision of comprehensive, quality care to all.
c) The exclusive use of technology-driven treatments over traditional care methods.
d) The prioritization of acute care services over preventive and primary care.

Answer: b) Cost containment with the provision of comprehensive, quality care to all.
Explanation: An effective health care system strives to balance the need for cost containment with ensuring that all individuals have access to comprehensive, high-quality care. This includes a focus on preventive and primary care services, equitable access to care regardless of financial status, and the integration of technology to enhance, not replace, the quality and reach of health care services. Achieving this balance is essential for promoting the health and well-being of the entire population.

555. Integrated health care models are designed to:
a) Separate mental health care from physical health care to specialize treatment.
b) Increase the administrative burden on health care providers.
c) Coordinate primary care, mental health, and social services for holistic patient care.
d) Focus solely on the physical aspects of health while ignoring mental and social factors.

Answer: c) Coordinate primary care, mental health, and social services for holistic patient care.
Explanation: Integrated health care models aim to provide a coordinated approach to patient care that includes primary care, mental health services, and social support services. By integrating these various aspects of care, the model seeks to address the whole person, recognizing the interconnection between physical health, mental health, and social determinants of health. This holistic approach improves health outcomes, enhances patient satisfaction, and can reduce health care costs by preventing the escalation of untreated conditions.

556. Barriers to health care access in underserved populations might include all of the following EXCEPT:
a) Comprehensive health insurance coverage.
b) Transportation difficulties.
c) Language and communication barriers.
d) Lack of awareness of available services.

Answer: a) Comprehensive health insurance coverage.
Explanation: Comprehensive health insurance coverage is not a barrier but rather a facilitator of access to health care services. Barriers to health care access, especially in underserved populations, often include issues such as transportation difficulties, language and communication barriers, and a lack of awareness or understanding of the available health care services and how to navigate the health care system. Addressing these barriers is crucial for improving health care access and equity.

557. A social worker receives a friend request on their personal social media account from a current client. The MOST appropriate response would be to:
a) Accept the friend request to build a stronger therapeutic relationship.
b) Ignore the friend request and discuss the social media policy in the next session.
c) Accept the request but limit the client's access to personal posts.
d) Recommend the client follow the professional social media account instead, if available.

Answer: b) Ignore the friend request and discuss the social media policy in the next session.
Explanation: Maintaining professional boundaries is crucial in social work practice. Accepting a friend request from a current client on personal social media can blur these boundaries, potentially affecting the

therapeutic relationship. The best course of action is to ignore the request and use the situation as an opportunity to discuss the agency's social media policy with the client, emphasizing the importance of keeping personal and professional relationships separate to maintain the integrity and effectiveness of the therapeutic process.

558. A social worker in a school setting is asked by a teacher to share information about a student's counseling sessions. The social worker should:
a) Share all information with the teacher to support the student's educational needs.
b) Refuse to share any information, citing confidentiality concerns.
c) Share relevant information only after obtaining written consent from the student's parents or guardians.
d) Discuss the request with the student before deciding what information, if any, can be shared.

Answer: c) Share relevant information only after obtaining written consent from the student's parents or guardians.
Explanation: While collaboration among school professionals can be in the student's best interest, the social worker must adhere to principles of confidentiality and only share information about counseling sessions with other school staff when it is relevant to the student's educational needs and with the proper consent. Obtaining written consent from the student's parents or guardians before sharing any information ensures that confidentiality is maintained while also allowing for necessary collaboration.

559. In a community mental health setting, a social worker is approached by a former client in a public place. The client starts discussing personal issues related to past therapy sessions. The social worker should:
a) Engage in the conversation to show support for the former client.
b) Politely explain that it is not appropriate to discuss therapy issues in public and offer to schedule a time to talk in a more private setting.
c) Immediately walk away to avoid any breach of confidentiality.
d) Encourage the former client to seek help from another therapist.

Answer: b) Politely explain that it is not appropriate to discuss therapy issues in public and offer to schedule a time to talk in a more private setting.
Explanation: The social worker should handle the situation with tact and professionalism, acknowledging the former client's needs while also maintaining professional boundaries and confidentiality. Politely explaining that it is not appropriate to discuss therapy issues in a public place and offering to schedule a time to talk in a private, professional setting respects the client's dignity and the professional's ethical obligations.

560. A social worker who provides counseling services at a substance abuse treatment center is asked by a client for a personal loan to help with rent. The social worker should:
a) Provide the loan as a gesture of goodwill to support the client's recovery.
b) Decline the request and explore other resources or services that can assist the client with their financial needs.
c) Offer a smaller amount than requested to avoid creating dependency.
d) Lend the money if the client signs a contract agreeing to repay the loan.

Answer: b) Decline the request and explore other resources or services that can assist the client with their financial needs.
Explanation: Providing a personal loan to a client is a clear violation of professional boundaries and can create a conflict of interest and dependency. The social worker should instead maintain professional boundaries and explore other resources or services, such as community programs, social assistance, or housing support services, that can help the client address their financial needs in a more appropriate and sustainable manner.

561. When a client gifts a social worker with an expensive item as a thank-you for the services provided, the social worker should:
a) Accept the gift to avoid offending the client.
b) Politely decline the gift and explain the agency's policy regarding gifts.
c) Accept the gift but report it to their supervisor to avoid any ethical issues.
d) Suggest that the client donate the item to charity instead.

Answer: b) Politely decline the gift and explain the agency's policy regarding gifts.
Explanation: Accepting expensive gifts from clients can create ethical dilemmas, potential conflicts of interest, and boundary issues. It is important for the social worker to politely decline the gift and explain the agency's policy on gifts, which typically discourages accepting gifts that could affect the professional relationship. This approach maintains the integrity of the therapeutic relationship and adheres to ethical standards.

562. A social worker serving on a committee that awards community grants discovers a close friend has applied for funding. To handle this situation ethically, the social worker should:
a) Vote in favor of awarding the grant to the friend to strengthen their personal relationship.
b) Abstain from the discussion and voting on the friend's application due to a conflict of interest.
c) Advocate strongly for the friend's application, citing their personal knowledge of the friend's integrity.
d) Review the friend's application more critically than others to avoid appearing biased.

Answer: b) Abstain from the discussion and voting on the friend's application due to a conflict of interest.
Explanation: The social worker should recognize the conflict of interest and abstain from any discussion, deliberation, or voting regarding the friend's application for funding. This action ensures that the grant awarding process remains fair, unbiased, and ethical. Disclosing the conflict of interest to the committee also highlights the social worker's commitment to maintaining professional integrity and ethical standards.

563. During a home visit, a client asks the social worker to stay for dinner as a thank you for their help. The MOST appropriate response is to:
a) Accept the invitation to build rapport with the client.
b) Politely decline the invitation, explaining the importance of maintaining professional boundaries.
c) Accept the invitation but insist on bringing the meal to share.
d) Decline and report the client's behavior as overly familiar to a supervisor.

Answer: b) Politely decline the invitation, explaining the importance of maintaining professional boundaries.

Explanation: While the client's invitation is likely well-intentioned, accepting such invitations can blur professional boundaries and potentially impact the objectivity and effectiveness of the therapeutic relationship. The social worker should politely decline the invitation, taking the opportunity to reinforce the nature of the professional relationship and the importance of maintaining clear boundaries.

564. A social worker in private practice receives a request to conduct therapy sessions with a colleague's child. The social worker should:
a) Agree to the request as a favor to the colleague.
b) Politely decline due to the potential for a dual relationship that could affect objectivity.
c) Accept but ensure sessions are strictly confidential and separate from the professional relationship with the colleague.
d) Agree, provided the colleague agrees not to discuss the child's treatment in the workplace.

Answer: b) Politely decline due to the potential for a dual relationship that could affect objectivity.
Explanation: Providing therapy to a colleague's child can create a dual relationship that may compromise the social worker's objectivity and professional judgment. It is best practice to avoid entering into therapeutic relationships where existing personal or professional relationships might impact the effectiveness of treatment. The social worker should politely decline and, if appropriate, offer referrals to other qualified professionals.

565. In supervisory relationships, it is critical for the supervisor to:
a) Encourage dependency from supervisees to strengthen loyalty and commitment.
b) Use the relationship to delegate personal responsibilities to supervisees.
c) Maintain clear professional boundaries while providing guidance and support.
d) Focus solely on administrative tasks, avoiding involvement in professional development.

Answer: c) Maintain clear professional boundaries while providing guidance and support.
Explanation: Supervisory relationships in social work should be characterized by clear professional boundaries, with the supervisor providing the necessary guidance, support, and feedback to foster the supervisee's professional growth and development. The relationship should be structured to promote learning, ethical practice, and the development of professional skills, rather than creating dependency or blurring the lines between professional responsibilities and personal interests.

566. Cognitive Behavioral Therapy (CBT) is particularly effective in treating depression because it:
a) Encourages patients to express their feelings in creative ways without addressing underlying thoughts.
b) Focuses solely on medication management without exploring thought patterns.
c) Helps patients identify and challenge negative thought patterns and behaviors contributing to depression.
d) Avoids discussing patients' past experiences, focusing only on future aspirations.

Answer: c) Helps patients identify and challenge negative thought patterns and behaviors contributing to depression.
Explanation: Cognitive Behavioral Therapy (CBT) is an evidence-based psychological treatment shown to be effective in treating depression, among other conditions. It operates on the premise that negative

thought patterns and maladaptive behaviors play a fundamental role in the development and maintenance of depression. CBT helps patients to identify, challenge, and modify these cognitive distortions and behaviors, thereby alleviating symptoms of depression. This approach is active, directive, and time-limited, focusing on current problems and practical strategies for change.

567. In a family therapy session, the therapist notices a pattern of enmeshment between a parent and child. An appropriate intervention would be to:
a) Encourage the family to spend more time together to strengthen their bond.
b) Ignore the dynamics and focus solely on individual therapy goals.
c) Facilitate boundary-setting exercises to help define individual roles and spaces.
d) Promote complete independence among family members to break the pattern.

Answer: c) Facilitate boundary-setting exercises to help define individual roles and spaces.
Explanation: Enmeshment refers to overly close and blurred boundaries between family members, leading to a lack of independence and individuality. In a therapeutic context, addressing enmeshment involves helping family members establish healthier, clearer boundaries. This can be achieved through exercises and discussions facilitated by the therapist that encourage each family member to identify and express their own needs, feelings, and identities separately from the family unit. This intervention aims to promote balance between connectedness and autonomy within the family.

568. For a community facing a significant increase in substance use disorders, an effective community intervention might include:
a) Isolating individuals with substance use disorders from the rest of the community.
b) Implementing broad punitive measures for drug use without offering support services.
c) Developing a community-wide education and prevention program, along with accessible treatment options.
d) Focusing solely on law enforcement without addressing underlying causes of substance use.

Answer: c) Developing a community-wide education and prevention program, along with accessible treatment options.
Explanation: Addressing substance use disorders in a community effectively requires a multifaceted approach that includes education, prevention, and treatment. Developing a community-wide education and prevention program can raise awareness about the risks of substance use, promote healthy behaviors, and reduce stigma. Additionally, ensuring that treatment options are readily accessible to those in need provides support for recovery and rehabilitation. This comprehensive strategy addresses both the prevention and treatment dimensions of substance use disorders within the community.

569. When working with a group of adolescents displaying risky behaviors, a social worker might employ which of the following interventions?
a) A psychoeducational group focusing on skills development, such as decision-making and problem-solving.
b) An approach that strictly enforces disciplinary actions without any educational component.
c) A policy of non-intervention, allowing adolescents to learn from their own mistakes without guidance.
d) Focusing only on individual counseling, ignoring the potential benefits of group dynamics.

Answer: a) A psychoeducational group focusing on skills development, such as decision-making and problem-solving.
Explanation: For adolescents displaying risky behaviors, participating in a psychoeducational group can be particularly beneficial. Such groups can provide a safe and structured environment for learning and practicing essential life skills, like decision-making and problem-solving. Through interactive activities and discussions, participants can gain insights into their behaviors, understand the consequences, and develop healthier coping mechanisms. This approach leverages the influence of peer dynamics to reinforce learning and promote positive change.

570. Motivational interviewing is a technique that is particularly useful for clients who are:
a) Completely ready to make a change and just need instructions on how to proceed.
b) Ambivalent or resistant to change, by helping them explore their own reasons for change.
c) Seeking advice on issues unrelated to change or decision-making.
d) Needing detailed information about their condition, rather than exploring feelings about change.

Answer: b) Ambivalent or resistant to change, by helping them explore their own reasons for change.
Explanation: Motivational interviewing is a client-centered counseling style for eliciting behavior change by helping clients to explore and resolve ambivalence. It is particularly effective with clients who are ambivalent or resistant to change, as it respects their autonomy and promotes self-efficacy. Through this approach, clients are encouraged to articulate their reasons for change, weigh the pros and cons, and consider how change aligns with their values and goals, thereby fostering a greater internal motivation to change.

571. When a social worker is planning an intervention for an organization experiencing high levels of staff burnout, a key strategy might include:
a) Increasing the workload to improve efficiency and distract staff from burnout.
b) Ignoring the issue, assuming it will resolve itself over time.
c) Implementing stress management and self-care workshops, along with organizational changes to address work-life balance.
d) Advising staff to seek individual therapy outside of work without addressing organizational issues.

Answer: c) Implementing stress management and self-care workshops, along with organizational changes to address work-life balance.
Explanation: Addressing high levels of staff burnout in an organization requires a proactive and comprehensive approach. Implementing stress management and self-care workshops can provide staff with the tools and strategies to manage stress more effectively. Additionally, making organizational changes that promote a healthier work-life balance, such as adjusting workloads, improving communication, and offering flexible working arrangements, can help tackle the root causes of burnout. This dual approach addresses both the individual and systemic factors contributing to burnout.

572. In the treatment of individuals with trauma histories, Trauma-Focused Cognitive Behavioral Therapy (TF-CBT) is effective because it:
a) Focuses exclusively on the physical symptoms associated with trauma.
b) Requires clients to relive their traumatic experiences repeatedly without coping mechanisms.
c) Combines cognitive and behavioral techniques to address the specific needs of trauma survivors.

d) Avoids discussing the trauma altogether to prevent re-traumatization.

Answer: c) Combines cognitive and behavioral techniques to address the specific needs of trauma survivors.
Explanation: Trauma-Focused Cognitive Behavioral Therapy (TF-CBT) is an evidence-based treatment specifically designed for individuals, especially children and adolescents, who are experiencing significant emotional and psychological difficulties as a result of exposure to traumatic events. TF-CBT combines cognitive and behavioral interventions to help clients process and cope with their traumatic experiences. Techniques include teaching coping skills, gradually exposing clients to thoughts and feelings associated with the trauma in a safe way, and helping to reframe unhelpful beliefs related to the trauma. This approach aims to alleviate symptoms of post-traumatic stress disorder (PTSD), depression, anxiety, and other trauma-related issues.

573. For a community struggling with the aftermath of a natural disaster, a social worker might coordinate which of the following interventions?
a) Encourage the community to forget the event and move on as quickly as possible.
b) Isolate affected individuals to prevent the spread of trauma.
c) Develop a community resilience-building program, including support groups and resource mobilization.
d) Focus solely on physical rebuilding efforts, ignoring the psychological impact.

Answer: c) Develop a community resilience-building program, including support groups and resource mobilization.
Explanation: In the aftermath of a natural disaster, addressing both the psychological impact and the physical rebuilding efforts is crucial. Developing a community resilience-building program can provide essential support, helping community members to cope with their experiences, foster a sense of solidarity and collective recovery, and mobilize resources for rebuilding. Support groups offer spaces for individuals to share their experiences and feelings, while resource mobilization helps to address practical needs and challenges faced by the community, thereby promoting healing and resilience on both individual and community levels.

574. Transformational leadership is best described as a style where the leader:
a) Focuses primarily on completing tasks and adhering to strict rules.
b) Motivates followers by setting a vision and inspiring them to achieve beyond expectations.
c) Makes decisions based solely on organizational policies, without considering employees' input.
d) Uses rewards and punishments as the primary means to achieve compliance from followers.

Answer: b) Motivates followers by setting a vision and inspiring them to achieve beyond expectations.
Explanation: Transformational leadership is characterized by leaders who inspire and motivate their followers to exceed their own self-interests for the good of the organization or team. They do this by setting a vision that is inspiring, challenging the status quo, and encouraging creativity and innovation among followers. Transformational leaders focus on developing their followers' potential and fostering a high level of commitment towards the organizational goals.

575. Situational leadership theory suggests that:

a) The most effective leadership style is consistent and unchanging, regardless of the situation.
b) Leaders should adapt their style based on the maturity level of their followers and the demands of the situation.
c) Leadership effectiveness is determined solely by the traits a leader possesses.
d) A hands-off approach is always the best way to lead, as it empowers team members.

Answer: b) Leaders should adapt their style based on the maturity level of their followers and the demands of the situation.
Explanation: Situational leadership theory posits that there is no single "best" style of leadership. Instead, effective leadership is achieved by adapting one's style to the maturity level of the followers (their readiness and competency in relation to a specific task) and the specific requirements of the situation. This approach suggests that leaders need to be flexible and versatile in their leadership styles to be effective in different contexts.

576. Authentic leadership is primarily concerned with:
a) The leader's ability to act in a genuine and transparent manner, based on their true self.
b) Following established leadership formulas without deviation.
c) Emphasizing traditional roles and hierarchies within the team or organization.
d) The leader's capacity to maintain distance from followers to ensure authority.

Answer: a) The leader's ability to act in a genuine and transparent manner, based on their true self.
Explanation: Authentic leadership focuses on the authenticity of leaders and their leadership, emphasizing honesty, integrity, and transparency. Authentic leaders are self-aware and act in accordance with their values and convictions, thereby fostering trust and respect among their followers. They are genuine in their interactions and encourage open communication, leading to a positive organizational culture.

577. The servant leadership approach is best described as a leadership style where the leader:
a) Prioritizes their own needs and goals over those of their followers.
b) Serves the needs of their followers, putting their development and well-being first.
c) Avoids making any decisions to prevent conflicts within the team.
d) Believes in using power and authority to command respect and obedience.

Answer: b) Serves the needs of their followers, putting their development and well-being first.
Explanation: Servant leadership is a philosophy where the main goal of the leader is to serve others. This type of leader focuses on the needs, development, and well-being of their followers before their own. They aim to nurture the abilities of their followers, helping them to grow both professionally and personally. Servant leaders are characterized by their focus on collaboration, trust, empathy, and the ethical use of power.

578. In the context of leadership theories, the concept of "emotional intelligence" is critical because it allows leaders to:
a) Ignore emotions in the workplace to maintain a high level of professionalism.
b) Understand and manage their own emotions and those of their followers effectively.
c) Focus solely on logical decision-making without considering the emotional impact.

d) Use emotions to manipulate followers into achieving organizational goals.

Answer: b) Understand and manage their own emotions and those of their followers effectively.
Explanation: Emotional intelligence in leadership refers to the leader's ability to recognize, understand, and manage their own emotions, as well as to recognize, understand, and influence the emotions of others. High emotional intelligence is critical for effective leadership as it enhances communication, conflict resolution, empathy, and the ability to motivate and inspire followers. Leaders with high emotional intelligence are better equipped to handle the complexities of social interactions and to foster positive relationships within their teams.

579. Cross-cultural leadership is important in today's globalized world because it:
a) Ensures that leadership practices conform to a single cultural standard.
b) Recognizes and values diversity, leading to more inclusive and effective leadership practices.
c) Advocates for the elimination of all cultural differences to streamline organizational processes.
d) Focuses exclusively on the leader's home culture, disregarding the cultures of followers.

Answer: b) Recognizes and values diversity, leading to more inclusive and effective leadership practices.
Explanation: Cross-cultural leadership emphasizes the importance of understanding, respecting, and valuing the cultural differences among individuals in a globalized workplace. It involves adapting leadership styles to be effective across different cultural contexts, fostering an inclusive environment where diverse perspectives are valued. This approach enhances collaboration, innovation, and team effectiveness by leveraging the strengths of a diverse workforce.

580. In the initial stages of assessment, a comprehensive biopsychosocial interview is essential because it:
a) Provides a diagnosis based solely on the client's self-report.
b) Focuses only on the biological aspects of the client's presenting problem.
c) Allows the social worker to prescribe medication.
d) Offers a holistic view of the client, including biological, psychological, and social factors.

Answer: d) Offers a holistic view of the client, including biological, psychological, and social factors.
Explanation: A comprehensive biopsychosocial interview is fundamental in the assessment phase as it gathers information across biological, psychological, and social domains. This approach ensures a thorough understanding of the client's situation, contributing factors to their presenting problems, and potential areas for intervention. It is a cornerstone of social work assessment because it recognizes the complex interplay of various factors in a person's life, rather than focusing on a single aspect.

581. When utilizing standardized assessment tools, it is important for social workers to:
a) Rely solely on the tool's outcomes for diagnosis and intervention planning.
b) Use the tools in combination with professional judgment and other assessment methods.
c) Consider the tools as optional and rarely integrate them into practice.
d) Focus only on the scores, disregarding the client's cultural and personal background.

Answer: b) Use the tools in combination with professional judgment and other assessment methods.

Explanation: Standardized assessment tools are valuable in providing objective data on a client's functioning and needs. However, they should be used in conjunction with professional judgment and other qualitative assessment methods. This approach ensures a comprehensive assessment that takes into account the client's unique circumstances, cultural background, and personal experiences, leading to more accurate and tailored intervention planning.

582. A social worker evaluating a child's developmental delays would MOST likely utilize:
a) The Diagnostic and Statistical Manual of Mental Disorders (DSM-5) solely.
b) An unstructured interview with the parents about their observations.
c) Developmental screening instruments and observation of the child.
d) Peer comparison without formal tools or assessments.

Answer: c) Developmental screening instruments and observation of the child.
Explanation: To assess a child's developmental delays accurately, a social worker would most likely use developmental screening instruments specifically designed for evaluating developmental milestones in children. In addition, observing the child in various settings and situations provides firsthand insight into their developmental status. These approaches offer structured and reliable methods for identifying developmental delays, which can then be compared to normative developmental milestones for a child of that age.

583. In the context of mental health assessment, the term "differential diagnosis" refers to:
a) Diagnosing only the most apparent mental health disorder.
b) The process of distinguishing between two or more conditions that share similar signs or symptoms.
c) Assigning multiple diagnoses to ensure comprehensive treatment.
d) Avoiding a diagnosis to prevent labeling the client.

Answer: b) The process of distinguishing between two or more conditions that share similar signs or symptoms.
Explanation: Differential diagnosis is a critical step in the assessment process, especially in mental health, where many disorders may present with overlapping symptoms. It involves systematically ruling out other conditions and considering a range of possible diagnoses before determining the most accurate one. This careful consideration ensures that treatment plans are appropriate and targeted to the client's specific needs.

584. A client presents with symptoms of anxiety. In assessing the severity and impact of these symptoms, a social worker should:
a) Focus exclusively on the physical manifestations of anxiety.
b) Utilize a validated anxiety rating scale along with clinical interview findings.
c) Disregard the client's subjective experience of anxiety as unreliable.
d) Assume the client's anxiety is not severe if they are functioning well in their job.

Answer: b) Utilize a validated anxiety rating scale along with clinical interview findings.
Explanation: To accurately assess the severity and impact of a client's anxiety, a social worker should use a combination of validated anxiety rating scales and findings from a clinical interview. This approach allows

for a comprehensive assessment that considers both the clinician's observations and the client's subjective experience of anxiety. Rating scales provide a standardized method to gauge anxiety levels, while the clinical interview offers deeper insights into the anxiety's impact on the client's life.

585. When assessing for substance use disorders, it is crucial to understand the concept of "substance dependence" as it:
a) Applies only to illegal drugs and not to alcohol or prescription medications.
b) Is characterized by occasional use of substances without significant impact on daily life.
c) Involves a pattern of compulsive use despite harmful consequences.
d) Automatically implies the individual is not capable of recovery.

Answer: c) Involves a pattern of compulsive use despite harmful consequences.
Explanation: Substance dependence is defined by a pattern of compulsive substance use characterized by a strong desire to take the drug, difficulties in controlling its use, persisting in its use despite harmful consequences, a higher priority given to drug use than to other activities and obligations, increased tolerance, and sometimes a physical withdrawal state. This definition applies to the use of alcohol and prescription medications, as well as illegal drugs. Understanding this concept is crucial for accurate assessment and effective intervention planning.

586. For a client experiencing symptoms of post-traumatic stress disorder (PTSD), an effective assessment technique would include:
a) Focusing solely on current functioning without exploring past trauma.
b) Using PTSD-specific assessment tools and exploring the client's trauma history in a safe and supportive manner.
c) Avoiding discussions of trauma to prevent re-traumatization.
d) Assuming that symptoms will resolve without direct intervention.

Answer: b) Using PTSD-specific assessment tools and exploring the client's trauma history in a safe and supportive manner.
Explanation: For clients showing symptoms of PTSD, it is essential to use PTSD-specific assessment tools that can accurately identify symptoms and severity. Additionally, exploring the client's trauma history is crucial for understanding the context and impact of their symptoms. However, such discussions must be conducted in a manner that is safe, supportive, and paced according to the client's readiness to minimize the risk of re-traumatization.

587. In assessing a client's risk of self-harm, it is IMPORTANT to:
a) Wait for the client to bring up the topic before asking direct questions about self-harm.
b) Assume that the absence of previous self-harm attempts means there is no current risk.
c) Directly ask about any thoughts, plans, or previous acts of self-harm in a nonjudgmental manner.
d) Focus the assessment exclusively on environmental factors, ignoring psychological aspects.

Answer: c) Directly ask about any thoughts, plans, or previous acts of self-harm in a nonjudgmental manner.

Explanation: Assessing a client's risk of self-harm requires direct and open questions about their thoughts, feelings, plans, and history regarding self-harm. This should be done in a nonjudgmental and empathetic manner to encourage honest disclosure and to build trust. Waiting for the client to bring up the topic or assuming there is no risk without direct inquiry can overlook critical warning signs and delay necessary interventions.

588. A key aspect of assessing for depression in clients involves:
a) Disregarding reports of physical symptoms, as they are not relevant to the diagnosis.
b) Assuming that high-functioning individuals do not experience depression.
c) Observing for both emotional and physical symptoms as well as the impact on daily functioning.
d) Solely focusing on the presence of sad mood without considering other symptoms.

Answer: c) Observing for both emotional and physical symptoms as well as the impact on daily functioning.
Explanation: An effective assessment for depression requires attention to both emotional and physical symptoms, as depression can manifest in various ways, including changes in mood, appetite, sleep patterns, energy level, concentration, and physical well-being. Additionally, understanding how these symptoms impact the client's ability to function in daily life is crucial for a comprehensive assessment. This holistic approach ensures that the social worker can accurately identify depression and its severity, informing appropriate intervention strategies.

589. Contingency theory of leadership suggests that:
a) The effectiveness of a leader is independent of the situational context.
b) A leader's effectiveness is directly related to their personality traits.
c) The success of leadership styles varies according to the organizational environment and task structure.
d) Leaders are most effective when they adopt a democratic style in all situations.

Answer: c) The success of leadership styles varies according to the organizational environment and task structure.
Explanation: Contingency theory posits that there is no one best way to lead. Instead, a leader's effectiveness is contingent upon how well their leadership style matches the context in which they are operating. This theory takes into account variables such as the organization's environment, the nature of the task, and the relationships between leaders and followers, suggesting that different situations may require different leadership styles for optimal outcomes.

590. Path-goal theory is primarily concerned with:
a) How leaders can ensure lifelong employment for their followers.
b) The leader's role in clarifying paths to help followers achieve work goals and personal satisfaction.
c) Establishing a clear hierarchy in an organization to ensure discipline.
d) The avoidance of any obstacles in an organization, ensuring a smooth path for the leader only.

Answer: b) The leader's role in clarifying paths to help followers achieve work goals and personal satisfaction.

Explanation: Path-goal theory focuses on how leaders motivate their followers to achieve their goals and perform at their best by clarifying the path to various rewards. Leaders adjust their style and strategies to fit the needs of their followers and the work environment, addressing obstacles and providing the necessary support. This approach enhances follower satisfaction and productivity by aligning leader behavior with follower needs in the context of achieving the task at hand.

591. The LMX (Leader-Member Exchange) theory emphasizes:
a) The transactional relationship between leaders and followers.
b) The creation of in-groups and out-groups within a team.
c) The importance of dyadic relationships between leaders and each of their followers.
d) Leadership as a shared process that evolves from group dynamics.

Answer: c) The importance of dyadic relationships between leaders and each of their followers.
Explanation: LMX theory focuses on the dyadic (two-way) relationships that leaders form with each of their followers. It posits that leaders do not treat all followers the same but rather develop unique relationships with each, leading to the formation of in-groups and out-groups. The quality of these leader-member exchanges influences various outcomes, including job satisfaction, commitment, and overall team effectiveness. High-quality relationships characterized by trust, respect, and mutual obligation tend to result in positive outcomes.

592. Understanding the concept of "complex trauma," it is essential to recognize that it:
a) Occurs from a single, isolated event that is easily overcome.
b) Is a result of prolonged, repeated exposure to highly stressful situations.
c) Only affects individuals with pre-existing mental health conditions.
d) Can be addressed fully in a few therapy sessions without long-term intervention.

Answer: b) Is a result of prolonged, repeated exposure to highly stressful situations.
Explanation: Complex trauma arises from prolonged exposure to stressful situations such as ongoing abuse, prolonged war conflict, or repeated exposure to traumatic events. It often involves direct harm, abandonment, or betrayal, particularly in situations where there is an expectation of protection. This form of trauma can lead to severe psychological distress and a wide range of emotional, cognitive, and behavioral issues, necessitating comprehensive, long-term therapeutic interventions to address the multifaceted impacts on an individual's mental health and well-being.

593. When assessing an individual's response to trauma, it's crucial to understand that reactions:
a) Are uniform across all ages, genders, and cultures.
b) May vary significantly due to factors like age, gender, and cultural background.
c) Are solely psychological and do not include physical symptoms.
d) Can only be accurately assessed several years after the traumatic event.

Answer: b) May vary significantly due to factors like age, gender, and cultural background.
Explanation: Trauma reactions are highly individualized and can be influenced by various factors including, but not limited to, an individual's age, gender, cultural background, previous experiences with trauma, and existing support systems. These reactions can manifest as a range of emotional, physical, cognitive, and

behavioral symptoms. Recognizing the diversity of trauma responses is essential for providing empathetic and effective support and intervention.

594. Secondary traumatic stress is most likely to affect:
a) Individuals who witness a traumatic event in a movie or television show.
b) Professionals who work closely with trauma survivors, such as social workers or therapists.
c) People who have no direct or indirect exposure to trauma but read about it in news articles.
d) Individuals who hear a story about a traumatic event from a friend of a friend.

Answer: b) Professionals who work closely with trauma survivors, such as social workers or therapists.
Explanation: Secondary traumatic stress (STS) occurs in individuals who are exposed to the traumatic experiences of others, particularly in a professional context. Social workers, therapists, and other professionals working closely with trauma survivors may experience symptoms similar to PTSD as a result of empathetic engagement with their clients' traumatic experiences. Understanding and addressing STS is crucial for the well-being of professionals in trauma-related fields.

595. Trauma-informed care in social work practice emphasizes:
a) Assuming that every client has a history of trauma.
b) Prioritizing physical health concerns over psychological impacts of trauma.
c) The use of confrontation to encourage clients to face their traumatic experiences.
d) Ignoring trauma histories to focus on present symptoms and issues.

Answer: a) Assuming that every client has a history of trauma.
Explanation: Trauma-informed care is an approach that assumes any client could have a history of trauma. It emphasizes understanding, recognizing, and responding to the effects of all types of trauma. Trauma-informed care aims to create a treatment setting in which clients feel understood, supported, and safe to discuss their trauma histories and symptoms, promoting healing and recovery in a way that avoids re-traumatization.

596. The concept of "resilience" in the context of trauma refers to:
a) The ability to be unaffected by any traumatic events.
b) A rare trait that only a few individuals possess.
c) The process of adapting well in the face of adversity, trauma, or significant stress.
d) The strategy of avoiding situations that might trigger memories of the trauma.

Answer: c) The process of adapting well in the face of adversity, trauma, or significant stress.
Explanation: Resilience refers to the process through which individuals demonstrate positive adaptation and recovery in the face of adversity, trauma, or significant sources of stress. It does not imply that a person is unaffected by trauma but rather highlights the capacity to recover and continue functioning psychologically and physically. Resilience can be strengthened through various means, including support systems, positive coping strategies, and adaptive therapeutic interventions.

597. The concept of "complex trauma" is best understood as:
a) Trauma that is complicated to treat due to the lack of available therapies.

b) A single, life-threatening event that has long-lasting effects on the individual.
c) Exposure to varied and multiple traumatic events, often of an invasive and interpersonal nature.
d) Trauma that only occurs in complex social systems and affects groups rather than individuals.

Answer: c) Exposure to varied and multiple traumatic events, often of an invasive and interpersonal nature.
Explanation: Complex trauma refers to the experience of multiple traumatic events that are of an invasive, interpersonal nature and the wide-ranging, long-term impact of this exposure. These events often occur within the context of relationships, contributing to their complexity. Unlike single-incident traumas, complex trauma affects various aspects of the individual's life, including emotional regulation, self-concept, and the ability to form secure attachments.

598. In assessing the impact of trauma on children, it's important to consider:
a) Only the physical injuries sustained.
b) The child's age, developmental stage, and the presence of a supportive environment.
c) That children are resilient and typically unaffected by traumatic events.
d) Trauma affects all children in the same way, irrespective of individual differences.

Answer: b) The child's age, developmental stage, and the presence of a supportive environment.
Explanation: The impact of trauma on children can vary significantly based on several factors, including the child's age, developmental stage, and whether they have a supportive environment to help them cope. These factors can influence how a child perceives and processes the traumatic event, as well as their recovery trajectory. Recognizing these individual differences is crucial in providing appropriate support and interventions.

599. The role of a social worker in supporting a client experiencing trauma may include all of the following EXCEPT:
a) Acting as the primary therapist for the client's PTSD without any additional training.
b) Providing psychoeducation about trauma and its effects.
c) Facilitating referrals to trauma-informed mental health services.
d) Offering support and advocacy to navigate social systems.

Answer: a) Acting as the primary therapist for the client's PTSD without any additional training.
Explanation: While social workers play a crucial role in supporting clients experiencing trauma through psychoeducation, referrals, and advocacy, acting as the primary therapist for PTSD or other specific trauma-related disorders requires specialized training in trauma-focused therapies. Social workers without this specialized training should refer clients to qualified mental health professionals for therapeutic interventions.

600. The concept of "secondary traumatic stress" (STS) is most relevant to:
a) Clients who have experienced multiple unrelated traumatic events.
b) Professionals who experience trauma symptoms due to exposure to clients' trauma stories.
c) Individuals who witness a traumatic event but are not directly involved.
d) Families of individuals who have experienced trauma.

Answer: b) Professionals who experience trauma symptoms due to exposure to clients' trauma stories.
Explanation: Secondary traumatic stress (STS) refers to the emotional duress that results when an individual hears about the firsthand trauma experiences of another. It's particularly relevant to professionals like social workers, therapists, and first responders who are exposed to the trauma stories of the people they help. Symptoms of STS can mirror those of PTSD, affecting professionals' well-being and their ability to provide care.

601. A trauma-informed approach in social work practice emphasizes:
a) Avoiding any discussions of trauma to prevent retraumatization.
b) Understanding the widespread impact of trauma and integrating knowledge about trauma into policies, procedures, and practices.
c) Focusing exclusively on providing trauma-specific therapies to all clients.
d) The assumption that only clients with a trauma diagnosis require a modified approach.

Answer: b) Understanding the widespread impact of trauma and integrating knowledge about trauma into policies, procedures, and practices.
Explanation: A trauma-informed approach is based on the understanding of the prevalence and impact of trauma and the need to incorporate this understanding into all aspects of service delivery. It involves recognizing the signs and symptoms of trauma, avoiding retraumatization, and promoting environments of healing and recovery rather than practices that may inadvertently cause harm.

602. The presence of resilience in individuals who have experienced trauma indicates:
a) The absence of any trauma-related symptoms.
b) An innate ability that prevents the individual from experiencing trauma.
c) The process of adapting well in the face of adversity, trauma, tragedy, threats, or significant sources of stress.
d) That trauma has not significantly impacted the individual's life.

Answer: c) The process of adapting well in the face of adversity, trauma, tragedy, threats, or significant sources of stress.
Explanation: Resilience is the process through which individuals exhibit positive adaptation despite experiences of significant adversity or trauma. It does not imply that the individual is unaffected by trauma or that they do not experience distress. Instead, resilience reflects the capacity to recover from difficulties, utilize adaptive coping strategies, and perhaps emerge stronger than before. It is a dynamic process that can be fostered and developed over time.

603. Incorporating a strengths-based perspective when working with trauma survivors involves:
a) Identifying and solely focusing on the client's weaknesses and areas of improvement.
b) Recognizing and building on the client's inherent strengths, resources, and coping skills.
c) Assuming all trauma survivors possess the same strengths and resilience.
d) Disregarding the impact of trauma on the individual's life.

Answer: b) Recognizing and building on the client's inherent strengths, resources, and coping skills.

Explanation: A strengths-based perspective in trauma work focuses on the client's resilience, resources, and any positive coping mechanisms they have developed. This approach acknowledges the impact of trauma but also emphasizes the individual's capacities and abilities to overcome challenges. It is about partnering with the client to identify and amplify existing strengths and resources to support recovery and empowerment.

604. The long-term effects of unaddressed childhood trauma can include:
a) Immediate resolution without any interventions.
b) Enhanced emotional resilience by adulthood.
c) Increased vulnerability to a range of mental health disorders, including PTSD, depression, and anxiety.
d) A guaranteed development of specific phobias related to the trauma.

Answer: c) Increased vulnerability to a range of mental health disorders, including PTSD, depression, and anxiety.
Explanation: Unaddressed childhood trauma can have profound and lasting effects on an individual's mental health, increasing their vulnerability to various mental health disorders such as PTSD, depression, and anxiety. The impact of childhood trauma can extend into adulthood, affecting emotional regulation, self-concept, and the ability to form healthy relationships. Early intervention and support can mitigate some of these long-term effects.

605. In the treatment of trauma, "safety and stabilization" are prioritized in the initial phase because:
a) It is assumed that all clients are in immediate physical danger.
b) Long-term therapy goals cannot be achieved without addressing immediate safety concerns and stabilizing the client's emotional state.
c) Trauma treatment is most effective when prolonged exposure techniques are applied from the start.
d) All trauma survivors require hospitalization.

Answer: b) Long-term therapy goals cannot be achieved without addressing immediate safety concerns and stabilizing the client's emotional state.
Explanation: The initial phase of trauma treatment focuses on ensuring the client's safety and emotional stabilization. This foundational step is crucial because clients need to feel physically and psychologically secure before they can effectively engage in further therapeutic work related to processing trauma and building coping skills. Addressing safety and stabilization helps to create a therapeutic environment where clients feel supported and prepared to explore and work through their trauma experiences.

606. The first step in effective crisis intervention typically involves:
a) Immediately solving the problem that caused the crisis.
b) Conducting a thorough assessment of the individual's past psychiatric history.
c) Establishing rapport and ensuring the individual's safety.
d) Advising the individual to avoid stressful situations in the future.

Answer: c) Establishing rapport and ensuring the individual's safety.
Explanation: The initial step in crisis intervention involves establishing a connection with the individual to ensure they feel supported and understood, and assessing their safety. This foundational step creates a

trustful relationship necessary for effective intervention. Ensuring the individual's safety is paramount, as it addresses any immediate risk of harm to themselves or others before proceeding with further intervention strategies.

607. When working with a client experiencing a panic attack, the priority intervention is to:
a) Discuss long-term coping mechanisms for stress.
b) Help the client to focus on slow, deep breathing techniques.
c) Immediately start psychotherapy to address underlying issues.
d) Encourage the client to ignore the symptoms and distract themselves.

Answer: b) Help the client to focus on slow, deep breathing techniques.
Explanation: In the midst of a panic attack, the most immediate and practical intervention is to assist the client in managing acute symptoms through slow, deep breathing techniques. This approach helps to reduce the physiological symptoms of panic by calming the nervous system, providing immediate relief, and helping the client regain control over their breathing and heart rate.

608. A critical component of working with survivors of natural disasters is:
a) Encouraging them to quickly forget the event and move on with their lives.
b) Offering solutions to all of their problems during the first meeting.
c) Providing psychoeducation about common reactions to trauma and stress.
d) Delaying any intervention until they reach out for help on their own.

Answer: c) Providing psychoeducation about common reactions to trauma and stress.
Explanation: Providing psychoeducation to survivors of natural disasters is crucial as it helps them understand their reactions, normalizes their experiences of trauma and stress, and reduces feelings of isolation and confusion. Educating individuals about common responses to trauma can also empower them to identify their needs and seek appropriate support, thereby facilitating the healing process.

609. In the context of crisis intervention for a person experiencing suicidal thoughts, it is important to:
a) Avoid discussing suicide directly to not encourage those thoughts.
b) Assure the person that their feelings will quickly pass and are not significant.
c) Directly and openly ask about suicidal thoughts and feelings.
d) Leave the topic until they bring it up in conversation.

Answer: c) Directly and openly ask about suicidal thoughts and feelings.
Explanation: Directly asking about suicidal thoughts and feelings is a critical step in assessing risk and intervening appropriately. Open communication provides an opportunity for the individual to share their experiences and feelings, breaking through isolation and shame that may be associated with these thoughts. This approach allows the professional to evaluate the immediacy of the risk and to develop an intervention plan that ensures the individual's safety.

610. When a family is in crisis due to a member's substance abuse, an effective strategy is to:
a) Focus solely on the family member with substance abuse issues, ignoring the wider family dynamics.
b) Immediately refer the family member for inpatient treatment without assessing their willingness.

c) Facilitate a family meeting to discuss the impact of substance abuse and explore support options.
d) Suggest that the family cut ties with the member until they decide to seek help.

Answer: c) Facilitate a family meeting to discuss the impact of substance abuse and explore support options.
Explanation: Facilitating a family meeting provides a structured environment for open communication about the impact of substance abuse on the family and allows for the exploration of support and treatment options. This inclusive approach acknowledges the systemic nature of substance abuse, promoting understanding, support, and collective action towards recovery and healing, respecting the readiness and willingness of the individual with substance abuse issues.

611. In dealing with a community experiencing a traumatic event, such as a mass shooting, a social worker's role includes:
a) Waiting for community members to individually seek out services.
b) Providing immediate, on-site psychological debriefing to all affected individuals.
c) Assessing the community's needs and coordinating with other agencies to provide resources.
d) Advising the community to move on as quickly as possible to restore normalcy.

Answer: c) Assessing the community's needs and coordinating with other agencies to provide resources.
Explanation: In the aftermath of a mass traumatic event, a social worker's role involves a proactive approach to assess the community's immediate and long-term needs and to coordinate with other agencies and services to provide comprehensive support. This may include mental health services, crisis counseling, and logistical support, aiming to address the wide range of impacts such traumatic events have on communities.

612. The concept of "psychological first aid" in emergency services is best described as:
a) A long-term therapeutic intervention aimed at resolving deep-seated psychological issues.
b) A set of practices aimed at reducing initial post-trauma distress and supporting short-term adaptive functioning.
c) An intervention where individuals are encouraged to analyze their feelings and reactions to the crisis deeply.
d) Providing medication to manage the psychological effects of trauma immediately.

Answer: b) A set of practices aimed at reducing initial post-trauma distress and supporting short-term adaptive functioning.
Explanation: Psychological first aid is a humane, supportive response to a fellow human being who is suffering and who may need support. It involves evidence-informed strategies designed to reduce stress symptoms and assist in a healthy recovery following a traumatic event, disaster, or crisis. It focuses on basic, non-intrusive support with a focus on safety, comfort, and helping affected individuals to meet their immediate needs and to connect them with additional support if necessary.

613. When addressing crises related to domestic violence, it's essential to:
a) Convince the survivor to leave the abuser immediately, regardless of their readiness.
b) Validate the survivor's feelings and experiences, while providing options for safety planning.

c) Focus on the reasons why the survivor may have provoked the violence.
d) Encourage the survivor to confront the abuser as a form of empowerment.

Answer: b) Validate the survivor's feelings and experiences, while providing options for safety planning.
Explanation: In cases of domestic violence, it is crucial to validate the survivor's feelings and experiences, acknowledging the complexity of their situation. Providing a non-judgmental, supportive space for them to share their story is vital. Offering options for safety planning empowers the survivor to make informed decisions about their next steps, respecting their autonomy and readiness to change their situation.

614. For individuals experiencing homelessness and a mental health crisis, an effective approach would be to:
a) Immediately focus on solving their long-term housing needs before addressing mental health.
b) Insist on hospitalization for mental health treatment as a prerequisite for housing assistance.
c) Provide integrated services that address both immediate shelter needs and mental health support.
d) Suggest they find stable housing on their own before seeking mental health services.

Answer: c) Provide integrated services that address both immediate shelter needs and mental health support.
Explanation: An effective approach for individuals experiencing both homelessness and a mental health crisis involves integrated services that address both needs simultaneously. This dual-focus strategy recognizes the interconnection between stable housing and mental health recovery, offering a more holistic and supportive path towards stability and well-being.

615. When working with clients from different socioeconomic backgrounds, it is important for social workers to:
a) Assume that clients' financial issues are the result of poor personal choices.
b) Apply the same interventions regardless of the client's economic situation.
c) Recognize how socioeconomic status impacts access to resources and shapes life experiences.
d) Avoid discussing financial matters to prevent embarrassing the client.

Answer: c) Recognize how socioeconomic status impacts access to resources and shapes life experiences.
Explanation: Socioeconomic status significantly influences individuals' access to resources, opportunities, and their overall life experiences. Recognizing this allows social workers to tailor interventions that are sensitive to and meet the specific needs of clients from diverse economic backgrounds. It's essential to consider these factors in practice to address and mitigate the barriers clients may face.

616. Incorporating an understanding of intersectionality in social work practice means acknowledging that:
a) Individuals belong to a single social category that predominantly shapes their experiences.
b) The intersection of various social identities, such as race, gender, and class, does not influence a person's life experiences.
c) People's experiences are shaped by the interplay of multiple social identities, creating unique modes of discrimination and privilege.
d) Only the most visible identity of a person should be considered when providing social work services.

Answer: c) People's experiences are shaped by the interplay of multiple social identities, creating unique modes of discrimination and privilege.
Explanation: Intersectionality is a framework for understanding how aspects of a person's social and political identities (gender, race, class, sexuality, ability, etc.) combine to create different modes of discrimination and privilege. It highlights the complexity of the compounding nature of disadvantage and recognizes that individuals face multi-faceted layers of discrimination based on their unique identity combinations.

617. In working with LGBTQ+ clients, a culturally competent social worker should:
a) Use the same approach as they would with heterosexual and cisgender clients, ignoring sexual orientation and gender identity.
b) Assume to know the clients' needs based on their sexual orientation or gender identity.
c) Avoid any discussions related to sexual orientation and gender identity unless the client initiates it.
d) Create a safe and affirming space for clients to explore and express their identities.

Answer: d) Create a safe and affirming space for clients to explore and express their identities.
Explanation: Culturally competent social work with LGBTQ+ clients involves creating a supportive environment where clients feel safe and affirmed in exploring and expressing their sexual orientation and gender identity. Recognizing and validating their experiences and identities can help build trust and facilitate effective support and intervention.

618. When addressing the needs of clients with disabilities, it's critical to:
a) Focus solely on the disability and its limitations.
b) Practice from a model that views disability primarily as a medical issue to be fixed.
c) Understand disability within the context of the social model, which focuses on societal barriers.
d) Assume what accommodations they need without consulting them.

Answer: c) Understand disability within the context of the social model, which focuses on societal barriers.
Explanation: The social model of disability suggests that disability is not caused by the individual's impairment but by the societal barriers and attitudes that exclude individuals with various impairments. This perspective encourages social workers to focus on removing societal barriers and advocating for changes that promote inclusivity and accessibility, rather than perceiving the disability as a problem to be fixed.

619. A social worker's awareness of their own cultural identity and biases is essential because it:
a) Eliminates all forms of bias in practice automatically.
b) Allows the social worker to adopt a universal approach to all clients, ignoring cultural differences.
c) Helps prevent the imposition of the social worker's values on the client.
d) Means the social worker no longer needs to engage in continuing education on cultural competence.

Answer: c) Helps prevent the imposition of the social worker's values on the client.
Explanation: Self-awareness of one's cultural identity and biases is crucial in social work practice as it helps professionals recognize how their own backgrounds, values, and biases might influence their interactions

with clients. This awareness prevents the imposition of the social worker's values on the client, promoting respect for the client's unique culture, values, and experiences.

620. Effective communication with clients who have limited English proficiency can be facilitated by:
a) Speaking louder and slower in English to ensure understanding.
b) Using complex technical jargon to sound professional.
c) Assuming their children can serve as adequate interpreters for all situations.
d) Utilizing professional interpretation services to ensure accurate communication.

Answer: d) Utilizing professional interpretation services to ensure accurate communication.
Explanation: For clients with limited English proficiency, using professional interpretation services is crucial for effective communication. These services ensure that both the client and the social worker understand each other accurately, facilitating clear dialogue and supporting informed decision-making. Relying on children or family members as interpreters can compromise confidentiality and accuracy, and may place an undue burden on them.

621. In serving racially and ethnically diverse communities, it is important for social workers to:
a) Implement a color-blind approach, treating everyone the same.
b) Recognize and address systemic barriers that disproportionately affect these communities.
c) Only focus on cultural differences and ignore other aspects of identity.
d) Assume that all members of a community share the same beliefs and experiences.

Answer: b) Recognize and address systemic barriers that disproportionately affect these communities.
Explanation: Recognizing and addressing systemic barriers is crucial when serving racially and ethnically diverse communities. These barriers, including racism, discrimination, and inequality, can significantly impact individuals' access to services, opportunities, and their overall well-being. A culturally competent social worker seeks to understand these systemic issues and works to advocate for equity and justice within these communities.

622. Acknowledging religious and spiritual diversity in practice involves:
a) Assuming all clients adhere to the same religious beliefs as the social worker.
b) Ignoring clients' religious and spiritual beliefs as they are not relevant to social work practice.
c) Imposing the social worker's spiritual beliefs on clients to guide them morally.
d) Respecting clients' religious and spiritual beliefs and considering how these beliefs impact their experiences and needs.

Answer: d) Respecting clients' religious and spiritual beliefs and considering how these beliefs impact their experiences and needs.
Explanation: Acknowledging and respecting clients' religious and spiritual diversity is fundamental in providing holistic and client-centered care. Understanding the role of these beliefs in clients' lives allows social workers to tailor interventions that honor their values and perspectives, contributing to more effective and meaningful support.

623. According to Bandura's Social Learning Theory, which factor is NOT considered crucial for learning through observation?
a) Attention to the behavior being modeled
b) Retention of the observed behavior
c) Physical punishment as a consequence of imitating the behavior
d) Reproduction of the observed behavior

Answer: c) Physical punishment as a consequence of imitating the behavior
Explanation: Bandura's Social Learning Theory posits that learning occurs through observation, imitation, and modeling. Key factors that contribute to learning include attention, retention (remembering what one has observed), reproduction (the ability to replicate the action), and motivation. Physical punishment is not a fundamental aspect of learning within this theory; instead, the focus is on how positive and negative reinforcements can influence the likelihood of a behavior being repeated.

624. The Ecological Systems Theory, proposed by Bronfenbrenner, emphasizes the importance of which of the following in understanding an individual's development?
a) The genetic makeup of an individual
b) The individual's IQ level
c) Interactions within and between various environmental systems
d) The individual's ability to adapt to any environment without influence

Answer: c) Interactions within and between various environmental systems
Explanation: Bronfenbrenner's Ecological Systems Theory highlights the complex interactions between an individual and the different layers of their environment, including the microsystem (immediate surroundings), mesosystem (interconnections between microsystems), exosystem (external environmental settings that indirectly affect the individual), macrosystem (broader cultural values, laws, and customs), and chronosystem (dimension of time). This theory suggests that understanding an individual's development requires considering all these interconnected systems rather than focusing solely on intrinsic factors like genetics or IQ.

625. In the context of operant conditioning, reinforcement is used to:
a) Punish undesirable behaviors so they are not repeated.
b) Increase the likelihood that a behavior will be repeated.
c) Provide negative feedback to reduce certain behaviors.
d) Randomly reward behavior to create confusion and variability.

Answer: b) Increase the likelihood that a behavior will be repeated.
Explanation: Operant conditioning, a concept introduced by B.F. Skinner, involves using reinforcement to increase the likelihood of a behavior being repeated. Reinforcement can be positive (adding a desirable stimulus following a behavior) or negative (removing an aversive stimulus following a behavior). Both types of reinforcement aim to strengthen a behavior, making it more likely to occur again in the future, as opposed to punishment, which aims to decrease or eliminate unwanted behaviors.

626. Which of the following best represents the concept of "classical conditioning" as proposed by Ivan Pavlov?
a) A dog learns to sit to receive a treat.
b) A child learns to avoid a hot stove after being burned.
c) A bell rings every time before a dog is fed, and eventually, the dog salivates at the sound of the bell alone.
d) A student learns to solve math problems faster with the help of a tutor.

Answer: c) A bell rings every time before a dog is fed, and eventually, the dog salivates at the sound of the bell alone.
Explanation: Classical conditioning, a theory developed by Ivan Pavlov, involves learning through association. In Pavlov's famous experiment, a dog learned to associate the sound of a bell (a neutral stimulus) with food (an unconditioned stimulus), eventually responding to the bell alone (now a conditioned stimulus) with salivation (a conditioned response). This process demonstrates how a previously neutral stimulus can elicit a conditioned response through association with an unconditioned stimulus.

627. The theory that suggests behavior is motivated by the desire to meet specific needs, progressing from basic to more complex, is known as:
a) B.F. Skinner's Operant Conditioning
b) Abraham Maslow's Hierarchy of Needs
c) Erik Erikson's Stages of Psychosocial Development
d) Jean Piaget's Stages of Cognitive Development

Answer: b) Abraham Maslow's Hierarchy of Needs
Explanation: Abraham Maslow's Hierarchy of Needs is a motivational theory in psychology comprising a five-tier model of human needs, depicted as hierarchical levels within a pyramid. From the bottom of the hierarchy upwards, the needs are physiological (food and clothing), safety (job security), love and belonging needs (friendship), esteem, and self-actualization. Maslow suggested that the most basic level of needs must be met before the individual will strongly desire (or focus motivation upon) the secondary or higher-level needs.

628. In Behaviorism, the term "extinction" refers to:
a) The introduction of a new behavior to replace an old one.
b) The revival of previously extinguished behaviors due to changes in environment.
c) The process by which a conditioned response decreases after repeated exposure to the conditioned stimulus without the unconditioned stimulus.
d) An increase in aggressive behaviors when a desired outcome is not achieved.

Answer: c) The process by which a conditioned response decreases after repeated exposure to the conditioned stimulus without the unconditioned stimulus.
Explanation: In the realm of classical conditioning, extinction occurs when a conditioned stimulus is repeatedly presented without the unconditioned stimulus, leading to a decrease in the conditioned response over time. For example, if the sound of a bell (conditioned stimulus) no longer predicts the

arrival of food (unconditioned stimulus), the conditioned response (salivation) will eventually diminish and cease.

629. The attachment theory, primarily developed by John Bowlby, suggests that:
a) Children are born as blank slates, and their personalities are entirely shaped by their environment.
b) The bond formed between caregivers and their children in early childhood has profound effects on an individual's social, emotional, and cognitive development.
c) Attachment is a learned behavior that only develops if the caregiver provides food.
d) Children form attachments only with their biological parents.

Answer: b) The bond formed between caregivers and their children in early childhood has profound effects on an individual's social, emotional, and cognitive development.
Explanation: Attachment theory posits that the emotional bond formed between a child and their caregiver in early childhood is crucial for the child's development. This theory emphasizes that secure, anxious, and avoidant attachments formed in childhood influence an individual's ability to form healthy relationships throughout life. Attachment experiences affect a wide range of developmental outcomes, from emotional regulation to interpersonal dynamics.

630. Vygotsky's Sociocultural Theory of Cognitive Development emphasizes that:
a) Children's cognitive development is an autonomous process, unaffected by social interactions.
b) Learning and development are influenced by culture, language, and social interactions.
c) Cognitive development stops in early childhood.
d) Peer influence has minimal impact on cognitive development.

Answer: b) Learning and development are influenced by culture, language, and social interactions.
Explanation: Lev Vygotsky's Sociocultural Theory asserts that an individual's development cannot be understood without referencing the social and cultural contexts in which learning takes place. He argued that cognitive functions are the products of social interactions and that learning is deeply embedded within and influenced by one's culture and the use of language. Vygotsky highlighted the importance of the "Zone of Proximal Development" and the role of more knowledgeable others in facilitating learning.

631. The Transtheoretical Model of Change, developed by Prochaska and DiClemente, is useful in understanding:
a) The static nature of personality traits over the lifespan.
b) The universal stages of grief that all individuals experience identically.
c) The process by which individuals progress through a series of stages when changing behavior.
d) The immediate transformation that occurs when individuals decide to change a behavior.

Answer: c) The process by which individuals progress through a series of stages when changing behavior.
Explanation: The Transtheoretical Model of Change outlines a sequence of stages individuals typically move through when changing a behavior, including precontemplation, contemplation, preparation, action, maintenance, and sometimes relapse. This model recognizes that change is a process, not an event, and that individuals at different stages benefit from different types of interventions. It is widely used in

counseling and health promotion to tailor strategies that support individuals at various stages of readiness to change.

632. When developing a new program within a social service agency, what should be the FIRST step in human resources management?
a) Assigning tasks to existing staff members without assessing their current workload
b) Conducting a needs assessment to determine staffing requirements for the program
c) Hiring new staff members based on the estimated budget before defining program goals
d) Purchasing new software for program management before determining staff needs

Answer: b) Conducting a needs assessment to determine staffing requirements for the program
Explanation: The first step in human resources management when developing a new program is to conduct a needs assessment. This process involves evaluating the program's goals and objectives to determine what human resources are needed to achieve them effectively. By understanding the specific skills, knowledge, and capacities required, the agency can make informed decisions about staffing, training, and development needs, ensuring that the program has the appropriate support to succeed.

633. In addressing staff burnout in a high-demand social service agency, which strategy would be LEAST effective?
a) Increasing the number of staff to reduce individual caseloads
b) Implementing mandatory overtime to ensure all work is completed
c) Providing access to professional development and self-care resources
d) Offering regular supervision and support meetings for staff

Answer: b) Implementing mandatory overtime to ensure all work is completed
Explanation: Mandatory overtime, especially in a high-demand setting, is likely to exacerbate staff burnout rather than alleviate it. Burnout occurs from prolonged exposure to stressful work conditions, and increasing work hours adds to this stress. Effective strategies to address burnout include reducing caseloads, offering resources for professional development and self-care, and providing supportive supervision. These approaches help manage workload, promote well-being, and support staff resilience.

634. What is an essential consideration when integrating volunteers into a social service organization's workforce?
a) Treating volunteers significantly differently from paid staff to emphasize their temporary status
b) Ensuring there is a clear distinction in the quality of work expected from volunteers versus paid staff
c) Providing comprehensive training and support to volunteers, similar to that offered to paid staff
d) Limiting the responsibility and autonomy of volunteers to only basic, menial tasks

Answer: c) Providing comprehensive training and support to volunteers, similar to that offered to paid staff
Explanation: Volunteers are a valuable resource in social service organizations, and providing them with comprehensive training and support is essential for their effective integration into the workforce. Training ensures that volunteers are well-prepared to contribute meaningfully to the organization's goals, while support helps maintain their engagement and satisfaction. Treating volunteers with the same respect and

professionalism as paid staff, including appropriate levels of responsibility and autonomy, enhances their experience and the quality of service delivery.

635. In managing conflicts within a social service team, what is a key step for a supervisor?
a) Ignoring the conflict in hopes that it will resolve itself over time
b) Encouraging team members to vote on the best solution to the conflict
c) Addressing the conflict directly through facilitated discussion and problem-solving
d) Automatically siding with the most experienced team member to expedite resolution

Answer: c) Addressing the conflict directly through facilitated discussion and problem-solving
Explanation: Addressing conflicts directly through facilitated discussion and problem-solving is a key step for supervisors in managing team dynamics. This approach involves actively listening to all parties involved, understanding their perspectives, and collaboratively working towards a mutually acceptable solution. Ignoring conflicts or siding with one party without a fair process can lead to resentment, decreased team morale, and a toxic work environment. Effective conflict resolution supports a positive and productive team culture.

636. When evaluating the performance of social service staff, it is important to:
a) Base evaluations solely on the quantity of work completed
b) Use a one-size-fits-all approach to assessing performance across different roles
c) Include both qualitative and quantitative measures of performance
d) Conduct evaluations as a surprise to get the most honest assessment of performance

Answer: c) Include both qualitative and quantitative measures of performance
Explanation: Including both qualitative and quantitative measures in staff performance evaluations provides a more comprehensive and accurate assessment of an employee's contributions and areas for improvement. While quantitative data might include caseload numbers or service delivery metrics, qualitative measures assess the quality of work, client feedback, and the employee's collaborative and problem-solving abilities. This balanced approach ensures that evaluations are fair, holistic, and conducive to professional growth.

637. In fostering a diverse and inclusive workplace within a social service agency, it is crucial to:
a) Focus solely on diversity in hiring without addressing workplace culture
b) Implement policies and practices that support diversity at all levels of the organization
c) Assume that diversity will naturally lead to inclusivity without deliberate efforts
d) Limit diversity initiatives to certain times of the year or special occasions

Answer: b) Implement policies and practices that support diversity at all levels of the organization
Explanation: Fostering a diverse and inclusive workplace requires implementing policies and practices that support diversity in recruitment, hiring, retention, and promotion at all levels of the organization. This approach goes beyond just diversifying the workforce; it involves creating a culture where all employees feel valued, respected, and empowered to contribute their best. Efforts must be ongoing and integrated into the organization's core values and operations, rather than being sporadic or symbolic.

638. When planning professional development opportunities for social service staff, what factor is critical to consider?
a) The most expensive options to ensure perceived value
b) One-time events rather than ongoing learning opportunities
c) The specific learning needs and career goals of individual staff members
d) Exclusively external training programs without considering in-house expertise

Answer: c) The specific learning needs and career goals of individual staff members
Explanation: Considering the specific learning needs and career goals of individual staff members is critical when planning professional development opportunities. This personalized approach ensures that the professional development offered is relevant, engaging, and beneficial for each employee's growth and advancement. It acknowledges that staff members have unique skills, interests, and aspirations, and supports them in achieving their potential. Ongoing learning opportunities, rather than one-time events, contribute to sustained growth and job satisfaction.

639. In addressing high turnover rates among social service staff, which strategy would be MOST effective?
a) Increasing workload to improve efficiency and reduce the need for a larger staff
b) Offering competitive compensation and benefits, along with a supportive work environment
c) Reducing training opportunities to minimize costs
d) Limiting feedback to annual performance reviews to reduce staff anxiety

Answer: b) Offering competitive compensation and benefits, along with a supportive work environment
Explanation: High turnover rates in social service settings can often be attributed to factors like inadequate compensation, excessive workloads, and lack of support. Offering competitive compensation and benefits, along with creating a supportive and positive work environment, can significantly enhance job satisfaction and retention. This strategy recognizes the importance of valuing staff, both financially and professionally, and investing in their well-being and development.

640. In implementing a new client management system in a social service agency, what step is essential to ensure staff adoption and effective use of the system?
a) Choosing the most complex system to ensure it has all possible features
b) Providing comprehensive training and ongoing technical support to staff
c) Implementing the system all at once without a pilot phase
d) Excluding staff from the decision-making process to expedite selection and implementation

Answer: b) Providing comprehensive training and ongoing technical support to staff
Explanation: To ensure the successful adoption and effective use of a new client management system, it is essential to provide comprehensive training and ongoing technical support to staff. This approach facilitates a smooth transition, addresses potential challenges and resistance, and enhances staff confidence in using the new system. Involving staff in the selection process and considering their feedback can also promote buy-in and ensure that the system meets the actual needs of both staff and clients.

641. What is the primary goal of integrated health care models in social service settings?
a) To increase the profitability of health care services by combining resources

b) To provide care that is isolated to either physical or mental health, but not both
c) To deliver coordinated physical and mental health services to better meet client needs
d) To make health care services more complex and specialized

Answer: c) To deliver coordinated physical and mental health services to better meet client needs
Explanation: Integrated health care models aim to provide comprehensive care that addresses both physical and mental health needs in a coordinated manner. By combining resources and services, these models seek to improve overall client outcomes, increase satisfaction, and potentially reduce costs by preventing the exacerbation of health issues through early intervention and holistic care.

642. Which factor is most crucial in determining an individual's access to health care services?
a) The individual's level of education
b) Geographic location and availability of health care providers
c) Personal preferences for health care providers
d) The individual's career choice and workplace benefits

Answer: b) Geographic location and availability of health care providers
Explanation: Geographic location and the availability of health care providers in the area are crucial factors in determining an individual's access to health care services. People living in rural or underserved areas may have limited access to primary care and specialist services, affecting their ability to receive timely and appropriate care. This barrier can lead to disparities in health outcomes between different populations.

643. What is the significance of cultural competence in health care provision?
a) It ensures that all patients are treated with the same standardized approach, regardless of their background
b) It involves adapting health care practices to conform to the provider's cultural norms
c) It emphasizes understanding and respecting patients' diverse cultural backgrounds to provide effective care
d) It mandates the use of interpreters in all patient-provider interactions, irrespective of need

Answer: c) It emphasizes understanding and respecting patients' diverse cultural backgrounds to provide effective care
Explanation: Cultural competence in health care involves recognizing and respecting the diverse cultural backgrounds, beliefs, and needs of patients to provide effective and personalized care. By understanding cultural differences, health care providers can better communicate with patients, respect their preferences and beliefs, and improve health outcomes by ensuring care is accessible and relevant to all individuals, regardless of their cultural background.

644. In the context of social work, what role does advocacy play in improving health care access?
a) Advocacy is primarily focused on promoting pharmaceutical companies' interests
b) It involves lobbying for lower health care standards to make services more widely available
c) Advocacy aims to influence policies and practices to remove barriers and improve health care access for underserved populations

d) Social workers engage in advocacy to eliminate all forms of health insurance, promoting a cash-only system

Answer: c) Advocacy aims to influence policies and practices to remove barriers and improve health care access for underserved populations
Explanation: Social workers engage in advocacy to address systemic barriers and inequalities that impede access to health care services. Through advocacy efforts, social workers strive to influence policy changes, improve health care delivery systems, and ensure that all individuals, especially those from underserved communities, have equitable access to the health care services they need. This may involve advocating for policy reform, increased funding for health services, and the implementation of programs designed to improve access and outcomes.

645. How does the Affordable Care Act (ACA) aim to improve health care access in the United States?
a) By mandating that all citizens receive care exclusively from private insurers
b) Through the introduction of health insurance marketplaces and expansion of Medicaid eligibility
c) By requiring all health care services to be provided free of charge
d) By decreasing the regulation of health insurance companies to increase competition

Answer: b) Through the introduction of health insurance marketplaces and expansion of Medicaid eligibility
Explanation: The Affordable Care Act (ACA) sought to improve access to health care in the United States by introducing health insurance marketplaces for individuals to purchase insurance and by expanding Medicaid eligibility to cover more low-income individuals and families. These measures were designed to reduce the number of uninsured Americans and make health care more accessible and affordable for a broader segment of the population.

646. What challenge does the social determinant of housing play in accessing health care services?
a) Individuals with stable housing are less likely to seek preventive health care services
b) Unstable housing or homelessness can complicate access to health care services and follow-up care
c) Housing stability increases the risk of chronic health conditions
d) There is no correlation between housing status and health care access

Answer: b) Unstable housing or homelessness can complicate access to health care services and follow-up care
Explanation: Unstable housing and homelessness are significant barriers to accessing health care services. Individuals facing these challenges may find it difficult to schedule and attend appointments, receive consistent treatment, or follow up on care due to lack of transportation, inability to receive communication from providers, or prioritization of immediate survival needs over health care. Addressing housing stability is a critical step in improving access to health care and overall health outcomes.

647. How do language barriers impact health care access and quality?
a) They ensure that health care services are provided in the most widely spoken language only
b) Language barriers can lead to miscommunication, misunderstanding of health information, and decreased satisfaction with care

c) Language barriers have no significant impact on health care outcomes
d) They increase the efficiency of health care delivery by simplifying provider-patient interactions

Answer: b) Language barriers can lead to miscommunication, misunderstanding of health information, and decreased satisfaction with care
Explanation: Language barriers in health care settings can significantly impact the quality of care and patient satisfaction. When providers and patients do not share a common language, it can lead to miscommunication, misunderstandings, and errors in medical care. It may also discourage patients from seeking care, following treatment plans, or accessing preventive services. Providing language access services, such as medical interpretation and translation of materials, is essential for improving access and quality of care for patients with limited English proficiency.

648. What is the role of telehealth in enhancing health care access?
a) To replace all traditional in-person health care services with online consultations
b) To provide an alternative means of accessing health care services, particularly for those in remote or underserved areas
c) To increase health care costs by introducing new technologies
d) To limit patient interaction with health care providers to improve efficiency

Answer: b) To provide an alternative means of accessing health care services, particularly for those in remote or underserved areas
Explanation: Telehealth has emerged as a valuable tool in enhancing health care access by providing remote consultations, health monitoring, and information sharing through telecommunications technology. It is particularly beneficial for individuals in remote, rural, or underserved areas where access to health care providers and services may be limited. Telehealth can help overcome geographical barriers, reduce travel time and costs, and support the delivery of timely and convenient care.

649. In managing health care for aging populations, what consideration is essential for social service professionals?
a) Assuming all older adults have the same health care needs and preferences
b) Focusing solely on acute care needs and ignoring long-term care planning
c) Integrating services to address both medical and social needs, such as transportation, housing, and caregiver support
d) Limiting access to new medical treatments due to age

Answer: c) Integrating services to address both medical and social needs, such as transportation, housing, and caregiver support
Explanation: Managing health care for aging populations requires an integrated approach that addresses the comprehensive needs of older adults. This includes not only medical care but also social services that support their overall well-being, such as accessible transportation, stable housing, and caregiver support. Recognizing and addressing the interconnected nature of these needs is essential for promoting health, independence, and quality of life for aging individuals.

650. When a school social worker is informed that a student is experiencing homelessness, their FIRST step should be to:

a) Notify all the student's teachers about their living situation for awareness.
b) Assess the student's immediate needs for shelter, food, and clothing.
c) Encourage the student to change schools for a fresh start.
d) Postpone any action until the student's academic performance declines.

Answer: b) Assess the student's immediate needs for shelter, food, and clothing.
Explanation: The first step for a school social worker when informed of a student's homelessness is to assess the student's immediate basic needs. Ensuring the student has access to shelter, food, and clothing is critical to providing stability and support, enabling them to focus on their education. School social workers play a crucial role in connecting students and their families with community resources and services to meet these immediate needs.

Made in the USA
Coppell, TX
11 March 2025